LIVERPOOL PORCELAIN

TO
MY WIFE

First edition published 1957
by B.T. Batsford Ltd   London

This edition published by Portman Press
an imprint of B.T. Batsford Limited
1989

ISBN 0713 4 6189 6

Printed and bound in Great Britain by
Courier International Ltd, Tiptree, Essex
for Portman Press
4 Fitzhardinge Street, London W1H 0AH

PLATE I

Jug of Chaffers' porcelain, painted in under-glaze blue and enamels, inscribed
THE UNION REIN VOS and dated 1764. *Height 11¾ in.*
The Trustees of the Victoria and Albert Museum (Crown Copyright)

LIVERPOOL PORCELAIN

*of the eighteenth century
and its makers*

By

KNOWLES BONEY

"To purchase a clear and warrantable body of truth
we must part with and forget
much that we know."
—*RELIGIO MEDICI*

PORTMAN PRESS
LONDON

PREFACE

URING THE PAST FIFTY YEARS, much information about eighteenth-century Liverpool china and its makers has come to light. Yet together with much in addition, this has never been published and it can truly be said that no chinaware of comparable importance, made in any centre in this country, is less well known. The first aim of the author has been to make this information available to the interested public.

In this task, the size and diversity of the records has presented difficulty. For any errors and omissions arising therefrom, the author seeks the reader's indulgence. Regarding the views which have been expressed some follow lines along which a few minds have been moving for years past. These, and some others for which the author accepts responsibility, now receive support from the Chaffers–Christian–Podmore Agreement. Their general acceptance will partly depend on the extent to which they will be found to conform to the new alignment which the publication of this Agreement makes necessary.

The illustrations, unless otherwise stated, are from photographs taken by the author of pieces in his collection. In recording the results of their examination in detail, full advantage has been taken of the benefit which this circumstance permits. The camera used in this work was the property of the author's friend and colleague, the late Samuel Saxon Barton, Liverpool gynaecologist, to whose memory as doctor, poet and artist, a posthumous tribute is gratefully paid.

The grateful thanks of the author are tendered:
To the Corporation of Liverpool's Libraries, Museums and Arts Committee for facilities granted for research and to Mr H. A. Taylor of the Liverpool Record Office, wherein are lodged the Entwistle MSS; to Mr E. S. Barnard of the British Museum; to Mr R. J. Charleston and the Staff of the ceramic department of the Victoria and Albert Museum; to Mr Rollo Charles of the National Museum of Wales and members of the Staff of the Department of Art, among whom Mr Collier's services are particularly remembered; and to Mr Cyril Shingler of the Museum of the Worcester Royal Porcelain Company, who has given valuable advice and help on many occasions.

To Mr A. J. Bartram Kiddell for his early encouragement and his gift of Gatty's rare monograph on the Liverpool potteries, which has been of inestimable value; to Mr Ernest Allman of Bootle, with whom many of the problems involved have been discussed and whose loans of ceramic literature have assisted the work; to Mr H. R. Marden King, M.A., for reading the draft of the book, giving it friendly criticism and according the benefit of his scholarly attainments on innumerable occasions; to Messrs Josiah Wedgwood & Sons, Ltd, for permission to make full use of the Sadler-Wedgwood letters. To his publishers for their suggestions and advice in the arrangement of the work and for their courteous and ready co-operation at all times; and lastly to his wife, who, knowing nothing of English china, is the possessor of an unrivalled knowledge of the English language which she has placed unreservedly at his disposal.

CONTENTS

		PAGE
Preface		v

CHAPTER

One	Introduction	1
Two	Worcester Connection	12
	Sources of Information	16
	Map showing the sites of Liverpool potworks	22
Three	The Ware	24
	First Period: Native Liverpool Characteristics	29
	Oriental and Worcester Characteristics	34
	The 'Scratch-Cross' Group	41
	Second Period	48
	Third Period	53
Four	The Decoration of the Ware	59
	Blue-and-White Decorated Ware	75
Five	Printed Ware	81
	The First Five Years	86
	The Association with Wedgwood	91
	Signed Wares	93
	Classification of Liverpool Prints	94
	Trends in Development	103
	The Sources of the Prints	104
	Reversed Prints	107
	Liverpool Ceramic Prints in Perspective	111
Six	Short Biographical Notes	113
	Richard Chaffers	114
	Philip Christian	119
	Robert Podmore	124

CHAPTER		PAGE
Six	Samuel Gilbody	125
	Reid & Co.	127
	William Ball	129
	Edward Chaffers	130
	The Pennington Family	132
	John Part	141
	Robert Pennington	141
	John Pennington, Jnr	142
	Zachariah Barnes	143
	John Sadler	147
	Guy Green	151
	Jeremiah Evans	152
	Thomas Billinge	154
	Richard Abbey	156
	Henry Baker	157
	Thomas Lawrenson	159
	Lawrence Harrison	160
	The Liverpool Johnsons	160
	Peter Perez Burdett	162
Seven	Factory Wasters and Marks	164
	Analysis	165
	Notes on the Plates	167
	The Plates	*Between pages* 192 & 193
Appendix I	The Agreement	193
II	Letter from John Rosson, of Moor Hall, Ormskirk, Lancashire, to the Editor of the *Liverpool Mercury*, dated 12th May 1854	196
IIIA	Letters referring to the 1755 Agreement	200
IIIB	Extracts from *Marks and Monograms*, Fourth Edition, 1874, by William Chaffers	202
IVA	Extracts from Sadler's letters to Wedgwood	203
IVB	Josiah Wedgwood	207
V	From Gore's *General Advertiser*, 1st May 1767	208
VIA	Extracts from Wedgwood letters: Transfer Printing	209
VIB	Extracts from Wedgwood letters: Robert Wilcox	211
VIC	Extracts from Wedgwood letters: Miscellaneous	212
VII	A note on the Liverpool burgesses or freemen	214
	Bibliography	215
	Index	217

CHAPTER ONE

INTRODUCTION

I N T H E Y E A R 1755, a small private company for the manufacture of porcelain was formed in Liverpool. In that year, Robert Podmore, for some time previously in the employment of the Worcester Porcelain Company, came to Liverpool and entered into an agreement with two local potters, Richard Chaffers and Philip Christian. This agreement provided in effect that he, Podmore, would teach them how to make porcelain, in the making, painting and burning of which he 'is said to be very knowing and expert' and be entirely responsible for the technical details of its manufacture and decoration from start to finish. Chaffers and Christian were to subscribe the capital necessary for the new venture.

There are some grounds for thinking that this event may not have marked the beginning of porcelain manufacture in Liverpool and that earlier attempts had been made. The matter will be considered later. Here, it is only necessary to remark that, at a time when porcelain-making was so much in men's minds and had already been attempted with success in other parts of the country, it seems unlikely that the possibility of such a development had been overlooked by the enterprising Liverpool potters. At this date, Liverpool was the centre of an extensive and flourishing pottery industry which had been in existence many years and which, in size and importance, ranked high among its craft industries in the eighteenth century. Indeed, the size of this was such as to confer on the town a prominent place among other centres of the industry in this country and had an important bearing on the develop- ment of the porcelain manufacture now taking place.

No definite date can be assigned to its beginnings. As in so many other localities in days before industrial development had occurred when simple wants could be met in simple ways from local resources, rude vessels, bricks, and maybe tiles were doubtless made from local clay found suitable for the purpose. The records of Liverpool town before 1600 show many entries dealing with the digging of clay for brick-making and regulations were made which show clearly that the practice was sufficiently prevalent to need proper control. As a result, the sites whereon digging was allowed were specified. A minimum distance from the highway was laid down as one of the conditions and filling in afterwards was enforced.[1] Apparently a man could not even dig clay on his own land without permission and the payment of certain dues; and fines were imposed for infringements.

Gatty tell us that[2] 'the earliest records concerning pottery I have at present found are amongst the Municipal documents and refer to brick making. There is one in 1618, concerning the getting of marl on the common by one Mossock of Toxteth Park; and in 1693, an order occurs concerning brick-making, "that all persons allowed to get marl to make bricks on the common shall dig to the bottom of the clay and marl and make the ground level before they carry off their bricks".'

Liverpool was a port, even in these far back days and among the goods handled for export were crates of 'muggs' on which an export duty had to be paid. This fact may well have acted as a stimulus to the production locally of similar goods in competition. That Liverpool was making mugs in the seventeenth century seems probable from various orders regulating the passage of carts laden with mugs through the town. Thus, in 1663, 'carts laden with muggs for export shall not go through the streets, but keep to the water side'. This, of course, might refer only to an export trade from outside sources; but in 1685 we find that there was a toll charge of sixpence per cartload 'put on board anie shipp by "forreiners", reduced to twopence if the Potts be a freeman's';[3] and when we read in 1690 that 'Richard Mercer, a freeman of this town, being supposed to defraud it by countenancing and protecting Muggs and pipes of strangers as if they were really his own, is to be enquired into and taken notice of the next Qrter Sessions',[4] the inference that mugs and pipes were made in Liverpool at this date is reasonably certain.[5]

The bracketing of pipes with mugs in this paragraph provides further proof where mugs are concerned, because we know that pipe-making was carried on in seventeenth-century Liverpool.[6] In the Holt & Gregson MSS. quoted by Gatty, we read, 'There are seven pipe manufactories in Liverpool and about sixty men employed by the masters in this business and about as many women, since every labourer has a female to finish off'.

There is an oft-quoted paragraph from the same source which reads, 'To stone buildings (1660) there succeeded in the seventeenth century brick and slate buildings in Liverpool. To the brick-making succeeded the clay potteries; to them, delft ware made of pipe clay and glazed with salt. The clay was glazed with lead ore. To the delph ware succeeded the whole flint or Queen's ware

---

[1]Town records, October 1577. [2]Gatty, *The Liverpool potteries* page 3, 1882.
[3]Town records, quoted by Gatty, op. cit. [4]Ibid.
[5]Gatty thinks that these excerpts 'need have no connection with wares made in Liverpool, but may refer to those carted from Staffordshire . . . .'
[6]Richard, son of James Atherton, pipe-maker, baptized St. Nicholas Church, 29th July 1679.

in 1760 by Wedgwood.' This is a confused statement, doubtless the result of the writer possessing insufficient knowledge of the technical details of his subject, but is not without its value. One may not be entitled to infer much from it, but the reference to 'ware made of pipe clay and glazed with salt', even though it be incorrectly described as 'delph' should not escape notice. It is the use of these materials in this particular way, rather than the name that matters and it can hardly be doubted that a reference to saltglazed ware is indicated.

But confused though this statement is, it may be considered to afford some assistance in getting the development of the pottery industry in Liverpool into its proper perspective. The chief product of this development was undoubtedly delftware, the manufacture of which reached considerable proportions during the eighteenth century, but it seems to have been a growth of that century entirely. A critical examination of the extracts I have given do not lend support to a belief that anything more elaborate than bricks, pipes and rude mugs were made before that time, the latter made from local clays and possibly slip-decorated. Gatty tells us that in 1701 'Josiah Poole of Liverpool received permission from the Corporation to make tiles and pantyles and bricks from local clay'. Of painted earthenware — the article which later was to become known as delftware — there is so far no mention and expert opinion now favours the view that this was not a development from pre-existing conditions but an importation from London, which may be dated about the time of Richard Holt's association with the Lord Street pothouse in 1710.[1]

The proof of this is interesting. In a short list of a dozen potters' names which Gatty extracted from the registers of St. Peter's parish church, Liverpool, between 1710 and 1720,[2] four or five are new to Liverpool,[3] but they are found, also as potters, in the parish registers of St. Olave's and St. Saviour's, Southwark,[4] prior to 1710, after which date they do not recur.[5] In such circumstances, complete identity of names leaves little room for doubt that migration from Southwark took place about this time.

From these beginnings, the growth of the industry went forward rapidly, reaching such dimensions, in fact, that we learn from the Catalogue of the

[1]Professor F. H. Garner (Trans. E.C.C., No. 4, 1937, page 47) tells us that the Brislington pottery arose in the same way, more than half a century earlier.
[2]Op. cit., page 7.
[3]They do not occur in any of the town records of the seventeenth century, *viz:* the Burgesses Roll, Hearth Tax Roll, the Free Present Money list of 1661 and the list of the Association of 1696. The Liverpool Dunbabin family, although not in Gatty's list, was also undoubtedly a Southwark family originally (first Liverpool mention, 1708) and maintained Southwark connections during a great part of the eighteenth century (Apollo, May 1955, page 151).
[4]Subsequently Southwark Cathedral, London.   [5]Ent. MSS.

Geological Museum[1] that, at one time 'pottery appears to have been the staple manufacture of the town.'

Support for this rather remarkable statement is provided by the import records of potters' clay from Carrickfergus on Belfast Lough. The Bristol delftware makers did not use clay from this source and obviously, had they required it, direct importation would have taken place. It is therefore not an unreasonable assumption that the Liverpool potteries absorbed the greater part of the 641 tons of this clay which passed through the town's Custom Offices in the year 1751.[2] This amount of clay would patently enable a great quantity of ware to be produced.[3]

Reference may also be made to the statement which occurs towards the end of the certificate signed by Alderman Thomas Shaw and Samuel Gilbody (both potters) which describes the title-printing experiment of Sadler and Green on 27th July 1756. In this, the words occur, 'The Town of Liverpool in particular, where the Earthen ware manufacture is more extensively carried on than in any other Town in the Kingdom'. The importance of this lies in the fact that, while adding little of value to the certificate as such, it is contemporary with the events described and could have been so easily refuted if untrue.[4]

Further proof of the size of the industry is furnished by reference to the *Poll and Squib* book, published by Sadler after the memorable Parliamentary election of 1761. From this we learn that one hundred and two potters voted for Sir William Meredith, which carried the Election. This was the occasion commemorated by the saltglaze mug with its inscription in 'scratch-blue' which read, 'Ser William a plumper'.[5] This will receive mention again later. But perhaps the most reliable proof of the point it is sought to make is provided by the census figures for the year 1790 which show that 74 families, totalling 374 persons were then living on Shaw's Brow, 'all of whom were connected with the potteries'.[6] Shaw's Brow (now William Brown Street) was the centre of the Liverpool potworks, but many lay outside this area; and,

---

[1]Quoted by Turner, *Transfer Printing on Enamels, Pottery, Porcelain* (1906), page 13.

[2]Toppin, Trans. E.C.C., No. 3, 1935, page 56.

[3]Dudley Westropp, *Catalogue of Irish Pottery and Porcelain*, Nat. Mus. Dublin, 1935, page 11, referring to an award of £10 in 1747 to J. Crisp & Co., delftware makers of Worlds End, Strand, Dublin, states that they used Carrickfergus clay, 'as did the Liverpool potters'.

[4]See Plate IV. The three documents concerned in this incident will receive consideration later.

[5]Chaffers & Co. took a great interest in this election and undoubtedly made both the salt-glaze 'plumper' mug and the commemmorative one in porcelain recording the fact that 982 persons voted for Sir William. The *Poll and Squib* book gives a lively picture of the manner in which elections were conducted in these days.

[6]Mayer, *Art of Pottery in Liverpool*, page 24.

bearing in mind that, at this date, the decline to which I have referred had been in progress many years, these figures, perhaps more than anything else help us to realize the size and importance of this once great industry.

Altogether the sites of about twenty potworks have been identified and there were doubtless others, all trace of which has been lost.[1] Figures of the number of persons engaged in the industry will of necessity vary considerably according to the basis of reckoning. Entwistle stated that he had been able to trace the names of some fifteen hundred persons who had at some time or other been connected with it, a figure which would doubtless include those engaged in allied occupations (tile making, pipe making, etc). The number of persons described as pot painters who could be shown to have been working between the years 1720 and 1800, alone totalled nearly one hundred. But if we consider solely those in control of the industry, the master-potters and those whose interest may have been no more than financial, we come down to smaller figures which probably more nearly correspond with those of the potters with voting rights.[2]

The twenty potworks, or thereabouts, to which allusion has been made, were connected with the names of some fifty potters and their families over the years. Of these, ten engaged in the making of an artificial porcelain during some part of their career; and it is noteworthy that these china makers, with one or two possible exceptions, began as makers of earthenware.

Quickly following Chaffers was the firm of Reid & Co. who began a manufacture on Brownlow Hill. In actual fact, Reid's seem to have succeeded in marketing their product before Chaffers was able to do so, probably as a result of the long delay suffered by Chaffers in his search for soaprock supplies. Closely following Reid's was Samuel Gilbody, a potter whose name has already been mentioned as one of the witnesses of Sadler's affidavit. He owned a pottery on land adjoining Chaffers on the east side and he had a retail shop over the way. Neither Reid nor Gilbody, however, met with great success, both having to close in 1761–2.

Fourth on the scene was William Ball, described as a china maker with premises in Ranelagh Street during the 1760's; and during this decade the names of two of the brothers Pennington, namely James and John, must be added to the growing list of Liverpool potters who took up china making.

[1]Entwistle put the total number of potteries at about twenty-five, but I am unable to confirm this without including such premises as those occupied by Sadler & Green (three at different dates), by Thomas Bridge in Cable Street (Gore, 1774), Gilbody's retail shop and other similar establishments.

[2]In some cases, businesses were controlled by merchants with little or no potting knowledge. 'Every merchant was concerned in a pot-house made of delft (*sic*) until 1785' (Holt & Gregson MSS., quoted by Gatty, op. cit., page 4.

The Christians, father and son (after Chaffers' death), the partners Barnes and Cotter, and finally, Seth Pennington, prominent during the last quarter of the century and probably the greatest of them all, complete the list.

The names of many streets and places remain to remind us of this time in Liverpool's past. One may instance Delf Side, Old Pottery Yard, Pothouse Lane, Shaw's Brow, Christian Street, Livesley Place, Barnes Court and Pennington Court, while the town records bear witness to the part played by many of these old potters in the public life of the town. In the latter connection, it is recalled that Alderman Thomas Shaw was Mayor in 1747 and that among the holders of less important offices may be mentioned Thomas Radcliffe and Edward Patton, constables, 1773; William Hartley, change keeper, 1774; William Dickson, town beadle, 1776; Joseph Fisher, deputy clerk of the market, 1778; John Fisher, sword bearer, 1781; and Edward Chaffers, chief overseer of the poor.

While it may be stated that the manufacture of delftware was always predominant, a considerable amount of lead-glazed earthenware of all kinds was made and also saltglaze; and it is worth recording that Liverpool was the only potting centre in this country where the manufacture of 'china' and of every type of earthenware was carried on contemporaneously.

The effect of this, with the unavoidable intermingling of ideas and methods which resulted, gives a character to much Liverpool china which is unmistakable and which may be of assistance in identifying it. We find not only great variety in potting shapes, some of which reflect strongly an earthenware influence, but we see also the hand of the delft painter or of the saltglaze decorator only too plainly visible in many cases. It is true that the Staffordshire porcelain of Littler may exhibit this to some extent, but only where saltglaze influences are concerned. The Liverpool potter always had good reason to use tin enamel when he took up china-making.

With such strong 'native' influences always at hand to assert themselves and in circumstances so essentially different from those prevailing in any of the other growing centres of a porcelain industry in this country, development in Liverpool was hardly likely to follow routine lines. It is probable that many potters, on taking up the manufacture of china, continued to make earthenware. We have no certain knowledge on this point and little or no direct evidence. Even the newspaper advertisements, from which we get so much information about the potters and their wares, fail us here, but it would probably be correct to include Philip Christian, Seth Pennington and Zachariah Barnes among those who carried on business in this way.[1]

Still considering the industry as a whole, it would appear that the peak of

[1]In including Barnes among the number I refer to the firm, Barnes & Cotter (see Z. Barnes).

prosperity was reached about the year 1760 and was maintained for the next few years. But by the middle 1760's a decline began to manifest itself and by the end of the decade we find, at a meeting of the Conversation Club held in January 1769, that the subject for discussion was 'The causes of the Decline of the Potters' business in this town and by what means it might be made to flourish'.[1] Evidently the rot had set in.

A glance at the poll books gives interesting information on this point. Whereas that for the 1734 election shows that seventeen potters recorded their votes, in 1761 the number had risen to one hundred and seventeen, but in 1790 it had fallen to no more than seventy-eight and this in spite of the fact that it was common practice at this time for an enfranchised potter who had migrated to return to Liverpool to record his vote.[2] To be enfranchised was a privilege in those days and valued accordingly. The downward trend is equally well shown — in reverse — by the increasing number of retailers appearing in the Liverpool directories as 'Staffordshire Merchants''.[3] In 1766 there are none, but in 1790 there were twenty-three and by the end of the century this number had doubled.

Writing in 1774, Enfield makes this interesting statement.[4] 'English porcelain, in imitation of foreign China, has long been manufactured in this town; and formerly with success. But of late this branch has been much upon the decline, partly because the Leverpool artists have not kept pace in their improvements with some others in the same way; but chiefly because the Staffordshire ware has had and still continues to have so general a demand, as almost to supersede the use of other English porcelain. The great perfection to which this art, both in works of utility and of ornament and taste, is carried at the modern Etruria, under the direction of those ingenious artists, Messrs Wedgwood and Bentley, at the same time that it is highly serviceable to the public and reflects great honour on our country, must be unfavourable to other manufactories of a similar kind.'

There can be no doubt that the competition of the Staffordshire potters with Josiah Wedgwood at their head was keenly felt in Liverpool at this time, as was also the threat from foreign competitors, anxious then as now to undersell us in our markets. We find Christian writing to Wedgwood on this matter in 1767 and trying to enlist the support of the Staffordshire potters for a Bill to make foreign china dutiable.[5] That he was unsuccessful in his object is not surprising when we recall the story that Wedgwood so successfully met this

---

[1] *W.L.A.*, 27th January, 1769.
[2] The poll book figures should be read in the light of total population figures — in 1734 about 12,500, in 1761, 26,000; in 1790, 55,800.
[3] The first directory was published in 1766. [4] Enfield. *A History of Liverpool* 1774, page 90.
[5] Referred to by Wedgwood in a letter to Bentley dated 14th February, 1767.

competition himself that the traveller could dine off Wedgwood ware at every hotel between London and St. Petersburg.

Wedgwood was not only a good potter, he was an extremely able business man; and he made it part of his business to know what the Liverpool potters were doing. It is unlikely that any event of importance occurred in these potteries without his knowledge. Most of the potters were personally known to him, indeed, in one or two instances he had a financial interest in their potworks.[1] For many years he maintained a selling and distributing agency in the town and he relied almost entirely on the facilities afforded by the port for his growing export trade.[2] Bearing these facts in mind, the quotation from Enfield's *History* assumes added importance. It is unstinted in its praise of the superiority of the Staffordshire products and is valuable as showing a contemporary appraisement of a situation which was gradually developing in Staffordshire's favour. The introduction of an improved creamware by Wedgwood about the year 1760 seems to have marked the turning point. Technically excellent and backed by Wedgwood's salesmanship, it quickly captured the world's markets. In this, no doubt, the greatest assistance was afforded by the newly discovered art of transfer printing on pottery and porcelain, thus making possible a means of decoration that was both rapid and cheap, while offering variety combined with a neatness of finish that was hitherto unknown. There can be little doubt, however, that the business arrangements which were quickly entered into between Wedgwood and John Sadler, the Liverpool printer who undertook to decorate the ware in this way, were gravely detrimental to Liverpool pottery interests as a whole and hastened the decline of the local manufacture.

But the Liverpool potters, as was only to be expected, were not long in coming into the field with a creamware which they produced in considerable quantity during the next two decades.[3] In Liverpool, as elsewhere, it was gradually replacing saltglaze in popular favour, finally superseding it, although, as far as Liverpool was concerned, the last battle in the long struggle was against delftware; and tolerably good though readily identifiable examples of Liverpool creamware may be, this battle was won by Wedgwood.[4]

Staffordshire competition was increased by the opening of the Trent-

[1]Reid & Co., bankrupts in 1761. 'Persons desirous of viewing the premises to apply to Mr Wedgwood at Burslem in Staffordshire'. He also assisted financially John Dunbabin.
[2]Bentley & Boardman, King Street, Bentley subsequently joining him in partnership. Bentley-Boardman partnership dissolved May 1779.
[3]The makers were Okill & Co., Flint Mug works and later at Park Lane Pottery: Messrs Rigg & Peacock at the latter works and, possibly, Richard Abbey at 11 Cleveland Square.
[4]Much Liverpool creamware has a decidedly green glaze, unmistakable when present–Examples bearing the town arms are known and provide proof of identity.

Mersey canal (Grand Trunk) which was completed in 1777,[1] the Staffordshire–Worcester canal having been opened some three or four years previously. It is not difficult to estimate the effect of these waterways in providing easy and safe transit for breakable goods, for which hitherto only the hazards of transport over rough unmetalled country roads had been possible. By these means, the interior of this country, especially perhaps the Potteries, was at once opened up; and Liverpool's advantageous position as an exporter of her own wares which she had enjoyed so long, was discounted.[2]

No explanation of the causes involved in the decline of this industry would be complete without taking into account the war with the North American colonies which broke out in 1775, affecting every branch of Liverpool's trade and bringing commercial ruin to the town. The general effect of such a war had been clearly foreseen and meetings had been widely held up and down the country protesting against the Government's treatment of the Colonists, in the hope of averting a war which, by the beginning of 1775 seemed inevitable. The Liverpool merchants took an active part in these proceedings.[3] That their efforts were unsuccessful is a matter of history, but it is interesting to note that six months after this unjust and disgraceful war had started, we find them still petitioning the King on the subject.[4] The young and active took to privateering, a poor substitute for the benefits of a steady trade and no compensation whatever to the merchants who received no share of any prize money.[5] With its commerce destroyed, its shipping captured or idle and 10,000 of its 40,000 inhabitants dependent on public relief or charity for support, Liverpool's plight was desperate.

[1] That a section of this canal had been in use for some time previously is shown by a letter from Green to Wedgwood in 1774 in which he complains about delays resulting from its use. (App. IV A, 26).

[2] *Per contra*, the opening up of the country by a network of canals greatly assisted in the development of Liverpool as a port.

[3] *W.L.A.*, 20th January 1775. Meeting of protest at the King's Tavern, Cornhill, London when three to four hundred merchants trading with North America expressed strong views on the attitude of the Government towards the Colonists and petitioned for the repeal of all Acts which had interfered with our friendly relations with them. Also (ibid., 27th January) a further meeting of Liverpool West India merchants with others interested in this trade, at the London Tavern forecasting commercial ruin for the whole country if the Government persisted in its policy.

[4] *W.L.A.*, 6th October, 1775, when the petition bore the names of a dozen Liverpool potters, *viz:* John Drinkwater, Edward Rigg, John Dunbabin, John Roscoe, Thomas Shaw, Ambrose Lace, Edward Chaffers, George Drinkwater, Thomas Deare, William Leadbeater and Philip Christian, both father and son.

[5] The attractions afforded by privateering at such times had doubtless always played a part in the life of this seaport town. Twenty years earlier, when the French were the enemy, we read of 'useful remarks on Privateering addressed to the laudable Association of Anti-Gallicans' (*W.L.A.*, 5th November 1756).

On the signing of peace in 1783, prosperity quickly returned. The blow to the pottery trade, however, had been unduly severe[1] and although it shared in the general improvement which took place after the war, very largely owing to the outstanding ability of its chief representative, Seth Pennington, recovery was incomplete and its final extinction no more than delayed. For the economic life of a community can only remain healthy under competitive conditions if the balance of these remains favourable to its continued growth. Here a changing complexity of factors turned the scale against the Liverpool potters and the industry died a natural death.

Foremost among the causes bringing this about must be reckoned the rapid growth of Liverpool as a port during the latter half of the eighteenth century. The great industrial development now beginning to take place in the Midlands and the North of England, following the improvement in internal communications already noted, found in Liverpool a natural gateway for a growing trade with the North American continent and the West Indies. The first twelve years of the reign of George III saw a great advance in this respect and were years of prosperity to the town. During this time, the number of ships paying dock dues nearly doubled, as did also their gross tonnage. Immediately the American War was over, the rate of increase mounted so rapidly that the figure of 450,000 tons was reached by the close of the century, representing nine times the volume of trade in 1760. Such progress indicated clearly the lines of development Liverpool's future was destined to follow and contributed materially to the changing scene. The actual date on which the last of Liverpool's indigenous potworks closed down is a little obscure, but the honour probably goes to Seth Pennington in the year 1806.

With the virtual extinction of this old industry in the manner I have attempted to outline and with nobody to carry on the tradition, it is not surprising to find that Liverpool's great potting past began to be forgotten. People naturally lost interest in something which, at that date, seemed of little importance. New developments were claiming their attention and they turned to making money more easily in other ways. Their attitude might not unfairly be described as 'off with the old, on with the new'. Before long, identification of the products of the various potteries must have become a difficult matter and soon even the general characters of Liverpool wares would be forgotten. No doubt the delftware manufacture suffered less in this respect than did the other earthwares and porcelain, in both of which the effects were far reaching. Of these, strange as it may sound, it almost came to be doubted that such were ever made at Liverpool. That state of affairs is happily long past. Much has been learned as a result of the painstaking labours of

---

[1]Much Liverpool ware was exported to America throughout Liverpool's potting history.

10

Gatty, Entwistle and many others and work on the subject is continuing. Fresh discoveries continue to be made, or rather, old and forgotten facts are brought to light and given new meaning; and there are signs that Liverpool is beginning to regain her right to be regarded as one of the important centres of the ceramic industry in this country during a great part of the eighteenth century.

CHAPTER TWO

WORCESTER CONNECTIONS
SOURCES OF INFORMATION

IT HAS LONG BEEN SUSPECTED that the beginnings of porcelain making in Liverpool were closely associated with the defection of Robert Podmore from the service of the Worcester Porcelain Company.[1] It is true that Joseph Mayer[2] speaks of him as coming to Liverpool from Wedgwood's employment, but, as we shall see, there is no support for this statement. It was later copied by the author of *Marks and Monograms*.

The substance of Mayer's account of this matter, as given to the Historical Society of Lancashire and Cheshire in 1855, is contained in a letter published by Chaffers' grandson, John Rosson, a year earlier and this must therefore be regarded as the foundation of our knowledge.[3] From the circumstances in which this letter was written, it is now possible to form an opinion on the general credibility of the account; while the discovery and publication of the Liverpool Agreement referred to in the opening chapter shows the closeness of the link with Worcester and makes possible an estimate of its consequences.

Mayer gave no dates and we were therefore completely ignorant of the duration of Podmore's Liverpool connection. We now know that it began in 1755 and lasted some twenty years, which means that he must have spent the greater part of his potting life there. But the part played by this man in the developing industry before he came to Liverpool and the conclusions which it seems to justify are so important, that his relations with the newly formed Worcester Porcelain Company first require to be examined in some detail.

We first hear of Robert Podmore in the Partnership Deed of this Company, which is dated June 1751. In this (*Clause 20*) he and a certain John Lyes are referred to as 'workmen who have for some time been employed by the inventors of the said Manufacture'. It has been assumed that the inventors were Dr John Wall and William Davis, an apothecary, two of the subscribers to the new Company, which was being formed to exploit their invention. Subsequent additions to our knowledge showed that this Company was taking over the business of a small factory which was engaged in making a

---

[1]Honey, O. E. P., 1946, page 199.
[2]*History of the Art of Pottery in Liverpool*, pages 25, 26, 27, 28.
[3]*Liverpool Mercury*, 12th May 1854; see Appendix II.

soaprock porcelain by a secret process in Redcliff Backs, Bristol. Both Wall and Davis had an interest in this concern.[1] That would explain their claim to have been the employers of Podmore and Lyes and at the same time establish the fact that both these men had been working at the older factory.

The idea that Wall and Davis invented, in the ordinarily understood meaning of the word, any process for making artificial porcelain, has long since been discounted.[2] R. L. Hobson made it clear that 'there was no real ground for supposing that Dr Wall did more than test in company with W. Davis, his collaborator, certain methods of porcelain making which were submitted to him'.[3] A moment's reflection entitles one to say that it is extremely doubtful if they did as much; and that their rôle of 'inventors' may be considered to be sufficiently covered by their possession of some knowledge of the secret process, such as their interest in the affairs of the older company would guarantee them.

It is otherwise with Podmore and Lyes. Clause 20 of the Partnership Deed, of which mention has already been made, discloses reference to a secret clearly connected with the process of manufacture about to be employed by the new Company and these two men were in possession of it. At least, they were in possession of sufficient knowledge to guarantee to them special pay and privileges and, as Dr Severne Mackenna adds, to make it imperative that their fidelity be assured. The conclusion that the secret refers to the method of making a soaprock porcelain seems inescapable. The new company was going to make it and Podmore and Lyes were going to show the way.

It has hitherto been assumed that this 'merger' could be dated from the Partnership Deed of June 1751 and that the final absorption of the older Company was represented by the announcement in July 1752 that 'it was now united with the Worcester Porcelain Company'.[4] Documents discovered by Mr A. J. Toppin seem to show that was not so.[5] From this source we learn that: (1) no sale took place until February 1752, when £300 was paid, this sum to include the remaining stock, the utensils and effects *and* the process of manufacture; (2) the sale of the remainder of the lease of the soaprock mine

[1]*John Wall and the Worcester Porcelain Company*, by C. W. D. Perrins in Trans. E.C.C. 1942, page 127.
[2]Ibid., where the remark is made 'china is the last thing which lends itself as the subject of small trial experiments carried out in the back premises of a shop'.
[3]*Worcester Porcelain*, R. L. Hobson, page 10.
[4]*Bristol Intelligencer*, 24th July 1752, quoted by Pountney in *Old Bristol Potteries* 1920.
[5]*The Proprietors of the Early Bristol China Factory* (Trans. E.C.C., volume 3, part 3, page 129 et seq. The documents deal with a petition in bankruptcy of Rd. Holdship in 1761. Holdship negotiated the transfer in February 1752, retaining the lease of the mine himself and entering into agreements with the company that he would sell and the Company would buy not less than 20 tons a year for twenty years at £18 per ton.

was the subject of a separate agreement between the Bristol Company and Richard Holdship of Worcester, who paid no less than £1,400[1] for it.

Of John Lyes there is no further mention and nothing is known of his subsequent history. Our sole concern, therefore, is with Podmore and his rôle at this time in the service of the Worcester Company. It can hardly be doubted that he was not a workman, as we understand the meaning of the word today, but a highly skilled arcanist who was probably in full possession of the secret of manufacture, notwithstanding the distinct implication to the contrary in Clause 20 of the Partnership agreement. In this connection, the possibility that Podmore had already deserted from his Bristol employment cannot be ruled out; and the wording of this clause can be read as an attempt by the Worcester proprietors to protect themselves against a contingency to which, in any case, they were particularly liable. It is easy to see that, by inferring that Podmore was only in possession of part of the secret of manufacture, breach of trust would be easier to prove and any penalty incurred thereby more easily enforceable.

We do not know how long he remained at Worcester, nor the circumstances of his leaving, but being described in the Liverpool Agreement as 'of the City of Worcester', it is likely that he had but recently left when he arrived in Liverpool in 1755. That there could have been an intervening period during which he was employed by Wedgwood, as both Mayer and Jewitt state, seems impossible. Not only is there no record of such employment at Messrs Wedgwood's, but to have taken place its date would have to fall during the period of the Whieldon partnership (1754-9). The importance of this lies in the fact that, were it true, the time he spent at Worcester would be correspondingly shortened. As it is, this can be limited to four years and may well have been less. The duration of his presumed period of employment at Bristol's Redcliff Backs factory seems to have been another two years[2] and it follows that, assuming continuous employment, something less than six years of Podmore's life could have been passed as a maker of soaprock china before he finally settled in Liverpool, where the records show he lived for

[1]The amount paid for the lease of the mine is in striking contrast with that paid for all the other assets of the Company and clearly shows the value of a soaprock supply and the difficulty in getting it. A royalty per ton was also payable to the mine owners.

[2]Probably rather less. The soaprock licence granted to Benjamin Lund of the Redcliff Backs factory in March 1749 was the first of its kind (Morton Nance, *Soaprock licences*, Trans. E.C.C., No. 3, 1935); and, as A. J. Toppin remarks (loc. cit.), production in the summer of that year is as early as could be expected. The possibility that Podmore could have gained soaprock experience elsewhere, e.g. at the earlier Limehouse factory with which a Bristol connection is reported to have existed (Dr Pocock's diary) must be borne in mind. No ware from such a source has been identified and its composition is unknown.

over twenty years. It is, therefore, likely that he produced correspondingly more ware in that town.

Turning to the Liverpool Agreement, we again find Podmore selling his services, though now somewhat differently. On this occasion his contract is with two practical potters of considerable experience, who clearly recognise his ability 'in the making painting and burning of earthenware in imitation of and to resemble china' and his importance to the success of the undertaking which they had in mind. As a result, he was made completely responsible for all the technical processes involved, from start to finish, as will be seen from a later clause which provides that he 'will at all times during the said term of seven years use his utmost care diligence skill knowledge and judgment in the making painting and complete finishing of the said Earthenware'.

The importance of determining the exact meaning which should be attached to these words needs no stressing. They can only mean that Podmore's duties were to include the exercise of his skill as a decorator, in which art the Agreement, in its preamble, has already affirmed his proficiency. It would have been as easy matter in the circumstances to have limited his responsibility to potting, in which he was also admittedly expert, had Chaffers and Christian so wished. The fact that they agreed otherwise and were at some pains to say so, shows that they recognized his ability as a decorator and wished to make use of it.

There is nothing remarkable in such a state of affairs and instances abound in which the arts of potter and decorator were combined. It may have been of commoner occurrence in early days, before 'specialization' was advanced[1] and in this case it may hark back to small beginnings at Bristol. In this particular case, also, it may be thought that, in actual practice, Podmore's responsibility in the matter would turn more on the ability which he could command and that, while no doubt he contributed personally to the decoration of the ware, his influence was shown mainly in the work of his 'school'. In this way, many pieces are accounted for which show early Worcester influences while seeming to belong to a later date.

But it will be seen that Podmore's responsibility extended far beyond the purely technical side of the new undertaking. He is placed 'in charge of all matters of direction management and superintending of the said work with authority over the laboureres servants and others engaged in it'. Chaffers and Christian are to receive instruction in the secret and in the method of use and are clearly responsible for the provision of all necessary capital, but the measure of control seemingly exercised by either in the early days of the venture was limited. In this way the workman of the Worcester Porcelain Company became the Managing Director of Chaffers & Co. and with

[1]Although Billingsley's name serves to remind us that it was not unknown fifty years later.

the change, Liverpool china emerged from obscurity into the broad light of day.

SOURCES OF INFORMATION

The available sources of information about the porcelain-making industry of the eighteenth century in Liverpool are abundant; and it is not easy to understand the confusion with which the subject has hitherto been so much surrounded. In order to get a clearer picture of what happened, it will be necessary to retrace our steps and examine the foundations of our knowledge.

For general information on the subject, we can refer to the usual miscellany of sources — the town records, which will include the Burgess Rolls, the voters' lists and the apprentice books; the newspapers, the parish registers, the Registry of Wills and numerous plans and leases of property. In addition, there are certain sources of information which are specifically concerned with the porcelain-making industry and it will be necessary to examine these in some detail for a proper understanding of what took place.

On 12th May 1854, John Rosson of Ormskirk, Lancashire, grandson of Richard Chaffers, wrote a letter to the *Liverpool Mercury* in circumstances which are therein stated, in which he gives certain information about Chaffers and the early days of china making in Liverpool (*Appendix II*). About this time or shortly afterwards, Rosson was visited by Joseph Mayer a silversmith of Lord Street, Liverpool with antiquarian tastes, member of a family of potters, himself interested in the art of the potter and conducting a research into the old Liverpool potteries. On 3rd May 1855, Mayer's monograph *The History of the Art of Pottery in Liverpool* was read before the Historic Society of Lancashire and Cheshire. In this, he mentions having visited John Rosson 'who related to me many particulars of his (Chaffers) career' and from whom he received authenticated examples of the potter's work.

A reprint of this paper appeared in 1871. As its title indicates, it deals with all the Liverpool potteries and has formed the basis of our knowledge of the subject, a great part of the information it contains being incorporated later into the account of these potteries given by the author of *Marks and Monograms*. This monograph does not state that practically all the information provided about Chaffers had been copied verbatim from Rosson's letter, the actual amount being indicated by the words *underlined* in the transcript which is here given.[1]

It is quite possible there is a simple explanation of this somewhat remarkable occurrence, but here it does not concern us. The necessity for drawing attention to it arises from the fact that it enables us to know the origin of the 'story' and assess its credibility.

[1]Appendix II.

John Rosson, living at Ormskirk and describing himself as the last surviving grandson in England of Richard Chaffers, was the son of Andrew Rosson who married Chaffers' daughter Elizabeth in 1770. It will be seen that his letter was the result of an article on *The Arts and Manufactures of Liverpool from 1769 to 1780* which the *Mercury* had recently published. In this, the pottery industry had received scant notice, which Rosson did not approve, but in proceeding to give the enlightenment which he thought necessary, he lays bare the very insecure foundation on which this portion of Mayer's *History* rests. For Rosson must have been born many years after Richard Chaffers died and, to quote his own words, he simply related what he had heard from an excellent mother.

In the light of this knowledge, how much of this narrative, so oft repeated, can we believe? What are we to make of that chance meeting between Chaffers and Podmore, then on his way to seek his fortunes in America, with its happy ending for Chaffers?; and of the subsequent heroic journey to Cornwall to obtain a supply of soaprock, when Chaffers, with a thousand guineas in his saddlebags with which to pay the wages of the miners and a brace of pistols in his holsters to meet the hazards of the journey, so nearly met with failure; and then the last minute success which rewarded his efforts, ending with the rejoicings at Liverpool when the first shipment of the precious mineral entered the dock?

Many of us may feel the disillusionment akin to that experienced by the child compelled to abandon long cherished beliefs no longer tenable, for the story is an epic in its way and well worth the telling. But against this feeling of loss must be set the solid gain which results from knowing exactly the value of our records. While the details do not matter the story in its essence must be true because it fits in with and explains all the known facts. Podmore undoubtedly came to Liverpool, met Chaffers and entered into an agreement with him and with Christian to 'make earthenware in imitation of and to resemble china'. The agreement exists in proof of it. The journey to Cornwall subsequently took place and a source of soaprock supply was secured. Teppit's letters exist in proof of this, for, so difficult was it to obtain soaprock at this time — and for many years afterwards — that nothing less than the personal approach was likely to effect it.[1] Teppit's letters are invaluable in this matter. In many instances they show the quantity of soaprock dispatched, its quality and the dates of shipment and conclude with a résumé and the state of the account at the date of Chaffers' death. Ten years after this event, the remainder of the mine lease was sold for £500 and with this transaction the association

---

[1]Guaregan Teppit, the miner-foreman of Chaffers' mine. The letters have been lost, but extracts are given in *Marks and Monograms*. See Appendix III B.

of Liverpool with Cornish soaprock ended. The story in its essentials is therefore more than inherently probable; it bears the imprint of truth.

Its improbabilities are fortunately of less importance. While it is likely that Chaffers had turned his attention to making china before Podmore's appearance on the Liverpool scene and may even, as John Rosson's letter informs us, have come to the conclusion that the use of soaprock for this purpose was desirable, we may not feel so inclined to accept the view of the purely accidental nature of the meeting between these two men which is put forward. Podmore, expert in the making of soaprock porcelain and on his way to America to try his fortunes there, called on Chaffers and had a talk. He is described as 'a very clever person, who, although not a scientific chemist or geologist, was nevertheless a very superior practical man'; and the result of this talk was that Podmore decided to forego his project and throw in his lot with Chaffers. One might have expected perhaps, that Podmore's previous association with Bristol and its nearness to Worcester would have inclined him to the use of that port for an intended journey to America, rather than Liverpool, where the facilities for such a journey at that date were no better. We do not know. We can only conclude that a purely chance visit by Podmore in the circumstances was a lucky 'turn up' for Mr Chaffers.

Reference has been made to the statement (originally Rosson's) that Podmore had been in Wedgwoods' employment and reasons have been given for discrediting it. This not only gives him longer service at Worcester, but avoids having to account for the inherent improbability of a man possessing such specialized knowledge of porcelain-making seeking employment where his talent would be of so little use. The list of improbabilities may be rounded off by referring once again to Wedgwood's praises and the final impossibility of Podmore having died in 1765.

But if the strength — and the weakness — of this portion of Mayer's *History* be thus exposed, we owe much to him for the researches he made at this time, the result of which he also incorporated in this published work. In addition to visiting John Rosson, he interviewed Miss Ann Pennington, the last surviving daughter of Seth Pennington and then living at Everton. From her, he was able to purchase a set of chimney ornaments, which she had kept 'as relics of her father's manufacture'.[1] These have proved invaluable as documents of Pennington's work. Mayer also visited Mrs Rockliffe of Edgehill, a grand-daughter of Philip Christian and from her he received some Whieldon-type plates;[2] while a visit to Barnes' youngest daughter Margaret

[1] Illustrated in the *History*, page 32. They formed part of the Mayer bequest destroyed by enemy action in 1941. Gatty (*Liverpool potteries*, 1882) describes them as underglaze blue painted with overglaze flowers in colour and showing traces of gilding.
[2] Similarly illustrated, op. cit., page 37., and described by Gatty later.

who had married Aaron Wedgwood, a grocer, in 1812, yielded what has proved to be, in all probability, the only badly authenticated piece of ware obtained by Mayer during these excursions.[1]

From all these persons, Mayer would receive such information as they were able to give on matters about which, admittedly, none would be likely to know much. Of far greater importance was the documentary evidence he was able to collect from three sources.

From Edward Eyes of Nantwich, Mayer purchased the original surveys with memoranda, of several Liverpool potworks. These had been made by an ancestor, John Eyes, a corporation surveyor of bygone days. Including as they did the draft surveys of fifteen or sixteen works, some of which had been remeasured under different owners, together with an old plan of[2] Liverpool, they form the basis of our knowledge of the old pottery sites and their changing ownership.

Then Mayer was able to visit Sadler's only surviving child, a daughter Elizabeth Mary, who was born in 1782. She would therefore be 72 years of age at the time and but seven years old when her father died. She was living at the farm she had inherited from her father at Aintree. From her Mayer obtained the original documents dealing with her father's experimental printing of tiles with Guy Green's help in 1756. These were: (1) the duly sworn affidavit; (2) the certificate given by Alderman Thomas Shaw and Samuel Gilbody; and (3) the petition for a patent by Sir Ellis Cunliffe and others. These documents are discussed elsewhere. Their present whereabouts is unknown, if, indeed, they still exist, but actual photographs which came into my possession are here reproduced with their signatures, as a permanent record.

Lastly, Mayer obtained certain letters from Lord Cross[3], a son of William Cross and Ellen Chaffers, who was a daughter of Edward Chaffers, one of the Executors of Richard Chaffers' Will. The date of this occurence is unknown, as also is the nature of the documents involved, but certain conclusions appear to be justified from a consideration of all the known facts.

Mayer died in 1886, but the fact that he had ever written to Lord Cross did not come to light until 1907, when it is revealed by Lord Cross himself[4] in reply to a letter from Charles Gatty, a former Curator of Liverpool Museum. Gatty's enquiries on this occasion refer to 'letters' and it seems likely that

[1]Referring to the so-called 'Barnes border' on a plate of underglaze-blue printed ware. The delftware items from this source are probably authentic.
[2]This plan was thought to date about 1760 by Sir James Picton. It has been used as the basis for the map of the Liverpool potteries.
[3]Richard Assheton Cross, first Baron Cross. See Appendix III A, for short biography.
[4]Appendix III A.

both he and Mayer before him had the idea of borrowing Teppit's letters, of which the author of *Marks and Monograms* had given extracts and which were known to be in Lord Cross' possession.[1] Mayer was apparently successful, but in the meantime the letters had been lost or mislaid and in their place Gatty received the Chaffers-Christian-Podmore Agreement.

Mayer exhibits no knowledge of this document at any time. In the *History*, both in its original form and in the reprint of 1871, his version of Podmore is that which John Rosson had learned at his mother's knee and the picture is dominated by Wedgwood rather than Worcester.[2] Had he learned of it at some later date, interested as he was in the Liverpool potteries and looked upon as their chief historian, it is unbelievable that he would have kept silent on a matter of such importance. Nor in such circumstances could Gatty's obvious ignorance be explained, for he was the Curator of the Mayer Collection soon after it was presented to the newly-erected Liverpool Museum and equally interested in everything connected with it.

It seems therefore safe to conclude that Mayer had never seen this Agreement and had no knowledge of its existence. Whatever he received from Lord Cross, this document was not included and when Gatty wrote many years later, it was produced by the merest chance for the first time. Lord Cross had no idea of its importance and his interest was even less;[3] yet it it not too much to say that an earlier knowledge of the existence of this Agreement would have prevented some of the confusion with which the subject of Liverpool porcelain has too long been surrounded.[4]

Brief mention has already been made of Teppit's letters which are of great value for the information they give about Chaffers' soaprock supplies and it is unnecessary to refer to them again. Long before Mayer died, he had presented to Liverpool Corporation the valuable collections of antiquities forming the Mayer Museum. These, which included his extensive collection of Liverpool pottery and porcelain were housed in the new Museum buildings which had been built on the site of the old potworks on Shaw's Brow. Charles T. Gatty (1851–1928) was the Curator of the collection from 1873 to 1884 and it is to him, probably more than to Mayer himself, that we owe the foundations of our knowledge of the old Liverpool potteries. Gatty was undoubtedly the first to

[1]*M. & M.*, 1874 edition, pages 733, 734, 735; and Appendix III B.

[2]It is interesting to note how the shadow of Josiah Wedgwood still hung over the subject of Liverpool pottery, even at this date, sixty years after his death, so great had been his interests in it and his influence. In fact, of course, at the date of the events spoken of, Wedgwood was of no importance.

[3]It will be appreciated that he was 84 years of age at the time.

[4]Even so, it could have been published in 1907–8. Why publication did not take place immediately the document was discovered is a question to which it is difficult to find an answer.

make a systematic study of the records. He published the result of his re-searches under the title *The Liverpool Potteries* in 1882. It deals chiefly with the potteries, as the title indicates, with but scant information of the potters themselves, but it still forms the basis of our knowledge on this matter and has been drawn upon freely by every writer upon the subject since. In addition, it contains a complete list of all the pieces originally comprising Mayer's gift, with notes of the manner in which they came into his possession, in the case of those of documentary importance. In some cases, this information is of the utmost value when we recall that the greater part of the collection was lost by enemy action during the 1939–45 war.

Although Gatty's curatorship ended in 1884, his interest in Liverpool ceramics was maintained, witness the correspondence with Peter Entwistle, the Assistant Curator and his efforts which resulted in unearthing the Agree-ment. One might add that but for him, we should never have known of John Rosson's letter. Peter Entwistle (1866–1939) continued the work at the Museum after Gatty left. He was an indefatigable worker and amassed a prodigious amount of information concerning the old Liverpool potworks, the potters and their families, realizing as do most students of the subject that Liverpool ceramics are one and indivisible and that to understand and appreciate one class of ware, a working knowledge of all is necessary. He seems to have had in mind the publication of a book dealing with the subject in this comprehensive way. It was an ambitious project and to marshal the vast amount of material he had collected and reduce it to the semblance of an orderly perspective may have proved too great a task. Whatever the reason, the long awaited and much needed authoritative account of Entwistle's accumulated knowledge did not appear and it was not until some time after his death that many of his papers and records came into the possession of the Corporation of Liverpool's Picton Library, where they are now available for reference. Most of the biographical data given here have been taken from this source, through the courtesy of the authorities concerned, as also have many of the contemporary references from local newspapers. For some of the latter, however, I am indebted to the late Francis Buckley, another ardent worker in this field who contributed much to our knowledge of this subject.

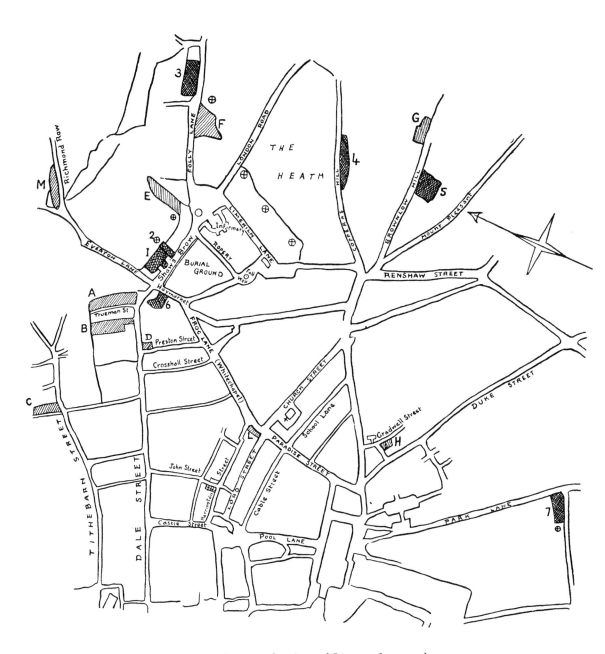

Map showing the sites of Liverpool potworks

MAP SHOWING THE SITES OF LIVERPOOL POTWORKS

From a Plan of Liverpool, dated by Sir James Picton at about 1760. It was among the Mayer MSS. and is now in the Picton Library, Liverpool. The marking of the sites is regarded by Gatty as contemporary, (*Liverpool Potteries*, C. T. Gatty, page 13). That of William Ball, in Ranelagh Street, is not shown; and I have omitted the Duke Street potworks and the Flint potworks (both earthenware), in order to save space.

An encircled cross denotes the site of a mill.

KEY: *China makers.*

1   Richard Chaffers, before 1755. Chaffers & Co., 1755–65.
      Philip Christian & Co. followed by Philip Christian & Son, 1765–75.
      Pennington & Part, 1776?–1799?
      Pennington & Edwards, 1799?–1805 or 1806.

2   Samuel Gilbody, 1756–61.

3   John Pennington, 1779–84.
      Jane Pennington. Probably also James Pennington and nephew John, 1786–96.

4   James and John Pennington, 1771–9.

5   Reid & Co., 1756–61.

6   Z. Barnes and J. Cotter, 1783–9. Z. Barnes, 1789–1800?

7   James Pennington, 1767–71. 1796–1801 (in Folly Lane, Islington).

Earthenware makers.

A   Thomas Shaw.

B   Unknown.

C   John Dunbibin. Thomas Deare & Co.

D   Richard Hillary & Co.

E   Philip Christian (reputedly).

F   Woods & Co. Jonas Bold & Co. Jonas Bold & Edward Chaffers.

G   Joseph Brooks.

H   James Bridge.

L   Josiah Poole (the Lord Street pottery). Later, Green & Thyer.

M   Livesley's Mug Works.

The Duke Street pottery stood on land whereon is now the North end of the Cathedral — 'Mr George Drinkwater's Mill on Mount Sion'. The Flint pottery (Mug Works), Okill & Co., was at the corner of Flint Street and Parliament Street. Another pottery, also not shown on this plan, adjoined Gilbody's on Shaw's Brow to the east of it. It was occupied by James Shaw and later by Roscoe & Rigby. The site of Sadler & Green's premises in Harrington Street is unmarked on the plan, numbers 14 and 15 being on the west side of John Street and number 16 on the east side of John Street. Excluding the last mentioned, the total number of sites amounts to twenty, of which eight were concerned with china-making during some part of their occupation.

CHAPTER THREE

THE WARE

THE QUESTION 'How can I tell Liverpool china?' is frequently asked. The answer is complicated by the fact, already mentioned, that there were ten separate manufactures in being over a period of half a century, as a result of which it is not possible to regard Liverpool china as an entity in quite the same way that we regard the products of other English factories. This must make for variety; indeed, in such circumstances it might be expected that the diversity of wares would be so great that no clear-cut picture of what should be regarded as typical Liverpool ware could emerge.

To a limited extent only is that true and, as in similar cases, the difficulty disappears on closer acquaintance, for influences were constantly at work tending to unify the wares. Attention has already been drawn to the earthenware background in which the Liverpool china-makers grew up and worked. As a unifying influence this must deserve a prominent place, for it runs through Liverpool china as a thread through fabric.

Next perhaps in order of importance is the fact the the potting community itself was compact and concentrated chiefly in the Shaw's Brow area and the adjacent district. Rarely can there have been fewer than three makers of china in production at any given time, a fact which alone would make for easy exchanges of labour and therefore of ideas and methods.[1] Local redistribution of labour was also constantly occurring from other causes, among which financial failure, as elsewhere in the industry, must unfortunately rank high. In Liverpool, owing to the size of the industry, the need for migration when this took place would be less pressing than in many other centres, while the accompanying local sales of plant and half-finished ware would add its quota to the general unifying effect. Lastly, of course, the outside potpainter put his stock patterns on everything. It is clear, therefore, that while there was scope for variety, there was likely to be enough underlying unity to establish a strong family relationship among Liverpool wares, a unity

[1]A possible exception to this may have been between 1761 and 1764, after the failures of Gilbody and of Reid & Co. in 1761. William Ball's name is in Gore for 1766 as a china maker, which means that he was in production in 1765, but how much earlier is uncertain. (*Gore's Liverpool Directory*, first issue in 1766.)

which may be observed to extend throughout the whole period of manufacture.

The effect of this would have been greater but for the sudden appearance on the developing scene of Podmore's 'alien culture', which quickly began to exert its influence, literally and very materially, on 'the shape of things to come'. Essentially this owned an Oriental origin. What Podmore brought to Liverpool in 1755 was an interpretation of Oriental ideas in potting and decoration as these had developed at Redcliff Backs and later at Worcester. There is reason to believe that, as time passed, the Liverpool potters drew inspiration more directly from the Orient, for when we come to consider the subject of decoration, we shall find many oriental designs which have no Worcester counterpart.[1] But it is convenient to refer to the 'early Worcester' ideas in potting and decoration which now began to show themselves, resulting in two types of ware, the one a product of local conditions, with its roots deeply in the soil; the other an importation giving rise to wares of early Worcester type and to wares blended of the two influences.

Porcelain of the first type was obviously made by the Liverpool potters outside the Chaffers combine — and by the combine itself if the supply of soaprock fell short or for other reasons unknown to us. Such ware may reasonably be regarded as non-steatitic, for Chaffers alone had a supply of this material.[2] But the dominance of the combine, and, particularly perhaps, the evidence afforded by the amount of soaprock used during these early years under Podmore's management, indicate that 'Podmorising' influences could make themselves easily felt, as undoubtedly they did. The result is that much early Liverpool porcelain has an early Worcester look and is frequently mistaken for the production of that factory, for Podmore was a true potter-artist and could only work in one way, producing at Liverpool what he had previously done at Bristol and Worcester.

The effect of this was increased by the undoubted fact that, over a considerable period of time, standard Worcester wares were deliberately copied. There is possibly an interesting reference to the part played by the Liverpool potters in this form of piracy, which is contained in a paragraph in the *Oxford Journal* for 1763, to which Mr George Savage drew my attention. This refers to 'A great abuse of it is the selling of other far inferior kinds of ware

[1]Liverpool's position as a seaport town would facilitate the import of Oriental ideas.
[2]The history of soaprock 'licences' supports the view that supplies of this mineral were very difficult to obtain. Holdship had to pay £1,400 for Lund's lease in 1752 (Toppin, Trans. E.C.C., volume 3, page 132), Christian obtained £500 for the remainder of his lease in 1775; and when Turner of Caughley tried to get a supply, he had to wait five years. Chaffers certainly made a non-steatitic porcelain, for analysis of a 'lady and parrot' mug showed that it is phosphatic, with a complete absence of steatite. Full analysis of a representative cross-section of early wares would provide the only satisfactory evidence on this point.

for Worcester'. The reference here might be to Lowestoft, which at this date was turning out much 'blue-and-white' ware, pirating Worcester patterns and copying its marks. The difference between Liverpool and Lowestoft practice in this matter would seem to be that, whereas the Lowestoft potters chiefly copied the crescent mark, at Liverpool the emphasis is on the pattern, and the use of Worcester marks, apart from painters' marks, was rarely adopted.

The impact of Podmore and his imported ideas on this earthenware-minded community did not last. The old ideas had never been entirely displaced; and with the death of Chaffers in 1765, possibly earlier, the old potting tradition re-asserted itself with the development of a type of ware under Philip Christian and the brothers Pennington which in time came to be regarded as representative of Liverpool china.[1] The conception which thus arose was later enlarged to admit two or three distinctive classes of ware which tradition had long associated with Chaffers' name; and in this way the gap in our knowledge implied by the question 'How can I tell Liverpool china?' was thought to have been filled.

It had, however, been filled in a way that left neither room nor need for other ideas on the subject, with the result that much early ware, dissimilar in appearance and frequently showing strong kinship with Worcester almost inevitably came to be excluded. This exclusion, moreover, took no account of the large amount of soaprock which had been imported by Chaffers between 1756 and the date of his death in 1765. This seems to have been something between twenty and thirty tons a year, sufficient to make a large quantity of porcelain.[2] Nor does it explain what Podmore was doing during all those years he was under contract 'to use his utmost care diligence skill knowledge and judgment in the making painting and complete finishing of the said earthenware, etc.,' in precisely the manner he had so successfully employed at Worcester and which his new associates, Chaffers and Christian, were so anxious he should continue to employ at Liverpool.

These are facts and no explanation which does not take them into account can be regarded as satisfactory. While the difficulty may be obvious, it is not easily overcome. There may be none in distinguishing between something made by Podmore at Bristol in 1750 and at Liverpool in 1765, but it is likely to be otherwise when we attempt to differentiate between wares which, because of similar composition, style of potting and decoration might equally well have been made at either place about the date of his migration to Liverpool. There is no doubt that intensive study of a large number of 'Podmore' pieces by modern methods will do much to clear up some of the

---

[1] The paper by Rackham (Trans. E.P.C., 1929, page 27) for many years the only good description of Liverpool china, is confined to a description of this type and no piece is discussed or illustrated to which a pre-1765 date can confidently be given.

[2] Appendix III B (2), where Teppit's letters are discussed.

confusion which at present exists. Here we should expect help from the fact that the development of the art of transfer printing as a method of decoration came into common use about this time. Employed at Battersea (on enamels) between 1753 and 1756 and possibly also at Bow, on porcelain, towards the end of this period, there is no evidence worth the name that decoration in this manner was used either at Worcester or at Liverpool before 1757, the date which modern research gives to Hancock's arrival at Worcester. It is therefore clear that in the matter we are pursuing, the year 1755, in which Podmore went to Liverpool, is critical; and that a *prima facie* case exists for stating that print-decorated ware of this type must, *ipso facto*, acquire Liverpool provenance.

The matter will be referred to again in discussing the 'scratch-cross' group and its 'Bristol-Worcester' associations. Here it may be said that in addition to any help afforded by the introduction of ceramic printing, a new Worcester 'body' was introduced about the same time. If we accept the analysis of the dated (1757) King of Prussia mug as representing the new standard in these matters,[1] an almost complete absence of lead, coupled with an increase in the soaprock content to fifty per cent are the principal changes. These may, perhaps, be correlated with W. B. Honey's statement that the decade beginning about 1755 shows a fully developed Worcester style in being, thereby implying that change had already taken place.[2]

It is probable that, having gone to trouble and expense in order to make improvements in the ware, the older type of body was abandoned, as happened elsewhere in similar circumstances; and consequently when we find ware of this type for which the decoration requires a later date, it is more likely to have been made at Liverpool than at Worcester. In saying this, due allowance will be made for the later decoration of undecorated stock on hand. Such an explanation is never entirely satisfactory and becomes less so the longer the period of time covered and the greater the number of pieces involved. It is possible also that old forms of decoration continued in use after Podmore's departure and we can only guess the extent to which this event brought about or coincided with the introduction of new ideas. Opinion on this point will vary with our estimate of his importance, but whatever may be the final judgment on this very complicated and interesting problem, it is probable that we shall be forced to recognize a marginal period of time during which attributions denoting locality will always be in doubt and may well prove impossible. 'A Podmore production' will be as far as we can get. Whether this is of much moment will depend on viewpoint, though it may be suspected that, where ceramics are concerned, 'the rose that smells as sweet' is less frequently met with than it should be.

[1]Hobson, *Worcester Porcelain*, page 104.   [2]Honey, *Old English Porcelain* 1946, page 169.

It is convenient to look upon Liverpool porcelain as falling into three periods. The first, lasting ten years from 1755, was dominated by Chaffers and ended with his death in 1765. It is the period of Worcester influence. The second, which lasted from 1765 to 1780, owed its greatness to the genius of Philip Christian and the two elder Pennington brothers, James and John. It witnessed the re-establishment of native Liverpool influences in potting and decoration. The third period, from 1780 to 1805, although marked by the work of Seth Pennington, the youngest member of this family and one of Liverpool's greatest potters, is the period of decline. These dates are approximate and the divisions arbitrary and of doubtful value. If the industry be considered as a whole, decline had certainly set in long before 1780.

In considering the wares of the first period, it will assist a proper understanding of the subject if the potting characteristics which own a purely Liverpool origin and those which, in common with Worcester, derive from the Orient, are dealt with separately, as far as possible.

Speaking generally, the wares of this period are well potted and proportioned, neatly finished and make use of simple forms without elaboration. Probably the most striking feature about all the wares dating from this time is their grey colour, frequently modified to greyish-green or greyish-blue in classes where a Liverpool 'native' background is present. Almost equally noticeable is the poor translucency of many of the specimens examined, seemingly irrespective of whether presumably of soaprock or phosphatic composition. On the other hand, thinly potted ware of almost eggshell quality was made, notably certain cups and saucers with everted rims, which will receive mention and which are close copies of the oriental.

Apart from noting varying degrees of opacity, valuable information can be obtained by the use of transmitted light, and although, for reasons which will appear shortly, the interpretation of the results may be difficult, it is an examination which should not be omitted. Many Liverpool wares of this period, probably the majority, exhibit a green or yellowish-green translucency, but in a considerable number a bluish-green or even a pure blue colour will be seen. This is not confined to any particular type or group. It might be explained by an absence of iron impurity in the materials used. Soaprock generally contains traces of iron, making it possible that these blue wares are non-steatitic.[1] If subsequent analysis confirms this, we may have here a valuable aid in making attributions. On the other hand, some samples of soaprock may contain no such impurity; and this might be held accountable for (1), the fact that every now and then one comes across a blue translucency

[1]The assumption here being that traces of iron cause a brownish translucency, changed to green by the addition of a blue salt of cobalt. In that case, any iron-containing clay would react in this way. Other possibilities cannot be ruled out.

in a piece with good early Worcester characteristics; and (2), even more rarely, the two components of a piece (e.g. teapot and cover), which show no signs of having been 'married', may show a contrasting translucency.

In the latter case, it might be thought that the use of different clays, steatitic or otherwise, must be held accountable. But there is evidence to show that, in the case of kaolinic clays, firing temperatures can affect colour by transmitted light considerably and this may apply to steatite. The matter clearly bristles with difficulty, and deductions if considered warranted, should be made with caution. From the examination of a limited number of pieces, it is permissible to state that for every acceptable Worcester example showing a blue translucency, it should not be difficult to find a dozen which are equally acceptable as Liverpool. In such circumstances, this feature may be regarded as presumptive evidence of a Liverpool attribution. It is perhaps unnecessary to add that a green colour is not proof of a soaprock body.[1]

In addition to relative opacity and colour effects, the use of transmitted light is of great value in revealing flaws in the paste. These are well known in the wares of (red anchor) Chelsea and Longton Hall, in both of which they occur in the form of 'moons'. No Liverpool wares that I have examined exhibit this feature, but many of early date do exhibit flaws which appear as lightish flecks in the paste, small in size and sometimes resembling comma marks.[2] In some cases they will be seen to correspond with surface irregularities (usually small depressions), but frequently no other defect is observable. Both 'native' wares and their more Worcester looking cognates may be affected in this way, but in wares of undoubted Worcester provenance their occurence is infrequent. Such defects may therefore also be considered to possess limited attributional value.

Regarding the general appearance of a piece, it is worth noting that while primarily this must be a glaze effect, the body of much of this early ware will be seen to have a grey look when broken or where unglazed surfaces present themselves for examination.

FIRST PERIOD
NATIVE LIVERPOOL CHARACTERISTICS

The glaze is thin, bluish-green and even. The thick starch-blue glaze which tends to collect in pools near footrings does not belong to this period.

[1] It is observable in much Longton Hall and early Derby ware, in neither of which has the presence of steatite been proved. The Swansea 'sodden snow' body contains steatite, whereas the 'duck-egg' body does not.

[2] Unlike 'moons', these appearances are due to tears in the paste. They are also a feature of some Longton Hall wares, as Dr Bernard Watney has shown, but in these they tend to be more linear, differing from the flecks of Liverpool wares.

Imperfections occur, noticeably a minute pin pitting which frequently has a very patchy distribution, but which causes little disfigurement unless blackening is also present. It is really quite remarkable how this defect — as may also be said about the blackening that so closely resembles smudgy finger marks — is so often confined to areas, such as bases or the insides of vessels, where the disfigurement is of little consequence and passes unnoticed. Areas completely devoid of glaze are sometimes seen. While these are generally within the footring, they may rarely occur elsewhere. Glaze shrinkage on the insides of footrings may or may not be present. It would probably be correct to say that, while the absence of this feature is the rule and is therefore of some assistance in distinguishing Worcester wares, in which, as is well known, it is commonly present, too much reliance should not be placed on it, unless blistering and other glazing effects are also visible. Among these, the 'peppering' caused by black specks and 'sanding' should be noted. The presence of a dry edge or 'scum line' is a feature of later date.

In proceeding to speak of potting characteristics in detail, the following may be noted among 'native' Liverpool features.

Handles may be of plain strap form, with the lower end back-turned and indented by upward pressure of the potter's thumb. As far as I know, this is peculiar to Liverpool.[1] In this form, both a thumb rest and grooving are absent. It is found thus on large jugs of baluster shape (Plate 1 (d)), on many coffee pots (Plate 4 (a, b)), and on some mugs, generally of large size (Plate 8 (f) and Plate 37 (a)). The scrolled handle with thumb rest is also met with in its simpler forms and is well seen on mugs of 'lady and parrot' type (Plate 8 (d, e)), but the more elaborate forms of this handle with its dependent tag (Plate 10 (a)) belong mainly to a later period. The plain round loop is found on small pieces such as coffee cups (Plate 23 (h, i)), and coffee cans (Plate 8 (c)), indeed, on the latter it is probably the commonest finding, but the grooved loop also occurs (shallow groove), (Plates 3 (i) and 7 (d)), as does the handle with D-shaped cross section (Plate 24 (h)) which is sometimes found with a mask decoration of its lower back-turned end. Both grooved and ungrooved handles may be found with an appearance, well shown in Plates 3 (i) and 25 (c), which is best described as U-shaped, the upper and lower limbs being nearly straight and parallel. This appears to be peculiar to Liverpool. The lateral grooving of handles is also observable on many Liverpool pieces, but less characteristic, as may also be said of an overlapping scale moulding which may sometimes be seen between the thumb-rest and body junction (Plate 20 (a)). Occasionally the back-turned lower end is pinched after the manner of the saltglaze potter.

[1] And probably confined to Chaffers' wares on which it is a very common finding.

The type of handle sometimes referred to as 'double-scrolled' is of considerable interest. It is found on mugs, either cylindrical or of inverted bell shape, the latter exhibiting the type of foot with Scotia moulding, shortly to be discussed and has been claimed both for Liverpool and Longton Hall. A similar type of handle, but without lateral grooving, is found on those heavily potted cylindrical mugs with a weak moulded decoration which have long been regarded as of Longton Hall make; and this may have contributed to the view that all mugs possessing this type of handle should be attributed to Longton Hall. While it is true that one occasionally comes across an example which does not lend itself to being classed as a product of either factory, the 'Longton view' received considerable support when it was discovered that a very typical example which happened to be decorated with a Sadler-signed print of that almost exclusively Liverpool institution, the 'Society of Bucks', contained no less than eight per cent of lead.[1]

This rather staggering fact nevertheless failed to shake the convictions of many knowledgeable Liverpool collectors in favour of a Liverpool origin for, at least, the printed mugs of this type.[2] They pointed out that, not only is the decoration of many very frequently a Sadler-signed print, but that in some cases the subject of the print itself demanded a date well after the Longton factory had ceased production. The difficulties raised in this way are not lessened by having to explain why Sadler should have taken the trouble and risk of buying from a distance what could have been bought more easily almost on his own door step;[3] and that he should do this at a time when local bankrupt stocks would be imminently available. It now seems likely that new light on this interesting subject will result from Dr Bernard Watney's recent finds on the site of the Longton Hall factory and judgment should be suspended until the evidence from this source has received due consideration.

Bases frequently yield valuable information about the provenance of a piece and therefore collectors pay great attention to an examination of these areas. It is hereabouts that one is most likely to find those little peculiarities, possibly inherent in the methods employed, which the potter, in his desire to produce an article in the popular taste, has disregarded as of no consequence. Foremost among these in importance is the undercut footring which is found on cups, saucers and bowls of every size. The external appearance of the piece which accompanies this feature is frequently characteristic enough to suggest its presence, for the footring may be seen to slope markedly inwards, having a slightly convex profile and making a very weak angle with the belly of the piece (Plate 11 (c), 19 (e)). Viewed from below, its inner face will

[1]*Analysed Specimens*, Eccles & Rackham, No. 9.
[2]Entwistle frequently referred to the handle as the 'Liverpool handle', (Ent. MSS.).
[3]See letter, Appendix IV A (24).

31

show varying degrees of undercutting from (and including) a vertical meeting with the base-line (Plates 34 (*e*), 50 (*b*)).

The type of base borne by mugs will be governed to a large extent by mug shape, which exists in considerable variety. The cylindrical mug of 'native' type may have a flat unglazed base (Plates 2 (*a*), 40 (*c*)). This is frequently spoken of as if it were found nowhere else (it is found on Longton Hall mugs) and even as if it were an indispensable feature for a Liverpool attribution. It is certainly a common finding on small mugs of the kind usually referred to as coffee cans, but less so on larger cylinders. A feature which I have not seen recorded is the chamfer at the junction of mug side with base on Chaffers' mugs of this type. It seems to be peculiar to that factory (Plates 8 (*c*), 2 (*b*), the latter showing it). Cylinders with wide footring and very shallow[1] counter, sinking occur, but these are probably of rather later date (1770 and later-Plate 21 (*d*)), in addition to the many with countersunk bases on the Worcester model. Of these, three are featured, viz: Plates 13 (*d*), 25 (*d*), 9 (*b*), the base of the last named being seen on Plate 50 (*c*).

Of all mugs, that which is most characteristically Liverpool is shaped like an inverted bell and usually provided with a 'Scotia' moulded foot.[2] This foot is typical of Chaffers' mugs of 'lady and parrot' type (Plate 8 (*d*)) and is seen in a modified form on the saltglazed 'Plumper' mug. In mugs of this type, the weight bearing surface of the footring is narrow and devoid of glaze, its inner edge falling abruptly at right angles to the base.

Plates 24 (*g*) and 24 (*h*) show another variety of the bell mug. Both have a deeply grooved foot and a recessed base which in this case is reached by a long sloping bevel. The bevel is a common feature of Liverpool bases and may be seen on mugs and jugs, coffee pots and vases, as indeed it may on much ware of other factories and therefore possesses no marked attributional value. This class of mugs is interesting and has already received notice in connection with its handles. It appears to be related to the 'scratch cross' group (*q.v.*).[3]

Many jugs are flat based, notably the baluster-shaped jug with its open splayed lip and absence of footring (Plate 2 (*c, d*)). In its early form, both lip and handle were perfectly plain, moulding in the form of foliate scrolls on the lip and elaborate scrolling of the handle being developments which belong to the close of the period we are now considering (Plates 10 (*a*), 39 (*e*)). A masked lip is more rarely present (Plate 41 (*a*)). Jugs of this type are among the most typical Liverpool productions. Easy to keep clean, pouring well

[1]The footring may be nearly an inch wide and the depth of countersinking no more than one sixteenth.
[2]The concave element in the moulding at the base of an Ionic column.
[3]The bases of these mugs and their marking are shown on Plate 50 (*k, l*).

32

and eminently practical, they long remained in favour, with versions in creamware by Wedgwood and the Staffordshire potters appearing later in the century.

While most of the smaller jugs (cream jugs) follow the pattern favoured by popular taste and turned out with little variation by nearly every factory in the country (pinched lip, wedge footring and grooved loop handle (Plate 23 (*d*, *e*)), we sometimes find these jugs with a grooved foot and flattened footring (Plates 6 (*k*), 26 (*e*)) in a manner recalling many 'scratch-cross' pieces.

Teapots exhibiting 'native' Liverpool characters are found in some variety, apart from those of ordinary globular shape which differ but little from those of many contemporary factories (Plates 19 (*d*), 22 (*a*)). Best known, perhaps, of the earlier types has a rather flattened body with fairly wide-spaced vertical reeding (Plate 21 (*a*, *b*)). Another form of globular teapot having an ear-shaped handle and possibly of Chaffers' make, is shown on Plate 22 (*f*), while yet another, more credibly from this factory because it belongs to the 'lady and parrot' group, is illustrated on Plate 26 (*d*). The teapots with palm tree mouldings belong more to the middle period and will receive mention later.

Teapot handles may be perfectly round in section, or ribbed and spouts also are sometimes found ribbed or faceted in an earthenware manner. The earthenware influence is shown to an unusual degree in the example furnished with crabstock handle and spout (Plate 17 (*b*)) and may be seen in yet another in the Victoria and Albert Museum (*C.1069/1924*) which has a round tapered loop handle with back-turned lower end and, curiously enough, an interior which is completely unglazed.

The early coffee pots compare favourably with those of any factory in combining good proportions with simplicity of design. Of pear shape, quite plain and devoid of all moulding, they are furnished with a strap handle, a rather curving spout, a grooved foot of characteristic shape and a recessed base which is reached by a short bevel (Plate 4 (*a*)). A deeply grooved handle, as in the example shown on Plate 31 (*a*) is sometimes present.

The covers of both tea and coffee pots resemble one another and present similar lines of development. At first flattened, as in the examples just noted, they tend to become deeper (Plates 4 (*b*), 20 (*a*)), until the high domed appearance so characteristic of later wares is reached. The cover knop broadly follows one of three patterns — turreted (Plate 21 (*f*)), conical (Plate 15 (*b*)), and mushroom-shaped with a projecting apex (Plate 15 (*a*)). A flat button is sometimes found (Plate 31 (*b*)), and, more rarely, the Worcester flower bud (Plate 21 (*a*)). The under side of the cover flange is glazed.

Many sauce boats which can be dated about the end of this period are attractively moulded in silver shape. Their open shape would doubtless make mould making easy, though whether on this account the cutting of a block was dispensed with is doubtful. This does not seem to have happened among the Staffordshire potters, for many blocks which correspond with saltglazed sauce boats can be seen at Messrs Wedgwood's Barlaston works. Yet at Liverpool, it seems possible that at times the actual silver article may have been used vicariously as a block, since a china cream jug is known to exist on which the silver marks are plainly visible (type Plate 21 (c)).[1] Whatever the method adopted, it is to be observed that sauce boats of this type, with their saltglazed counterparts, do not illustrate what has been referred to as 'earthenware influence'. They represent nothing specifically which is Liverpool property, but rather a method which was at the service of any factory wishing to employ it. These sauce boats are among the most charming examples of Liverpool china it is possible to meet. Moulded in relief with scrolls and sometimes with basket pattern sides, they are furnished with a wavy rim, projecting lip, scrolled handle and a flat base from which rises a graceful moulding of acanthus leaves. The base of these boats generally shows a patchy thin glazing most probably the result of volatilization (Plates 5 (e), 12 (d)). In most cases, the pleasing effect is enhanced by painted decoration.

That curiosity, tin glazed porcelain, may here receive brief notice. Pieces of this character are occasionally met with, painted in a pale smudgy blue — Mr Allman of Bootle had a cream jug of this type. Entwistle unearthed fragments of a plate, apparently similar, during excavations carried out on a pottery site (Plate VII), and there is no difficulty in accepting these as of Liverpool manufacture. Tin enamelled plates, of Chien Lung shape and painted in famille rose manner are also occasionally seen (Plate 42 (b)) and should, perhaps, be accepted with reserve. The shape, it is true, was much favoured by the Liverpool potters, but the decoration here follows the oriental mode too closely and does not suggest the delft painter's hand as one would have a right to expect.[2] Speaking generally, plates which can confidently be allotted to the early years of manufacture are uncommon and mostly exhibit oriental features in potting and decoration (Plates 3 (g), 31 (a)).

FIRST PERIOD
ORIENTAL AND WORCESTER CHARACTERISTICS

Among these, which may be contrasted with the foregoing, the following may be mentioned. The ribbed handle of many mugs, whether of cylindrical

[1] In the collection of Dr Statham of Bournemouth. The jug is referred to again in connection with its 'biting snake' handle. One very similar in shape is illustrated in the catalogue of Queen Charlotte's loan Exhibition of Old Silver, 1929, Plate LX, No. 622, strangely enough dated 1734.

[2] These are generally accepted as 'Liverpool' (Catalogue E.C.C. Exhibition, 1948, No. 497), but the possibility that they are of French make cannot entirely be ruled out.

or inverted bell shape (Plate 9 (*b*)) and the narrow-grooved loop handle, with which small mugs and coffee cups are frequently provided (Plate 32 (*k*)); the peaked form of scrolled handle which is sometimes found on small jugs and on bell-shaped coffee cups (Plate 3 (*c*)); the slight eversion of the rims of teabowls, coffee cups and saucers (Plate 3 (*a*, *e*)) and the somewhat squarish look of many of these same coffee cups. (Plate 32 (*g*, *k*)); the recessed bases of many cylindrical mugs (Plate 25 (*d*), 50 (*f*)); the rather weak and sometimes insignificant footrings of cups, saucers and teapots, some of which may be so poorly developed that they are hardly more than a beading (Plate 24 (*d*)); the depressed globular shape of many teapots of small size (Plates 6 (*j*), 21 (*f*)) some of which carry a particularly characteristic type of footring (Plate 16 (*b*)) many moulded patterns (Plate 3 (*a*, *b*, *c*)); and polygonal shapes (Plates 3 (*j*), 7 (*b*)).

Concerning many of the foregoing, it is clearly impossible to say whether they derive directly from oriental prototypes or arrived via Worcester. One must take into account the fact that Podmore's previous connection with that newcomer in the potting industry must have rendered easier the influx of ideas from that quarter. On the other hand, it must be remembered that in those days, as today, fashions determined sales and every potter copied the successful 'lines' of his competitors. It follows that some of the features just mentioned were common to other factories and would, in any case, have been adopted by the Liverpool potters. Their actual source matters but little. It is important, however, to remember that they are shared with Worcester, producing difficulties in this case which arise from similarities in paste and glaze and which are peculiar to that circumstance.

In dealing with these features separately, the ribbed loop handle so frequently seen on Worcester mugs of all types is a commoner finding on Liverpool mugs than is generally supposed, a fact which should be borne in mind when making attributions. In the specimen shown on Plate 13 (*d*) the ribbing fails to meet the point of handle attachment at the upper end. On teapots, a ribbed handle is almost as common as on Worcester examples.

The grooved loop handle on small mugs and coffee cups had a fairly wide use. The groove is frequently shallow, indeed, it may be so ill-defined as to be scarcely noticeable, particularly where an early date may be suspected (see Plate 3 (*i*), 32 (*k*) and compare with the grooving of similar handles on any Worcester cup). The singly fluted handle found on some Worcester mugs has no Liverpool counterpart except on a few examples of the 'scratch-cross' group (Plate 24 (*b*, *c*)).

No appreciable variation seems to exist in the peaked form of scroll handle and here, distinction between the products of the two manufactures must be sought elsewhere. In the case of the specimen featured on Plate 3 (*c*) this is not difficult, for it is of a pronounced blue-grey colour, shows a completely blue translucency and exhibits no glaze shrinkage; while the cream jug with this type of handle (Plate 32 (*f*)), apart from the nature of its printed decoration, includes among its un-Worcesterish potting features a large area on the neck devoid of glaze, other glazing defects, no shrinkage and a blue-green rather than a yellow-green translucency. Jugs of this type probably derive directly from silver shape. An interesting example, Liverpool printed, in which both the cut of the rim and the shape of the handle are unusual, may be seen on Plate 39 (*b*).[1]

Eversion of the rims of cups and saucers is one of the most important features of oriental origin which much early Liverpool ware shares with Worcester. It is associated with good potting, generally on thin translucent wares furnished with poorly developed footrings. In cups and saucers of this type (Plates 5 (*a*), 7 (*a*)), the efforts of our potters made a near approach to their exemplars, perhaps as good as any attained. Occasionally we find eversion of this type associated with a Liverpool footring showing undercutting which may be most marked (Plate 34 (*e*), (*f*)), or less so, as in the example shown on Plate 3 (*f*) which is blue painted and furnished with a well-known Liverpool border. Even saltglaze may exhibit the feature, which is perhaps surprising, but it can be seen on the bowl illustrated on Plate 18 (*d*) in connection with the subject of saltglaze decoration on Liverpool porcelain (*q.v.*). Teaware continued to be made in this way during the greater part of the period under discussion. I have seen one such cup and saucer dated 1764 and while this date does not necessarily coincide with that of manufacture, there is no doubt it was contemporary and an indication that, in Liverpool, the style prevailed well into the seventh decade of the century.

What may be regarded as a modification of the weak footring just spoken of is found on a certain class of Liverpool teaware. It is distinctive and therefore possesses attributional value. In this form, the appearances are those of a smallish footring, having a slightly convex profile. Viewed from beneath, this impression is seen to be false, for the footring then appears as little more than a beading of about one third the outside depth — or even less. The result is a very shallow — and often concave — depressed base (Plates 6 (*j*), 16 (*b*), 21 (*f*)).

Plate 50 (*a*) shows the base of such a teapot and that of a coffee cup from the same service. Other coffee cups of identical potting, all furnished with flat ungrooved strap handles, are shown on Plate 6 (*a*, *b*, *d*). This ware is characteristically Liverpool in many other respects[2] and its recognition

[1] Pure blue translucency.
[2] Grey colour, very poor translucency, no glaze shrinkage, flat and ungrooved strap handles, teapots with glazed cover flange and more than five holes in spout.

36

as a class is of importance in that it enables a whole group of pieces to be separated from Worcester wares which it superficially resembles and with which it has frequently been confused.

It is perhaps unnecessary to say that the shape exhibited by teapots of this group, generally referred to as 'depressed globular', is not peculiar to any factory. It was in common use at Worcester during the early years and many Liverpool examples are illustrated in these pages. One such from the de Winton collection (Plate 13 (c)), having a shallow depressed base, no glaze shrinkage, but with complete glazing of the cover flange, is of particular interest because of its mark — an incised saltire cross.[1] The decoration here gives good Liverpool support; and while the mark does not put it in the 'scratch-cross' group, to which clearly it does not belong, it provides an interesting link between this group and certain contemporary Liverpool wares.

One of the most interesting sub-groups of these 'depressed globular' teapots is characterized by a hump on the handle just above the point of its upper attachment. The late Arthur Hurst drew attention to this and pointed out that teapots of this type possessed certain other non-Worcester features, notably a beaded form of footring and more than five holes for the spout. He noted that, while the form taken by the cover knop was not constant, in some instances it was of a type not found on Worcester wares; and he could have added that the cover flange is almost invariably glazed underneath and that the spout has a somewhat unusually bulbous base. While the actual shape of teapots may not be of greater importance than that of mugs in determining provenance, it is, on the face of it, unlikely that a unit factory, such as Worcester at this date undoubtedly was, would be turning out simultaneously wares showing no uniformity in potting technique. Attributional values are largely based on the fact that this did not occur. Hurst advances reasons for thinking that this group may be attributable to Liverpool.[2] This, however, presents difficulties to which at present no satisfactory answer can be given and there the matter must be allowed to rest.

Fluted teapots of the type illustrated on Plate 6 (c) and Plate 10 (b) present unusual interest. Until recently always looked upon as Worcester, with the strong backing provided by a certain number of specimens which appear typical of that factory, even to the presence of the seal mark (Schr. I.520), there are good reasons for thinking that some should be regarded as of Liverpool make. In these, the ranking criteria are, greyish cast, bluish-green translucency, peppering and blistering of the glaze, no glaze shrinkage, glazing of the under surface of the cover flange and more than five holes for

[1]Referred to again under decoration.   [2]Trans. E.C.C., 1937, No. 4, page 42.

the spout. The combination of these, or of a majority of them, with saltglaze decoration, as in the example shown on Plate 10 (*b*) should be sufficient to exclude the claims of Worcester, assisted by the fact that this design, the 'beckoning Chinaman', already referred to, appears in the same form and painted by the same hand on that most egregiously Liverpool article, the tall coffee pot with scrolled 'tag' handle and moulded spout (type Plate 20 (*a*)).[1]

Teapots of this type may have either a rounded curved spout or a faceted spout, but it is always seated on a decagonal escutcheon, moulded in low relief. Careful measurement of about a dozen specimens has been made. They tally closely in every respect, apart from the fact that in one or two instances, a putative Worcester example was slightly smaller. This difference in size, which might be as much as three-sixteenths of an inch, combined with poor development of the escutcheon sometimes noted, is sufficient to show that different moulds are involved. Between the good Worcester features of some and the equally good Liverpool features of others, distinction may be easy. Borderline examples will, no doubt, continue to be attributed to Worcester, but few better illustrations could be found of the close parallelism which exists between the two manufactures and the difficulties which may be met with in distinguishing between them.

Most of the moulded patterns in use at Liverpool seem to demand a date rather later than we are considering, but a good example of an early ribbed moulding is seen on Plate 3 (*e*). The use of polygonal shapes, following the example of Chelsea, Bow and Worcester, is clear evidence of the oriental influence we are discussing. Hexagonal vases are occasionally met with and in this connection, those hexagonal cups which are sometimes found carrying the 'jumping boy' pattern (Plate 24 (*a*)) will be called to mind. These cups have a smallish footring with a slightly concave edge to each of the six panels which jointly form the rim and are very reminiscent of similar cups of early Worcester origin. In this particular instance, the decoration leaves no room for doubt concerning the matter of provenance, for the design is unknown on Worcester porcelain. The hexagonal cup illustrated on Plate 3 (*j*) is an example which, now firmly accepted, has had a somewhat precarious hold on Liverpool status in the past. In the case of the cup and saucer shown on Plate 7 (*b, c*), one still hears doubts expressed, but here again, recognition of a Liverpool origin is probably only a matter of time. Other good examples are provided by the 'red cow' print, of which an octagonal bowl and a coffee cup figure on Plate 32 (*a, j*).

The type of ware popularly known by the name of 'red cow' or 'red bull'

---

[1] The particular example referred to was exhibited by Messrs Tilley at the Antique Dealers' Fair in 1948. A Liverpool coffee pot showing half the design is in the Victoria and Albert Museum (*c.* 1192/1924).

may now receive brief consideration. The print itself will be dealt with when printed decoration is described, but here it may be stated that this print is found on two distinct types of ware, to each of which is reserved its own version of the subject. The first type, the commoner, will be seen to exhibit many of the features associated with 'Worcester type' Liverpool ware, e.g. it is grey looking, has a fair translucency which is usually bluish-green and exhibits glazing defects which will include bare areas, black specks and blistering, none of which we expect to find in Worcester wares of comparable date (1760–5). Its potting features also attract attention. Footrings of bowls may show a curving and inward sloping profile and are often undercut, while those of cups are smallish, frequently ill-defined and not quite circular. Further, many shapes are found which depart from ordinary Worcester standards. Coffee cups are squarish, with everted rims (Plate 32 (g)), and take on a squat look, teapots may be 'hump-handled', mustard pots have exaggeratedly concave sides and strange looking shoulder curves (Plate 32 (i)) while cream jugs often have a grooved foot (Plates 26 (c), 32 (h)). A flared beaker with ribbed sides is met with,[1] as also is a small covered cup of the shape seen on Plate 32 (d). But perhaps the most striking example of deviation from Worcester practice is provided by a spoon tray in my possession. The Worcester factory made its spoon trays carefully, never allowing glaze to stray on to the base. In this specimen, the glaze has been allowed to encroach on the base all round, at one place to a depth of about an inch, while the tray itself is short and slightly asymmetrical.

Ware of the second type on which this print is occasionally found has a more creamy appearance associated with very good pale green translucency. Technically it is a much better article than the ware just described and its provenance may be a matter of some doubt. The differences in the print, however, are not fundamental, but chiefly concern its colour treatment. They are described under that section. It should be noted that the cups and saucers found decorated in the style sometimes referred to as 'purple ruins' also belong to the type first mentioned.

In attempting to summarize the different points which should be taken into account in forming a conclusion on the provenance of any piece, it will be seen that, while none possess absolute value, some few come very near to that standard, so near that great reliance can be placed on their presence. Somewhat surprisingly perhaps, these are chiefly concerned with minor peculiarities in shape, rather than with matters involving the technique employed in potting and glazing, in spite of the fact that these are fundamentals with which the serious student of ceramics is primarily occupied. They may be stated as follows: Handles — the 'biting snake', the scrolled

[1] Worcester Royal Porcelain Company's Museum.

handle having a dependent tag at the lower end, the upthrust mark of the potter's thumb on the back-turned lower end of strap handles and the U-shaped loop handle. Bases — the chamfered bottom edge of cylindrical mugs (Plate 2 (*b*)), and the type of base shown on Plate 50 (*a, b*). Spouts — the cornucopia moulding of 'scratch-cross' jugs. The list is not meant to be exhaustive and no doubt many others could be added.

Among general potting characteristics, the importance of a grey appearance ranks high, particularly when associated with poor translucency. The value which should be attached to a blue colour by transmitted light has been discussed. As a means of distinction from Worcester wares I believe it has considerable weight, for I have but occasionally observed it in any piece which could with certainty be attributed to that factory, although it is by no means uncommon in both the groups of Liverpool porcelain which have been described. Exactly the same might be said regarding those small tears in the paste which show up as flecks by transmitted light. This feature also gains in importance from the fact that is observable in both groups.

There is yet another point to which attaches considerable value in these matters. Very rarely does one find a Worcester footring which does not present a perfectly regular circular outline, whereas on Liverpool wares a broken contour is of frequent occurrence (Plate 50 (*d*)). Whether the difference is merely the result of a little more carelessness on the part of the Liverpool potter in removing the piece from the wheel I do not know. If carelessness be the cause, it seems strange that it should be so unevenly distributed between the two factories.

The making of attributions may be likened in many ways to a doctor's diagnosis. A large number of points of varying importance are noted, compared and contrasted. The result is a balanced judgment, the value of which will depend largely on the experience behind it. In the majority of cases, no deep problems are involved; in others there will be the greatest difficulty in reaching a conclusion.

In this way, the provenance of a cylindrical mug with ribbed handle may be decided by the narrowness of the footring, the fact that this is glazed, that the other glazed portions of the countersunk base show imperfections due to firing and lastly, that glaze shrinkage is absent. The base of such a Liverpool mug is shown on Plate 50 (*c*); and the mug itself on Plate 9 (*b*). Combined in the way in which these features are found here, a Liverpool origin for the piece is more than a reasonable proposition, which is considerably increased when the method of decoration and the palette employed are taken into account. In the face of such evidence, the fact that it exhibits good potting with a Worcester 'duck egg' translucency need not receive undue weight.

The claim to Liverpool status of the cider mug (Plate 9 (a)) may be admitted by a greenish translucency which is marred by the presence of minute tears in the paste, by glazing defects (black specks) from faulty firing, which can be seen in the illustration, by its ground base ring[1] and by the fact that glaze shrinkage is absent. On the other hand, the decoration in this case does not help the Liverpool cause, for it is in good Worcester tradition and clearly, there is scope for the differences of opinion which have been expressed about this piece. However, it is not generally known that mugs of this type were made at Liverpool, the proof of which is afforded by the Liverpool handled and Sadler printed example shown on Plate 37 (a). This may make the proposition easier to accept.[2]

THE 'SCRATCH-CROSS' GROUP

Few collectors who have been following modern trends in research on English porcelain of the eighteenth century will have failed to note the changing views concerning the origin of this most interesting group which have taken place during the past thirty years. Long regarded as a product of the Bow factory, it became recognized as an established fact that it was essentially a soaprock porcelain, whereas 'specimens of Bow porcelain from 1748 onwards were proved on analysis to contain bone-ash'. Doubts about the importance which should be attached to chemical analysis, at the time we are considering a recent innovation, were finally resolved in favour of a soft paste Bristol — Lowdin's Bristol, as it was then called — or early Worcester origin for the whole of the group. Certain points of resemblance with early Worcester wares were noted, as indeed, were also certain divergences, the latter notably affecting mug shape and decoration. Somewhat later the attribution was slightly altered to 'Bristol-Worcester', as it became recognized that in many cases, the later date made possible by this conception fitted better with the requirements. On the whole, the solution thus afforded seemed satisfactory. The difficulty, however, which had apparently been so happily solved in this way, was not ended, for the significance of much printed ware which clearly belonged to the group began to obtrude. 'Bristol-Worcester' had its limitations, which might be said to be pin-pointed by the appearance at Worcester of printed decoration. This event is generally believed to have taken place in December 1757.[3] Had it taken place a whole year earlier, the difficulty,

---

[1] A ground base-ring must be almost as uncommon on Liverpool wares as on Worcester. It is present on the bowl, Plate 33 (e) and on the cup, Plate 14 (b).

[2] A bell shaped mug with ribbed loop handle was sold at Sotheby's (May 29th, 1956, lot 108) as Liverpool, with the footnote 'the attribution has been challenged', perhaps illustrating the difficulty here discussed.

[3] The Hancock engraved 'King of Prussia' mug, dated 1757.

which may be put briefly as the incongruity of early potting characters associated with a later type of decoration affecting a very large amount of ware, would still remain.[1] For these reasons, the many links between this group and early Worcester wares might begin to appear of less importance than the resemblances which could be seen to exist with those of Liverpool. Both were soaprock porcelains; and while it can be said that the relationship between the wares of Worcester and Liverpool was close enough to account equally well for any resemblances between the wares of either and those of the 'scratch-cross' group, the scale should turn in favour of Liverpool when decoration demands the later date which perhaps a Liverpool attribution alone permits.[2]

It is perhaps difficult to decide whether the group took origin at Worcester or at Liverpool. In favour of the former, there is the evidence of at least one dated example, a mug, which carries what must be regarded as a pre-Liverpool date (1754), although certain assumptions are necessary before this could be accepted as infallible proof of a non-Liverpool origin.[3] Then we have the evidence of the mug in the Dyson Perrins Collection, which in some way commemorates the Parliamentary Election at Worcester in 1747 and the ultimate victory of the Whig candidate, Mr R. Tracy.[4] Why this should be commemorated on a porcelain mug which, wherever made, must be dated considerably later than the event itself is by no means clear. But it must be admitted that whatever anomalies present themselves here, none would be more difficult to explain than that such a mug was made in Liverpool. To many, this might be accepted as good evidence of a Worcester origin for the whole group, although Dr Rhodes himself thinks it falls short of definite proof.

Better than either of these examples and shaped similarly to the first mentioned, is the armorial mug in Mr H. R. Marshall's collection, Case impaling Weston (Commemorative Catalogue E.C.C., No. 371), to which a date *circa* 1755 is assigned.[5] The Worcester link here seems assured, for Richard Case was High Sheriff of Worcestershire in 1761 and there is a monument to him bearing his Arms in Powick Church in the same county. Good reasons therefore exist for believing that the group took origin at Worcester. Indeed, in many ways these 'scratch-cross' pieces contrive to maintain a character of

---

[1] The amount is too great to permit of 'late decoration' as the explanation.
[2] The resemblances are not striking, but there are many links with early Worcester which embrace both decoration and painter's marks.
[3] Trans. E.P.C., 1931, No. III, page 82; and Catalogue E.C.C. Commemorative Exhibition, 1948, No. 370.
[4] Trans. E.P.C., 1931, page 82.
[5] Trans. E.C.C., No. 9, 1946, page 211, Marshall *Armorial Worcester Porcelain.*

their own and fail to exhibit the sort of fusion with accepted Liverpool types of the period which one would expect were they wholly products of that manufacture. In the description which follows, the points of resemblance to Liverpool wares will be discussed and attention drawn to differences where they seem to be of importance.

The name apparently arose in the course of informal discussions at the British Museum many years ago.[1] It seemed a happy description of a group of pieces having well-marked characteristics for which a name was needed; and from being a useful colloquialism it eventually acquired the dignity of sanction in print. These characteristics may be summarized:

1 The group is compact. Its potting features are remarkably consistent, regarding both paste and glaze and particularly in the shapes employed. The ware is of grey or greyish-blue colour and only occasionally when coloured enamels are used are creamy tones observable. The potting tends to be thick and heavy and has poor translucency of greenish hue. Firecracks, generally at the handle attachments, are often present. While pin-pitting, black specks in the glaze, sanding and areas bare of glaze are features rarely if ever seen, the surface in many places may show an orange peel effect, better seen by oblique illumination. Analysis shows that the paste contains about thirty per cent soaprock and up to four per cent lead.

2 The second characteristic is a matter of marks. The incised saltire cross from which the group takes its name, is one of three markings, the other two being an incised stroke, generally about half an inch in length and situated on the base at some distance from the cross, which is always beneath the handle; and a cut in the bevel of the footring. One or more of these marks may be present, generally two, more rarely all three. Occasionally the only marks are two incised strokes (jug, Plate 29 (c)), while sometimes there is no mark, although the piece clearly belongs to the group. In addition, on blue-painted pieces there may be a painter's mark in blue, which may be on the base or close under the handle.

Objection has been raised to the use of the name 'Scratch-cross' to designate the group, on the grounds that this cross is not a factory mark nor even characteristic of any particular group of pieces, being found on wares from many factories over a wide period of time; and that it is, in fact, nothing more than a device used by the potter who put on the handle in order to enable him to claim his own work (it is never found on pieces without handles).

While admitting the truth of this, it is generally agreed that the use of the term only denotes a group of pieces possessing certain well-marked characteristics and that the mere presence of such a mark does not denote identity

[1]Rackham, Trans. E.P.C., No. II, 1929, page 28.

with the group. In point of fact, if we consider marks alone, the incised stroke so frequently present on the bases of these pieces has much greater distinctive value and might well have suggested itself when a distinguishing name for them was needed.

The bulk of the ware which has survived, possibly as much as ninety-five per cent, is represented by mugs, jugs and coffee pots, a few cups and odd pieces making up the remainder.[1] The mugs conform to two types, (a) the 'spreading base' and (b) the inverted bell. The first named is an unusual shape. It is found on some Bow examples, fragments of at least one such having been found by Mr Aubrey Toppin in an unglazed state many years ago in conditions which clearly indicated a factory waster. This proved to be phosphatic.[2] The shape was also in use at Lowestoft, though less commonly, and at Liverpool; and something like it is occasionally found for which an early Worcester attribution would be a possibility. The 'scratch-cross' examples are furnished with a footring of moderate width, which is unglazed and yields to a shallow depressed base (glazed). The handle is of strap form, double grooved and has a back-turned lower end which is cut off square (Plate 28 (b, c)). The shape as in use at Liverpool is shown on Plate 36 (c) and Plate 39 (f). The former has a flat unglazed base and a plain strap handle back-turned and thumb-impressed in true Liverpool style. The latter has a narrow footring, depressed and glazed base and a handle with pottery associations. It will be seen, therefore, that while these four mugs show similarity in shape, neither the bases nor the handles of one pair have anything in common with those of the other. Although the shape is uncommon, this resemblance could be accidental and conclusions drawn therefrom unwarranted. It is otherwise with a small mug which I was recently shown. This was a slightly 'waisted', cylindrical mug, with flat unglazed base and grooved loop handle — a perfectly typical Liverpool coffee can. It was decorated with the 'stag hunt' and marked on the base with an incised cross and incised stroke in a manner indistinguishable from 'scratch-cross' pieces. It is perhaps necessary to say that careful examination of the marks failed to give evidence of being a late addition.

(b) The bell-shaped mug of the group is characteristic, being almost straight sided and showing little resemblance to the corresponding shapes of other factories (Plates 24 (b, c), 34 (c)). It has a small grooved foot an unglazed footring yielding to a shallow depressed base and a handle, reeded in the larger sizes, fluted in the smaller, which has a back-turned

---

[1]A teapot is shown on Plate 28 (a), marked with a single knife cut on the base beneath the handle. The teapot on Plate 13 (c) is marked with an insised cross but does not belong to the group.
[2]Wallace Elliot, Trans. E.P.C., 1929, page 16, where the group is discussed.

square cut lower end. There is an approximation to the shape at Liverpool (Plate 26 (c)), though with a different type of foot, which, however, is one very commonly found on jugs and coffee pots of the group, as we shall shortly see.

The jugs of the group are pear-shaped, with a tendency to a more pronounced waist than the shape usually carries and therefore expanding unduly towards the rim. The lip may be of the simple pinched type (Plate 29 (c)), but is sometimes masked (Plate 30 (a)), or may take on that characteristic form of a cornucopia with moulded foliate scrolls (Plates 27 (a–d), 29 (d)). It is of some importance to note that, whichever type is present, it may assume a slightly down-drooping look in profile which is not commonly observed in other wares. Some of these jugs are furnished with a grooved foot rather like that of the bell mugs, but more deeply grooved and having a much heavier rolled edge (Plates 25 (a), 27 (a)), while equally commonly found is a type of foot in which the rolled edge is replaced by an outward-sloping face making roughly an angle of 45 degrees with the base (Plate 26 (f)). In the larger sizes, these jugs have scrolled handles of oval section with a thumb rest and a rounded back-turned lower end. Their edges are frequently grooved while sometimes an overlapping-scale moulding is present between the thumb rest and the handle attachment (Plate 29 (d)). Smaller jugs may have a plain grooved loop handle (Plate 26 (f)).

Nothing resembling this 'waisted' appearance with down-drooping lip is found in the standard wares of either Worcester or Liverpool, as far as I have been able to observe, but it is significant that both features are present in the little cream jug decorated with a 'red cow' print, claimed for Liverpool on much other evidence. This jug will be seen also to carry the form of grooved foot with rolled edge, rarely found on Worcester cream jugs, but less uncommon on those of Liverpool (Plate 6 (k)), where it may be found on jugs of all sizes (Plate 14 (e)).

The other type of grooved foot just described must be of rare occurrence on Worcester wares of any date, whereas it is a normal finding on much early Liverpool. It is shown on the Liverpool bell-shaped mug, to which reference has already been made (Plate 26 (c)) and on innumerable coffee pots shortly to be described. The two types of foot can be studied on the two jugs shown side by side on Plate 26 (e, f), where some of the other points mentioned can be compared and contrasted.

Concerning handles, the scrolled handle with thumb rest is certainly less commonly found at Worcester than at Liverpool, where it was popular. Not much importance need be attached to that, for similar types were in use at Lowestoft and elsewhere. The presence of lateral grooving or of an overlapping scale moulding, in manner described, would seem to be better evidence of kinship, particularly perhaps the latter. Both features are shared by 'scratch-cross' (Plate 29 (d)) and Liverpool (Plate 20 (a)), but neither, to my knowledge, are found on Worcester wares.

'Scratch-cross' coffee pots vary somewhat in size but conform rigidly to an inverted pear shape and in having a grooved foot of the wedge type, a scrolled handle with a thumb-rest and a flattish cover with conical knop (Plate 26 (a)). The general resemblance of such a pot with the standard Chaffers' article at once attracts attention (Plate 4 (a, b)), the wedge foot of each being strikingly similar. The handles are different, but replace the flat strap handle with one from a Chaffers' mug (Plate 8 (d)) and the likeness increases. There is more dissimilarity in the spouts than elsewhere, but the gap is considerably reduced on looking at the Chaffers' teapot (Plate 26 (d)), with its spout so closely modelled on the lines of that carried by the pot shown on Plate 26 (a). The shape of this is so unusual that accidental resemblance is practically ruled out. In this way, it would not be difficult to construct a good 'Scratch-cross' coffee pot completely out of Liverpool spare parts; and the fact that this can be done is perhaps one of the strongest reasons for supposing that the two manufactures share a common inheritance.

From a consideration of the known facts, it seems likely therefore that the group originated at Worcester and subsequently underwent modification and development at Liverpool. Although membership is not a matter of marks, it will be noticed that only marked pieces, or examples of which marked pieces are known to exist, have been used in making this comparison with Liverpool wares, a necessary step in order to simplify the issue. The need for this is apparent when we pass in review the very large amount of ware which can be seen to exhibit relationship, in varying degree, with this comparatively small group. It is, in fact, nothing less than the entire conception known under the name of 'Bristol-Worcester' and the relationship is shown in every possible way — similarities in paste and glaze, in potting characters, in decoration and in the sharing of that legion of hieroglyphics which we refer to as 'Painters' marks'.

In one or two instances, all these criteria may be present, as, for example, in the case of that well-known type of sauce boat, mounted on a pedestal foot, with projecting lip, wavy rim, scrolled handle and exhibiting moulded decoration.[1] There is no difficulty in recognizing the near relationship of these to the group, although I do not know of a single specimen which bears an incised cross. The same might be said with rather less justification about those sauce boats in the form of folded leaves copied from Meissen.[2] In both these types, identity with the group is particularly a matter of paste, glaze and

[1]These are found blue painted with the design shown on Plate 28 and jade-marked.
[2]Noted by W. B. Honey, O.E.P., 1946, page 160.

46

potting characters. For the most part, however, Bristol-Worcester relationships are less a matter of actual resemblances than such links as can be provided by decoration — possibly identity of hand, but more often the use of the same motif in the same manner — and by painters' marks. A good example of the former may be seen when comparing the decoration of the scratch-cross-marked mug (Victoria and Albert Museum, *C.252/1915*) with that of a plate of dissimilar paste in the Schreiber Collection (Schr. I.457) and others will receive notice when decoration is discussed. Painters' marks, which are generally but by no means always in blue under the glaze, are so much a feature of early Worcester wares that they have almost come to be regarded as Worcester property. But there is no difficulty in supposing that their use was continued at Liverpool under Podmore's management, indeed, every reason exists for supposing that this would be so, particularly if, as is likely, other Worcester-trained workmen had accompanied him.[1] For these marks were in no sense factory marks, but the personal property of the painter and, as Hobson tells us, they owe their often unintelligible forms solely to the caprice of these people.[2] The so-called 'jade' mark, formerly regarded as the monogram of Thomas Frye, is one commonly found on 'scratch-cross' wares, as is another shaped rather like a backwardly-made letter F with a curving downstroke, while others include a mark like a trident, another like a script letter L (Schr. I.461) on a jug at one time regarded as 'Liverpool' and another which looks like a monogram in script of the letters J.H. (jug, Plate 30 (*a*)).[3]

None of these marks seems to be associated with any observable differences in the pieces which exhibit them and, assuming that the group did take origin at Worcester, one must look elsewhere for help in trying to decide, if indeed, it is possible to do so, the question of Worcester or Liverpool provenance in individual cases.

In any close study of early Worcester wares, it is interesting to note that we not infrequently find two 'versions' of the same object, very alike, yet dissimilar in that one is more heavily potted and opaque. A good illustration of this is provided by the coffee pots of the type Victoria and Albert Museum, *634/1925* which are found in two forms, identical in shape and employing the same moulding in exactly the same skilful way, but one is much greyer looking, more heavily potted and, although only slightly larger weighs nearly twice as much. The folded-leaf Meissen type of sauce boat provides

[1]Hobson (*Worcester Porcelain*, page 182) states that similar marks were used at other factories. The reference may be to Liverpool.
[2]Ibid, page 182.
[3]The jade mark may occur in paired association with others and seems to be the only one used in this way. The significance is not clear.

another example. Some of these are positively crude by comparison with others[1] in which potting and decoration reach the highest standards; and something similar might be said of some pedestal-mounted sauceboats with scrolled handle and splayed lip. Some explanation seems to be called for, since if these are all Worcester wares, there is no parallel to such a state of affairs in any other unit factory.

Narrowing the scope of this observation to the 'scratch-cross' group, it is significant that, among a group of pieces which is characterized by thick heavy potting and very poor translucency, the printed examples exhibit these properties in marked degree. Of possibly a dozen examples which I happen to possess, all but one are practically opaque, the exception being a very small mug with poor translucency for its size by any standards. The assistance that can be given by printed decoration in certain circumstances, by reason of its dating value, has been briefly indicated; and if the heavier pieces are so by reason of being Liverpool-made, the apparent anomaly of finding them associated with printed (and therefore later) decoration tends to disappear. Here I am reminded of George Savage's remark of making assumptions about a whole group of porcelains from the few we are able to study. He wisely concludes that, if we are conscientious, it would be difficult to see sufficient porcelain to justify every generalization. With that we can readily agree. But where a generalization may be unjustified, a suggestion may be permitted. The observed facts could be explained by supposing that the majority of all 'scratch-cross' pieces are thick and semi-opaque because they, including the printed examples, were made at Liverpool after 1755, where, generally speaking, a thicker and more opaque ware was favoured and where shapes tended to be clumsier and more 'provincial'. Conversely the much smaller amount of thinner ware may be given a pre-1755 date and early Worcester status.

SECOND PERIOD

With the waning of Podmore's influence towards the end of the first decade of manufacture, a more native style developed. As has been indicated elsewhere, Philip Christian, although a partner of Chaffers & Co. can never have been very actively engaged in the soaprock porcelain-making side of the business, which must have been entirely the concern of Chaffers and Podmore. With Chaffers' death in December 1765 and the expiry in January 1766 of Podmore's agreement, which apparently was not renewed, the trend of affairs of which we are speaking was hastened. Podmore's services may have been retained. We know that he was living as a potter in Preston Street

---

[1] The example on Plate 24 (*e*) has been chosen for that reason.

in 1767 and 1776, but while in any case, it is unlikely that the manufacture of a soaprock porcelain was abandoned — for the lease of the mine was not sold until ten years later — it is probable that at this time a bone-ash body began to be used increasingly with the introduction of the new styles.

This fits in with changes in the appearance of the ware which now began to show themselves. In place of the grey-looking rather opaque ware of greenish translucency, we begin to notice the appearance of a whiter china with a bluish cast, more transparent and showing dirty white or straw-coloured tones by transmitted light. A creamy look is sometimes seen, particularly in pieces where reasons exist for thinking that a later date is probable. The glaze is blue, 'starch-blue' is the name happily given to it and, indeed, the whole period we are now considering might well take its name from this fact, for it affects every Liverpool maker's wares.

This glaze tends to collect in the angle inside the base ring, although its distribution on bases — and sometimes elsewhere — is frequently patchy; it sometimes forms tears on the insides of cups, etc., and at times, it assumes a greenish tinge with a darkening effect which has been called 'thunder cloud', but the minute pin-pitting and the blackening, so characteristic of the earlier wares, is no longer seen.

Specimens of a glassy-looking porcelain are sometimes met with and belong to this period. They are characterized by good translucency and, frequently, by the presence of a 'scum line'. The mug shown on Plate 21 (d) is furnished with a plain loop handle and a shallow recessed base, countersunk barely more than one sixteenth of an inch within the confines of a wide footring. This is characteristic. The maker is unknown.[1]

At the time of Chaffers' death in 1765, it is probable that the Chaffers combine was the only china-making concern in Liverpool and had enjoyed this position since the bankruptcies of Reid & Co. and Samuel Gilbody five years earlier. The scene now underwent a change. In 1765,[2] William Ball, and very soon afterwards the brothers James and John Pennington started to make china; and while Ball does not seem to have remained more than four or five years, it was otherwise with the brothers, both of whom were in production in 1775. In that year James migrated to Staffordshire, but John continued to work a pottery for another ten years, during which time his younger brother Seth joined the ranks of the china makers. While this made for keen competition, it also meant that variety resulted and therefore no

[1]The falsely documented Hanley tea caddy probably belongs to the group. The painting of all these pieces, in which a 'strong pink' was first commented on by W. B. Honey (O.E.P., 1946, page 203) is equally characteristic.
[2]Liv. Dir., 1766.

more unified description of the wares of this period can be attempted than of those of the preceding. Where obvious links with these are observable — and there are many such — it is reasonable to apply a 'Christian' label, but there is little to be gained by attempting too much where one guess is as good as another.

Speaking generally, footrings become stronger, more wedge-shaped[1] and of smaller diameter. Undercutting becomes less marked and before long disappears; and with it goes the inward-sloping profile of the footring which has been mentioned as so characteristic of much early ware. The grooved foot on mugs (Plate 45 (e)), coffee pots (Plates 15 (a), 49 (c), 47 (a)), etc., tends to become more marked, anticipating the pedestal of still later days. Tea-bowls are still prevalent, for the handled teacup (Plate 14 (b)) never seems to have been much in favour at Liverpool, coffee cups become larger with straighter (Plate 23 (g)) sides and a form appears having a rather distinctive square look (Plates 10 (e), 16 (d)).

The plain flat strap handle disappears completely and handles generally become more scrolled. There is a marked increase in the use of moulded ornament in almost every class of article and the 'Liverpool' teapot makes its appearance (Plate 20 (e, f)). Well made and proportioned, this has a body moulded in relief with panels on either side formed by palm trees above a row of large fronds which spring from the base. There is a foliated spout, a ribbed handle and a domed cover with conical knop.[2] These 'palm-tree' teapots, as they are frequently called, may be found decorated in a great variety of ways. Formerly ascribed to Longton Hall, they are tied to Liverpool by numerous links which have long been recognized and accepted.[3]

The tall coffee pot with high domed cover (Plate 15 (d)) is generally provided with moulded ornament on the spout only, but occasionally an example is found in which the body of the piece is also relief moulded (Plate 15 (a, b)). An earlier example, with a remarkably ungainly spout is shown on Plate 20 (a) and may be taken as illustrating the development of the type. It has a flat base, thinly glazed and shows an overlapping scale moulding on the upper part of the handle which resembles that sometimes seen on big jugs of the 'scratch-cross' group, while the cover is still but slightly domed and a mere shadow of what it was shortly to become (Plate 15 (d)). The very elaborately scrolled handle is, however, present in its fully developed form, laterally grooved and tagged at the lower end in a way which, as far as I know, was not adopted by any other manufacture. It was in common use at Liverpool

[1]Plate 50 (j).
[2]Fragments of teapots of this type were unearthed on the site of Dunbibin's potworks, Smithfield Street (see plan).
[3]*Connoisseur*, May 1923, dealing with the Bulwer Collection, should be consulted.

on coffee pots and many large jugs between 1765 and 1780 (Plates 10 (*a*), 11 (*a*), 15 (*d*), 47 (*a*), 49 (*c*)).

Much of the moulded ware of the Liverpool potters is of a high standard and compares favourably with that of any other factory. As elsewhere, silver shapes in most instances provided the inspiration at a time when rococo scrollwork on the body of the ware and elaborately scrolled handles were fashionable. Mention has already been made of the sauce boats in this connection. Plate 5 (*e*) shows an uncommon type for which a date around 1765 seems permissible. A better-known variety is recognized by the presence of three arched panels on either side, resting on a row of acanthus leaves which spring from a slightly grooved foot (Plates 20 (*b*), 22 (*c*)). Boats of this type have a recessed base and a handle which may take the form of a biting snake. They seem to have been made in three sizes and are to be found painted in a variety of ways in which the decoration may or may not conform to the panelled reserves. As is well known, sauce boats of somewhat similar design were made at Lowestoft. The recognition of these should present no particular difficulty, but this can hardly be said of a blue-painted pair in the Museum of the Worcester Royal Porcelain Company, although these are crescent-marked. Attaching no undue importance to the mark, which on rare occasions was used by the Liverpool potters, slight differences in moulding observable on this pair may well justify their Worcester attribution and serve to illustrate the difficulty in these matters which is so frequently encountered.[1]

Before leaving the subject of these moulded sauce boats, generally so pleasing in appearance, it is to be observed that some, though well potted and showing good moulding, have a clumsy look. This is a fault which can be found, here and there, in Liverpool wares of any date. Technically expert, few of these potters can be credited with much artistic sense, providing the reason why their results are always better when they had a silver model for this type of work and why silver shape in porcelain is so much admired. The example shown on Plate 20 (*d*) illustrates this point; and it is of interest to note that this specimen is obviously from the same factory and decorated by the same hand as the coffee pot with the ungainly spout just described (Plate 20 (*a*)) to which the same remarks apply.

Mention has been made of the 'biting snake' handle. This derives from silver-shape. At first claimed for Longton Hall it has long been recognized as almost exclusively a Liverpool feature. Probably the earliest example of its use — and probably the most important, because of the evidential value of the

---

[1] The differences are not so much in design as in sharpness of outline, which compares unfavourably with that of the Liverpool examples. The latter are also less tub-shaped.

piece bearing it — is to be found on the porcelain sauce boat (Plate 41 (*d*)) to which reference has already been made. This displays a 'Liver',[1] a trailing vine and a smiling mask, all in moulded relief. While the three components of this moulding are reproduced with slight variation on one and the same saltglazed sauce boat in a manner which can hardly be a coincidence, I believe this sauce boat provides the only known example of the use of the 'Liver' on porcelain. It is of interest to note that the late Wallace Elliot, in referring to a specimen as 'decorated with the crest of the City of Liverpool' (Conn., July 1924, pages 163/164) was probably the first to draw attention to resemblances between it and the palm-tree teapots, at that time regarded by most expert opinion as products of Longton Hall.[2] This was an early step of great importance in our developing knowledge of the products of the long-forgotten Liverpool potteries.

Perhaps the best known example of the use of the 'biting snake' handle occurs on a cream jug of silver shape (Plate 21 (*c*), 45 (*c*)) to which reference has already been made (page 34). The use of this type of handle continued, sometimes in a debased form (Plate 20 (*b*)), on small jugs and sauce boats throughout this decade (1770–80) and later. A late example of its use, still easily recognizable, may be seen on Plate 43 (*g*).

Cream jugs with pinched lip and grooved loop handle in the prevailing style of Worcester and elsewhere continued to be made (Plates 19 (*f, g*), 23 (*c, d, e*)), but a new form copied from Chelsea models now made its appearance. Examples of these, with wavy rim, scrolled handle and an expanding spirally moulded body on which a moulded pattern of acanthus leaves rises from a nearly flat base, are found decorated in a variety of ways (Plate 23 (*j, k*)). It will be noticed that this acanthus leaf motif used in this way was much in favour with the Liverpool potters of this period. Other moulded wares include small leaf-shaped pickle dishes (Plate 24 (*f*)) and small sweetmeat trays sometimes made in the form of a shell and supported on peg-shaped feet.

Plates of any shape or size remain scarce, almost certainly because there is still no record of either dinner or dessert services being made. Those plates which have survived are generally of small size and exhibit a scalloped rim

---

[1]The 'Liver', heraldic bird, said to have taken origin from the Johannine eagle, when King John visited the town in 1207 and granted its first Charter. It figured on the Great Seal from earliest times and has been the crest of Liverpool City Arms for centuries. In this form, it was extensively used by the Liverpool potters as a motif in decoration and later by the Herculaneum manufactory as its factory mark.

[2]The 'palm-tree' teapots had been recognized as 'Liverpool' by the authorities at the Victoria and Albert Museum more than a year earlier (Conn., May 1923, pages 25, 26, *The Bulwer Collection teapots*).

(Plates 19 (*a*), 39 (*a, b*), 46 (*c*)). The Chien Lung shape, of plain circular outline, in which there is no proper footring excepting such as is obtained by slightly depressing the base, is still prevalent among the larger sizes (Plate 29 (*b*)). Dishes seem to be even rarer, probably because the Liverpool 'market' for these and similar articles required and preferred to use delftware during the whole of the period of manufacture so far considered (Plate 17 (*c*)).

In a general review of this post-Chaffers ware, little fault can be found with its potting. The experimental stages had been left behind and we no longer expect to find the mis-shapen footrings, the fire-cracks, the evidences of failure to maintain shape in the kiln and the glazing defects due to the faulty firing of earlier days. Yet it must be admitted that much of this chinaware never rises above mediocrity, while some, among which must be included much 'blue-and-white' is of poor quality and without artistic merit.

THIRD PERIOD

The ware of the third period, the longest of our arbitrary divisions which covers a span of some twenty-five years, is still marked by good potting. Seth Pennington, the youngest of the three brothers, was the chief potter during the greater part of this time, during the early part of which his brother John (*d.* 1786) and later John's widow Jane, assisted in some way by the returned exile and elder brother James, also contributed to the manufacture. The part played as a maker of porcelain by Zachariah Barnes (*q.v.*), must be discounted by a critical examination of the records. For the same reason, Wolfe & Co. (the 'Co' being Davenport), who occupied John Pennington's works in Folly Lane (Islington) towards the end of the century, although described as 'china manufacturers' in the 1796 Directory, are to be regarded as wholesale importers of Staffordshire goods only.[1] This might therefore be called 'the Pennington period'.

The changes which can be observed in the ware no doubt took place gradually but are none the less definite. The use of bone-ash had established itself completely. Crazing is frequently noticeable, but the tendency of the glaze, no longer so starch-blue, to collect in the angles of footrings is less marked. Perhaps the most notable potting feature is the development of the grooved foot which eventually became almost a pedestal. This can be seen on coffee pots (Plate 42 (*a*)), on mugs (Plate 45 (*e*)), on sauce boats, of which a new variety with a high angular handle, seemingly derived from the 'biting snake' now makes an appearance (Plate 48 (*c, d*)), and on jugs. The well-known 'Heinzelman' jug, dated 1779 (illustrated in Trans. E.P.C., 1929, page 27) is a good early example from the British Museum, where may be seen

---

[1] See under James Pennington.

also another, similar in shape and also blue painted, whereon is depicted a warship on one side and two warriors on the other. This is inscribed on the base $_W^M{}_E$ 1785. The example illustrated here is from the collection of Mr E. Allman (Plate 41 (a)) and is inscribed 'Robert Lewis' with date 1783.

Many of the older forms now disappear. Relief moulding, though still found, is sparingly used and even silver shape seems to have lost its appeal to the Liverpool potter. The scroll handle becomes less elaborate but the 'biting snake' remains, sometimes in fully developed form (Plate 43 (g)), but more often so modified that the handle terminal is merely cloven, as in the sauce boats just mentioned. Small jugs have taken on a new look and may be helmet-shaped (Plate 43 (g)), or exhibit ogee curves with a deeply grooved foot. The latter shape is also found in small mugs (Victoria and Albert Museum, *C.799/1924*), while the ovoid teapoy mounted on a pedestal makes an appearance (Victoria and Albert Museum, *C.1149/1924*).

The mask spout survives, as at Worcester and elsewhere (Plate 41 (a)). The tea bowl is still far commoner than the handled teacup and the straight-sided beaker, shaped like an inverted truncated cone, is now found (Victoria and Albert Museum, *C.806/1924*), although it seems possible that elsewhere porcelain examples had already appeared. At Liverpool, the shape is more commonly found in pottery. Many of these beakers are found bearing prints of the Bidston Hill signals and I have seen one such, dated 1788, made of opaque white glass, which is reasonably of Liverpool manufacture.[1] Plates are still scarce and when met with, rounded shapes seem to be commoner than those having fluted and scalloped rims (Plate 47 (c)).

The Liverpool potters had been famous for the large size of their bowls from early years. The majority of these were of delftware, including all those of the largest size. But there was a good sprinkling of examples in porcelain, chiefly belonging, however, to the period we are now considering and to the years immediately preceding. While there is nothing remarkable about them except their size, they include the ship bowls which were possibly intended for presentation to commemorate some successful enterprise. They will receive further notice when the subject of decoration is considered.

Vases, occasionally polygonal but usually of an inverted pear shape, had also been made in Liverpool for many years before the 'Pennington' period, now in review, established itself. The porcelain examples of the early years are of small size, being as a rule not more than five or six inches in height (Plates 13 (b), 17 (d), 40 (d)), but many later ones are considerably larger. A particularly fine specimen measuring twenty-one inches, in the collection of Mr Allman is featured on Plate 40 (e); another, one of a pair in the writer's collection, measures sixteen-and-a-half inches (Plate 41 (b)). Such vases

[1] Mr E. Allman's Collection. Perrin's Warrington Glass House seems to have closed in 1777.

almost certainly formed part of a set of five, consisting of three of pear-shape and two cylindrical beakers with flared rims, the whole modelled on the lines of the Chinese *garniture de cheminee*. Porcelain examples of the beakers are rare, although these may be found in earthenware; and there is reasonable sanction for attributing these and similar sets of 'chimney ornaments', as Mayer terms them, to Seth Pennington. Mayer tells us (op. cit., page 32, with illustration) that he purchased such a set in 1854 from Seth's last surviving daughter, then living in Everton Terrace, who 'kept them as relics of her father's manufacture'.

Ware of this class shows crazing and possesses a dirty yellowish translucency. In common with the bowls just discussed, its merit lies less in its potting than in its decoration, which is frequently of a high order. At a time when oriental influence in art form and decoration was still prominent, it is not surprising that the *garniture* should be copied by the English potters, not only at Liverpool but elsewhere (Plymouth). But the pear shape in single vases had always been a favourite with the Liverpool potters. It seems to have been used throughout the period of manufacture, not only in porcelain but in lead-glazed earthenware (creamware) and in delftware. In the latter medium, it was even adapted to commercial use, for we find it as the drug jar in but slightly modified form. Yet although a possible Liverpool origin for vases of this shape should always receive consideration, many similar were made elsewhere, notably at Lowestoft and distinction may not always be easy. Potting characters and, when blue-painted, the milky look of much Lowestoft blue, should assist.

Services, apart from teaware, were apparently not made. Presumably at that time those living in the style requiring such equipment would buy from Chelsea or Worcester, later at Derby. In this connection, I am reminded of an election address, recorded in Sadler's *Poll and Squib* book which was published just after the 1761 Parliamentary Election. In this, a plasterer called Nehemiah Lath asks the potters whether Sir William Meredith (a candidate) is not so fine a gentleman that he might think his table disgraced by having any Liverpool ware upon it?[1] Occasionally one comes across a flower-painted, lozenge-shaped dish, having the Liverpool marbled blue border, which may denote a remnant of a dessert service. As no other shaped dishes which could be fitted into such an idea seem to turn up, the probability is also that no dessert services were made.[2]

This leads to the question of figures. It could reasonably be argued that a public which did not require dessert services would have no use for figures.

[1] The reference here is presumably to the saltglazed 'Plumper' mug. The porcelain one was clearly not made until after the Election.
[2] Since writing this I have obtained existing proof of a dessert service of this pattern.

To that one might reply that Staffordshire made no dessert services until Wedgwood came on the scene, yet a considerable number of pottery figures were turned out. With the recognition that the Liverpool potters made salt-glaze and inferentially Astbury type and Whieldon type wares, it is likely they made figures of similar type also, although, with the possible exception of the little Grenadier, having a conjectural 'Liver' ornament in his hat (*Catalogue of British Museum, G36*) none have been identified. They will continue to remain hidden in the generic term 'Staffordshire' until a means of distinguishing them from the general run of figures of this class has been discovered.[1]

The case for earthenware figures is, indeed, so inherently probable that few would dispute it. With porcelain it is otherwise, yet the possibility should receive consideration for two reasons. Firstly, there are many porcelain figures whose attribution is far from secure; secondly, Liverpool as a possible centre of manufacture at the time these attributions were made was not considered. With our present knowledge of the Liverpool potters' attainments, to which it is hoped the pages of this book will bear witness, such attributions may have to be re-assessed. In other words, the advancement of a particular attribution on the ground that the figure was unlikely to have been made elsewhere would now have to take Liverpool into account.

The figures I have in mind may be thus grouped.

1   All figures for which there is a saltglaze counterpart, or which show a saltglaze influence. In a very thought-provoking paper read to the English Porcelain Circle in 1929, Mrs MacAlister had some interesting things to say on this subject.[2] Speaking of certain crude porcelain animals, she remarked that they could have but two possible sources of origin — 'One is William Littler, who made some of the models in saltglaze and the other is the unnamed potter from Limehouse, who was able to fashion animals in stoneware —'. From what precedes, it is clear that the statement about these particular saltglaze figures having been made by Littler is conjectural and it follows that the inference regarding similarly modelled figures in porcelain could apply with equal force to Philip Christian, a maker of saltglaze in a partnership which also made porcelain. Viewed thus they would but provide yet another instance of that dualism in design, examples of which have already been given from the productions of this factory.

2   The group generally regarded as 'late Longton Hall', which contains steatite but in insufficient quantity to satisfy a Worcester attribution. The great difficulty in obtaining supplies of this mineral has already been

[1]The author has a good earthenware figure of an officer of the Liverpool Volunteers, *circa* 1790, most probably of Liverpool make.
[2]Mrs MacAlister, Trans. E.P.C., volume II, 1929, page 49.

indicated.[1] While the Liverpool potters had overcome this, were skilled in the use of steatite and were using it in large quantities at this time, there is not the slightest evidence that the Longton potters had tried to get a licence which alone would guarantee a supply, or knew anything about its use. No analysis of Longton domestic wares has ever shown the presence of steatite. Worcester, of course, used it, but the scarcity of Worcester figures has been attributed to the unsuitability of the Worcester body for this purpose. Reasons exist for thinking that this may be true and it would be strange indeed if, with the imminent closing of the Longton factory, such a moment would be considered suitable for experimenting with an ingredient in the making of figures which had been found so unsatisfactory elsewhere for this purpose.[2]

The group referred to is briefly discussed in W. B. Honey's *Old English Porcelain*.[3] It is a small one and the difficulty this creates, wherever these figures may have been made must be viewed in the light of the degree of perfection which clearly has been attained. These are well-modelled figures which have long passed the experimental stage. The same applies to the figure of 'Britannia' (Schr. I.436), claimed for Longton Hall, for which the results of analysis are not available.[4] In this case, the figure carries printed decoration, long known to resemble that on certain Liverpool wares;[5] it seems to depict Britannia mourning the death of George II, which did not take place until October 1760;[6] and a somewhat similar Britannia sometimes occurs as printed decoration at Liverpool at this time.[7] It may be that the brown toned prints on the pedestal will some day provide the key to the secret of this lady's birthplace which, so far, she has succeeded in guarding in a manner more becoming the Sphinx. But whatever bearing these facts may be considered to exert on the perplexing question of the provenance of this figure, it can be seen that if some of the Longton Hall figure makers went to Liverpool after their own factory closed down, the steatitic figures just mentioned could be more easily accounted for, while Britannia's status in figure sculpture would appear more secure.

[1] Footnote, page 25.
[2] Hobson, *Worcester Porcelain*, pages 36, 96.
[3] Edition 1946, page 144.
[4] Previously attributed to both Bow and Chelsea.
[5] Trans. E.C.C., volume 2, No. 8, 1942, page 133; and Sotheby, catalogue of sale, 1st May, 1956, lot 26. Apart from the resemblences noted, no other centre readily suggests itself where printing could have been used in this way. In this respect, the figure is unique.
[6] See article by Frank Tilley, *Antique Collector*, June 1956, page 117.
[7] See Chaffers mug, Plate 38 (*a*). The Pitt portrait is found on a Sadler printed medallion (Schr. III. 403), the lettering on which corresponds with that of Houston's engraving and describes him as Secretary of State, which office he relinquished in 1761. While the engraving may reasonably be given an earlier date, the mug probably dates between 1759 and 1763.

3   There is yet another small group which calls for consideration. What can be said of those porcelain figures which are largely, if not entirely, tin glazed and which from time to time brighten, if indeed, they fail to illuminate the byways of the research student of ceramics? The admittedly small number of these is irrelevant. They require consideration solely for the evidence they may be considered to afford of the manufacture of porcelain figures in Liverpool. Those to which reference is made are almost certainly English and are only anomalous if attributed to any factory other than Liverpool, but, of course, the same might be said about the big 'Britannia' in virtue of its printed decoration.

Other groups spring to mind, but these few should be sufficient to show that the possibility of the Liverpool potters having made figures may not have received the attention which it deserves and the advancement of knowledge hampered thereby. If figures were made, one would certainly expect this to have taken place during those early years, when enthusiasm for the newly-discovered art was at its height and making a profit mattered less than the joy of making something new. The time may not be far distant when the results of examination by modern methods — ultraviolet light, chemical analysis and the use of the electronic computator — will be more extensively available than at present. When that time comes, we must be prepared to shed some of our cherished beliefs, while retaining the hope that the exercise of powers of observation and deduction will always find a place in the pursuit of collecting china.

CHAPTER FOUR

THE DECORATION OF THE WARE

LIVERPOOL PORCELAIN, it will be realized, ministered to no luxury taste and met no demands for purely decorative effects. The domestic wares which comprise the bulk of the output of the many factories at work, were not lavishly painted and their decoration is mainly confined to simple designs treated according to the prevailing conventions. Gilding was sparingly used.

While the biggest manufacturers, such as Chaffers & Co. undoubtedly had their own decorating rooms, which later would include a printing department, much 'outside' decorating was done. This was in the hands of independent decorators, among whom must be reckoned Sadler and Green and any other existing establishments of similar type.[1]

The pot painters, to give them the name by which they were known in eighteenth-century Liverpool, were a numerous class. If every person so described in contemporary records between 1720 and 1800 be included, we arrive at a list of nearly eighty names. Such a total, however, would not be a very reliable guide to their actual numbers, as the terms potter and pot painter were sometimes used indiscriminately. In a few cases, it may be that the potter was also the painter, in which event no error arises. But it might well happen that a pot painter would be described incorrectly as a potter, because his muffle gave a false impression, in which case the number of painters would be greater than the figures would indicate. There seems to be nothing to offset this and these figures therefore are more likely to be an understatement than the reverse.

Among this list of names, only ten are described as 'china painters' but again it is doubtful how much importance should be attached to this in a primarily delft-painting community, where terms were also frequently mis-applied. It may mean 'a distinction without a difference'. Bearing that in mind, the names of these ten persons are: Hugh Milligan, a painter at Reid's

---

[1]Sadler began as a pottery printer, but all the evidence goes to prove that his business developed into one which engaged in decorating every kind of ware in almost every kind of way. There are good reasons for thinking that Richard Abbey (q.v.) after leaving Sadler, conducted his own business in the same way.

China Works, 1756–61, with whom we are told the young William Roscoe was very friendly and from whom he obtained his first lessons in painting: Robert Wilcox and his wife, who was a daughter of Thomas Frye of Bow factory fame (1756–61): John Angel, living in Frog Lane (Whitechapel) in 1760: Edward Cranage, of whom there is no information except the baptism of a son at St. Nicholas' Church, 1768 and of a daughter in 1770: Joshua Driver, 1773, no information: Thomas Barrow, living in Preston Street, 1790: Robert and John Pennington, both sons of James Pennington, 1780–90: John Pennington, son of John and first cousin of the preceding, 1785–1800 and later. Of these, Wilcox and his wife are the subject of certain interesting correspondence between Wedgwood and Byerley.[1] The three Penningtons will receive further mention in the short biographical section of this book. The dates are approximate only.

Pottery decorating was not regarded as high art in the eighteenth century, indeed, it is doubtful whether even the best of it was regarded as art at all. The Liverpool pot painter would undoubtedly occupy a lowly position in the scale of craftsmen, paid for his hack work and kept in the background much in the same way as the hack engraver, whose labour was going to be put to similar use. As a result, we are rarely able to identify any decoration with its author, although it may be of high quality; and the most we can hope to do, in the overwhelming majority of cases, is to recognize a 'hand' and give a name to the particular style which it typifies. At other factories, the result has been such descriptive titles as 'the fable painter', 'the cotton stalk painter', 'the moth painter' and many others whose names are being added in this way to this gallery of unknown celebrities in increasing numbers. The usefulness of the convention, however, should not be allowed to obscure the fact that something which, after all, is only a style, tends to become invested with a personality; and that this enables us to talk as though such a person had not only existed, but as though we knew something about him, whereas, with the exception of those relatively rare cases in which great talent is clearly involved, we are probably looking at the product of a decorating establishment.

On Liverpool wares, it is possible to recognize many such 'hands', some of which, such as the 'dot artist' (Plate 11 (d)) and the 'spiky flower painter' (Plate 21 (a)) are already well known. Many more will be added as the characteristics of Liverpool china earn better recognition. For convenience, a few of these mannerisms may now be given, while others will be noticed elsewhere in the text. 1 The 'jointed branch painter', the inventor of the contrivance whereby a branch may be prolonged indefinitely by a succession of jointed curves (Plates 13 (e), 16 (e)). 2 The 'turreted bud painter' (Plate 21 (b)). 3 The 'knotted tree painter', with bare or almost bare branches (Plate 43 (a)).

[1] Appendix VIB.

4 The painter using horizontal red lines for ground treatment (Plate 43 (c)) and 5 the painter who prolonged the outline beyond the end of the leaf (Plate 31 (g, h)) in a curling manner. To these, but not quite in the same category, might be added the use of white enamel on ladies dresses[1] and, particularly, in delineating birds (Plate 13 (f)) and flowers (Plate 21 (f)); and the use, inside on the bottoms of cups and bowls, of a flower-leaf combination, in which a very distinctive purplish-red flower is found with a fleshy leaf like a marsh mallow. The drawing of flies with unequal antennae was commonly practiced by many Liverpool decorators.

No attempt will be made in what follows to describe decoration in detail, believing that more can be learned from a study of the pieces illustrated, which are representative of the whole manufacture. During the sixth decade of the eighteenth century, the period which witnessed the rise of china making in Liverpool, enthusiasm for oriental art forms was at its height. Unfortunately, this movement, which began in admiration of the artistic achievements of China and Japan many years earlier, had degenerated into such slavish copying that it became caricature. All sense of fitness and proportion was lost, and the taste of the wealthy classes showed itself in producing 'new designs for Chinese temples, triumphal arches and garden seats', by the installation of pagodas in Kew Gardens and the gift to posterity of Chinese Chippendale furniture.

As might be expected, oriental motifs, suitably adapted and following certain recognized conventions, were freely used by the pottery decorator wherever his art flourished. In this country, whether the designs were derived from Meissen versions or directly from Chinese and Japanese originals is frequently a moot point. Experts seem to agree that both means must have been used and that each case must be decided on its merits. But it is important to note that, where ceramic decoration is concerned, the pitfalls just referred to were avoided and the Chinese craze expressed itself with the happiest results. If copying was at times exact, it never appeared slavish and caricature, when present, was rarely unintentional but of the nature of a burlesque chinoiserie of great artistry and charm. More often, however, there was no attempt by our potters merely to imitate. Oriental influences are shown by clever adaptations which resulted in something possessing an appeal, peculiarly English, to which the qualities of our hybrid soft paste porcelain gave added effect.

The Liverpool potters followed the general trend in this matter and the early decoration, both on 'blue-and-white' and on coloured wares, is mainly on these lines. We find the usual Chinese landscape, with pagoda and trees (Plates 5 (e), 7 (f)), the river scene, with its impossible fisherman and his

[1]Practised at Worcester to a lesser degree.

incredible equipment, with hut, fence and root ornament completing the picture (Plates 5 (*a*), 7 (*g*)), and a great variety of decorative motifs in which 'Chinese' figures in a garden setting form a prominent feature (Plates 22 (*a*), 26 (*d*)). Most of the latter are versions of Chinese mandarin type porcelain made for export. The examples in enamel colours easily outnumber the others and the use of such designs continued almost throughout the whole period of Liverpool manufacture [Plate 15 (*d*) for the middle period and Plate 43 (*c*) for the last].

Most pottery decorators at this time were busily engaged in copying the work of their successful competitors. While one suspects that Liverpool's link with Worcester through Podmore may have made it easier for ideas to reach it from that direction than might otherwise have been possible, its position as a growing port through which merchandise from the Orient must pass favoured a more direct reception of oriental influences. One frequently comes across Liverpool pieces of first class quality which are obviously close copies of a Chinese original, but of which there is no Worcester counterpart (Plate 6 (*j*)). Yet again, one meets with others, owing little to Chinese influence and still less to Worcester, in which great originality in both subject matter and its treatment are shown. There is, for example, a small group characterized by a 'compact' greyish-green appearance and decorated in what may be termed a pseudo-oriental style, of which the subject known as the 'lady and parrot' may be taken as the type (Plate 9 (*c*)). With painting well done in a palette particularly suited to the grey background, these charming burlesques never fail to please, both by their humour and by the happy blending of the colours employed. I do not know of their like elsewhere; and if this group does not represent Liverpool china at its best, to me it represents it in its most typical form. There are two fine examples in the Wallace Elliot bequest (Victoria and Albert Museum, *C.21/38 and C.68/38*), in which the mingling of green and brown enamels with the production of a bronze effect, is particularly pleasing. Other examples will be found on Plates 8 (*a, b, e*), 9 (*d*).

The document for this group was a cup given to Mayer by John Rosson. Unfortunately, it seems to have been included among the war losses, but a good photograph remains (Plate 8 (*h*)) which can be compared with Mayer's illustration in the *History*. Its characteristic feature is the very distinctive looping of the border, which provides a certain means of identifying other members of the group, as, for example, the mug shown on Plate 8 (*e*). While the resemblances are not complete, they should be sufficient to establish relationship with 'lady and parrot' pieces.

Most of this 'Chinese figure' decorated ware is well done, the enamel colours being particularly bright and in some cases distinctive, a rich purple frequently occurring (Plate 25 (*d*)). Ware of this type has collected to itself many personages, each with his own particular setting. Some of these are so distinctive and restricted in use that they have almost come to be regarded as Liverpool property. One of the best known of these, the 'jumping boy', has already been mentioned. Commonly underglaze blue painted, it is sometimes met with having received additional decoration in red enamel and gold (Plate 24 (*d*)). The practice of treating underglaze blue patterns in this way was common among Liverpool decorators from early days and examples of most of them can be found in both states. Reference should be made to Plates 11 (*b*, *d*), 44 (*a*, *b*). This design has sometimes been claimed for Bow and I am credibly informed that examples are to be met with although I have not come across one.[1]

Another Liverpool character is popularly known as 'Old Bill', so called because of his walrus moustache and general resemblance to his prototype. In fact, he is a dignified Tartar mandarin. The origin of the design I do not know, but as, rarely, it may be found on Bow ware, it may be copied from the Chinese.[2] At Liverpool we find it on a wide range of pieces, all of which seem to belong to the post-Chaffers period. The design is completed with the assistance of court ladies amid a setting of garden furniture (Plate 15 (*d*)). It does not seem to have been used at Worcester.

Almost better known is the 'beckoning Chinaman', a monkish figure in a long purple robe with yellow trimmings, apparently engaged in beckoning to a flock of birds (Plate 10 (*b*)). The ware decorated in this way may be considered to belong to the early years. The design is reproduced in the same form on pieces of 'scratch-cross' type and it might therefore be held to lend support to the Liverpool origin of this group, in favour of which certain potting features have already been advanced (Plate 25 (*b*)). But this Chinaman, unlike 'Old Bill', is to be seen on pieces which also show reasonably good Worcester potting characters. I have in mind a cylindrical mug with ribbed handle in the possession of Mr H. Rissik Marshall, a type which was made both at Worcester and Liverpool and sometimes presents a problem of this nature.

It is true that decoration, unless it be in blue underglaze, affords insecure grounds on which to base attributions. In this case, however, the position is somewhat different, for the decoration is seen to be the work of a saltglaze painter. The field is thereby at once narrowed. This would easily be accounted for in a centre of a saltglaze manufacture, less easily where none such existed. At the date we are considering, the vogue for enamelled saltglaze had not begun to decline; and if for any reason, migration of such specialized labour took place, it would be to a town providing similar work. With this in mind,

[1]My informant is Mr H. R. Marden King.
[2]Mr E. Allman has a teapot so decorated, of Bow manufacture.

it is difficult to see what attraction Worcester could offer to a saltglaze decorator in competition for his services with Liverpool or similar centre of a saltglaze manufacture. There is, therefore, good reason for saying that where we find the hand of such a decorator on porcelain of this early Worcester type, if a Liverpool attribution is a reasonable proposition, it should commend itself more readily than a Worcester one. In this particular case it can be seen that this purple-robed Chinaman is found on so much Liverpool ware which could be selected as type pieces — on coffee pots of the type shown on Plate 20 (a)[1] and on the big Chaffers jugs (Plate 2 (d)), the issue is simplified thereby.

Saltglaze influence in the decoration of Liverpool porcelain belonging to the early years of manufacture is easily recognized and will repay consideration. In some few instances it may be possible to identify the same hand on porcelain and saltglaze, though it must be rare for the subject to be reproduced as closely as it has been on the saucer shown on Plate 18 (e) and on the salt-glaze bowl (Plate 18 (d)) which has been selected to replace the matching porcelain cup in this photograph. The painter of this particular example may be John Bowen, the Bristol delftware decorator who, it has been stated, left Bristol for Liverpool and there took up the decoration of saltglaze. Some of the characteristics of his style can be seen here — the crinolined lady, the landscape having a country house in the distance and the funny tufted trees flanking the scene, all are easily recognizable.

The 'beckoning Chinaman' in purple robe is frequently, though not always, associated with flower painting. This varies, but is always of saltglaze type and therefore probably by the same hand. The flower painting on the reverse side of the 'scratch-cross' jug bearing this figure is seen on Plate 25 (a). Reference should also be made to that on the teapot (Plate 10 (b)), where characteristically-painted flowers in the brightest enamels are seen; and again on a Liverpool coffee pot (C.1192-1924) in the Victoria and Albert Museum. As far as it may be permissible to make a judgment from an illustration, the flower painting seen on the last two examples is by the same hand as that on a coffee pot, formerly in the Solon Collection and, perhaps not surprisingly, attributed to Staffordshire (*Catalogue of a Collection of Pottery and Porcelain, 1912, No. 356*).

It will be noticed that in all these examples — and in others shortly to be mentioned — the method of indicating grass is by a wash of light green colour over rows of dots, more or less horizontally placed. This, as has been pointed out by W. B. Honey, is not infrequently observed on saltglazed wares. Whether it should be regarded as indicating the work of the same decorator is open to doubt. It may be seen on a group of pieces which custom has

[1]Footnote, page 38.

sanctioned as attributable to 'Bristol-Worcester' and even seems to have been claimed as support for that attribution, although it must be a doubtful asset for that purpose in view of its other associations. The fact that a similar technique can be seen on some Plymouth and early Newhall pieces does not help, but clearly does not disprove an earlier saltglaze connection, or even deprive it of a certain attributional value. Among the pieces illustrated here which show it, including those already mentioned, are the following: Plates 10 (b), 17 (a), 18 (b).

One of the best examples of the saltglaze decorator's art on porcelain is to be seen on another of those fluted teapots with which acquaintance has already been made (Plate 6 (c)). There is nothing unusual in the subject, which is a chinoiserie of pleasing character. The ground colour is a pellucid pink, with holes rather like those of a Gruyère cheese and shows considerable originality, but the great charm of the decoration lies in the transparency and brilliance of the enamel colouring, which must be seen to be believed. Other examples of saltglaze painting will be seen on the small vase (Plate 18 (b)), on the bowl from the same potworks (Plate 17 (f)), enamelled in a famille rose palette with a remarkably jewelled effect and on the large bowl similarly decorated in the famille rose manner (Plate 18 (a, c). Doubtless many more will be noticed among the illustrations of this book. With such evidence of painting of this type on Liverpool china, it must be regarded as somewhat remarkable that its possible significance should have aroused so little attention.

There is no difficulty in accounting for the hand of the delftware painter on Liverpool chinaware. Many pot-painters must have habitually decorated both delftware and saltglaze, turning to chinaware as circumstances demanded. The bowl already noticed (Plate 18 (a)) is a good example of a pattern found on all three classes of ware, the decorator being the 'dot artist', so called, from his habit of spattering numerous dots around the central peony-like flower. In its most characteristic form, the design occurs on blue-painted teaware and includes a meandering branch on which a kingfisher is perched (Plate 11 (d)). It is one of those frequently found with the use of additional over-glaze-red enamel.[1] A variation in which Chinese Imari features appear is seen on a dish (Plate 17 (c)) and is a particularly good example of delft painting on porcelain. The pattern is also seen on the vase shown on Plate 17 (d), close copies of which may be encountered in delftware.

Another design which enjoyed great popularity in this country among delft painters consisted of a large chrysanthemum, a much-jointed bamboo tree and a large rock-like root ornament. On Liverpool porcelain it may be seen in typical form on the big 'John Fell' jug, made by Chaffers and

[1]Compare Plate 11 (d) with Plate 44 (a).

65

dated 1762 (Plate 1 (*c*, *d*)). This piece is therefore of documentary importance. It possesses, however, additional interest from the fact that the design is found on a jug of 'scratch-cross' class (Plate 30 (*a*)) rendered in a manner so similar that if both are not the work of the same hand, it is hard to avoid the conclusion that they come from the same decorating rooms.[1] This would fit in with and even afford some support for the belief that Chaffers & Co., under Podmore's direction, were the makers of Liverpool's share of 'scratch-cross' wares. The delft painter's art can be traced on many other pieces here illustrated (Plates 5 (*b*, *d*), 23 (*m*), 31 (*b*), etc.).

Various adaptations of a Chinese Imari style were adopted by the Liverpool potters and are to be found on wares of every type (Plate 22 (*c*)). Treatment on these lines frequently seems to have resulted from the manner, already noted, by which standard under-glaze blue patterns received further embellishment with red enamel and gilding, although the untreated design may have been complete in itself. The pattern on the coffee can (Plate 8 (*c*)) should be compared with that on the Chaffers mug (Plate 8 (*d*)), the blue-painted portions of which are identical (thus incidentally affording proof of the factory of origin of this and similar coffee cans). As a rule, the general effect is pleasing and the many variations of the style, both in the hands of the china decorator and of others, form an interesting study. The porcelain teapot (Plate 17 (*b*)) already referred to from a potting standpoint and showing decoration in red and gold only, may receive notice here.

Versions of Imari patterns are also met with, Plates 22 (*e*), 31 (*e*), showing one of the best known. Generally mistaken for Worcester, they are easily recognized by the streaky appearance of the blue bands and the inferior quality of the gilding.[2] Other Japanese motifs were placed under tribute, of which mention may be made of the 'banded hedge', here represented on a flat-sided, delft-shaped bowl on which is depicted a battle between two fantastic dragons amid flowering shrubs (Plate 6 (*g*)). A teapot carrying the pattern (Victoria and Albert Museum, *C.1069/1924*) has already been mentioned in connection with its earthenware potting features.

The use of the fantail goldfish as decoration is interesting. The rarity of fish as the subject of porcelain decoration in Eastern art has been commented on by Mr W. W. Winkworth[3] and Dr Severne Mackenna finds that English examples are even more uncommon.[4] It is, therefore, perhaps surprising to

[1]Both are under-glaze (sometimes indicated by the contraction u/g) blue painted.
[2]The potting characters will usually provide a reliable guide. While in some examples they are unmistakably Liverpool, others may give rise to doubt, but the decoration does not seem to vary.
[3]*Antique Collector*, June 1954.
[4]*Antique Collector*, August 1954.

find that Liverpool can be credited with at least three of these, of all of which the provenance seems assured and doubtless there are others. One of these, a sauce boat of silver shape, is decorated in panels on the outside with a famille rose design, the inside depicting three Japanese goldfish in various colours (Plate 17 (e)). The potting and painting of this specimen are of a high quality. A somewhat less satisfactory use of a similar design is seen on the small bowl on Plate 7 (e), while a third example is to be seen on a mug in the Victoria and Albert Museum (1346/24) which we learn was once the property of Lord Nelson.[1] It seems likely that the use of this particular design, rendered in such a similar manner, was prompted by circulating Japanese prints rather than actually copied from Japanese porcelain.

The question whether the well-known 'quail pattern' was used by the Liverpool potters is uncertain. A possible example of its use may be seen on one of those fluted teapots characterized by a decagonal escutcheon at the base of the spout, in the National Museum of Wales at Cardiff (DW.2464). These teapots were made at both Liverpool and Worcester and distinction is sometimes difficult (page 38).

The use of a famille verte palette is not of frequent occurrence. The teapot shown on Plate 8 (g) is a good example, but as far as I can ascertain, nothing like the Worcester 'Bishop Sumner' pattern was ever attempted.[2] But copies of 'famille rose' are as often encountered as on contemporary Bow wares. The 'dot' artist's compositions derive from this source, as may easily be seen when looking at an example in enamel colours such as the bowl on Plate 18 (a). The style was also in favour with the saltglaze painter. A cursory glance at any representative collection of coloured saltglazed wares will provide many examples; and sufficient similarity between some of these and like-decorated pieces of Liverpool porcelain may be noted as to suggest the possibility of a common origin. In addition to the pieces already noted because of their saltglaze type of decoration, the reader is referred to Plate 13 (f), 21 (g)).

Most Liverpool flower painting in the English style is easily recognizable and while some of it is good, for the most part it does not rise above mediocrity. Well known and characteristic is the design which takes the form of a cabbage rose as the central feature of a tapering spray of small orange-coloured flowers. It is commonly found on tea ware traditionally associated with Chaffers' name, an attribution which is acceptable and fits in with other evidence on these matters (Plate 4 (c, d, e, f)). This ware is marked by the greenest of all glazes, so green that I once heard it likened to a coat of green paint. Equally well known is a manner of flower painting characterized by its

---

[1] An ink inscription on the base is the authority for this. Illustrated and described in *Connoisseur*, 1910, page 46.

[2] The 'kylin' pattern is occasionally met with.

hard black outlines and spiky leaves bent over at the tip (Plate 21 (*a, e*). The flowers include a bluish-red cabbage rose, a purple convolvulus, small bunched-up yellow rosebuds and sometimes a full-blown tulip with very splashed petals (Plates 15 (*c*), 19 (*a, c*)). The last named was reserved for the more important pieces and is nearly always associated with painting of good quality, being perhaps the work of the master hand, while the other may be that of the school. The indications are that painting of this type made its appearance towards the close of the first decade and prevailed over a considerable period of time, during which it is to be found linked, directly or indirectly, with a very wide range of other designs, decorative devices and potting shapes. The links include floral motifs and characteristic florets, distinctive borders, blue grounds treated in a variety of ways and reeded shapes; indeed, they are so extensive that it might be thought that so big and varied an assortment could not represent the output of one factory. That this was indeed so, however, seems clear from the proof afforded by the unifying evidence of the blue grounds which so many of these pieces exhibit. These are characteristically streaky and, being underglaze in every example I have been able to examine, must denote factory work and thus assist in establishing kinship in many cases where none might be suspected to exist.

Whether any of the flower painting of this great assemblage of wares is the work of 'outside' decorators is doubtful.[1] A careful study of the manner in which early patterns underwent change and reappeared later in combination with more mature styles assists the belief that all this ware is factory decorated in the only factory which could fulfil long term conditions, namely that of the Chaffers partnership and its successors.

A floral motif to which particular interest attaches consists of two stylized flowers, one red and the other blue, surmounted by a pair of pink turreted buds. It is found paired with other designs (Plate 20 (*b*)), is usually associated with a very distinctive quatrefoil floret in red, yellow and blue and is the decoration on a sauceboat (Plate 12 (*f*)), having a reeded moulding similar to that of the teabowl found as a factory waster by Entwistle (Rackham, E.P.C. Trans., 1929, page 31 and Plate 12 (*h*)).[2] It is also shown on the reeded teapot having a 'marbled' blue band on the shoulder (Plate 21 (*b*)) and decorated on the other side with the Chaffers' rose spray already mentioned.[3]

A study of the various specimens featured on Plates 12, 19, 21, etc, will repay the reader, but unfortunately it is impossible to show by means of

---

[1]Christian had an account with James Giles, the London decorator, between 1771 and 1776 (Toppin, Trans. E.C.C., 1933, No. 1, page 36), but the nature of the business done is obscure.
[2]The reeding is capped by a similarly feathered cresting.
[3]The floret is seen at the bottom left-hand corner.

illustrations more than a few of the links to which reference has been made. Illustrations are necessarily limited, are chosen for a variety of reasons, and, in any case, show only one side of the object. But one can spend long with the actual specimens, noting where similarities of one kind or another can be seen to exist and reflecting on the proof thus afforded of the size of the manufacture represented and the wide range of wares covered by its output.

In speaking of teapots of the depressed globular shape, mention was made of one showing an incised saltire cross (de Winton Collection, Cardiff), with a Liverpool decoration. This consists of a single rose with a projecting bud, very reminiscent of Jacobite engraved glass (Plate 13 (c)). A cylindrical mug painted by the same hand is shown on Plate 13 (d). I do not know the reason for the attribution of this decoration to Liverpool and I am unable to trace the hand on other wares. The mug has good Liverpool features and a similar teapot (unmarked) was sold at Sotheby's as Liverpool on 26th January 1954.[1]

There is a considerable amount of other quite undistinguished flower painting belonging to the middle period. A well-known design embraces a bluish-looking cabbage rose, a large dahlia-like flower with purple red centre and yellow petals, many small compact rosebuds and rather bright green leaves (Plates 19 (d), 23 (b, c)). The bowl (Plate 42 (c)) is interesting on account of its mark — an underglaze upright cross in dark red. Another design uses a peony as its chief flower, with which is associated a characteristic method of leaf veining and the 'jointed branch' technique (Plate 16 (d, e)). The flower painting of the last period, as elsewhere, degenerated into the use of stylized conventions of no artistic value. A good example is shown on Plate 23 (a).

When we come to speak of borders, Sadler seems to reflect the prevailing Liverpool view when he wrote to Wedgwood in 1763, 'We think that a red or other border around quarts would look tawdry', for in the early years, where Liverpool influences prevailed, borders were little used. We have no reason to think that Podmore shared this view, for to him we owe those charming little borders which show passages of trellis interrupted by formal floral ornament.[2] Somewhat later, borders came into general use; indeed, probably no centre in the country came to employ such a wide variety. Some of those most commonly employed are shown on Plate II, but many others will be encountered not shown here, as, for example, the deep trelliswork inside the rim of the late cream jug (Plate 43 (g)). One of the earliest, because ware exhibiting it is often found plain, is probably the 'beans' border (No. 27) of the cup and saucer in the Victoria and Albert Museum (C.1263/1924), on which the 'beans' are of large size — as they appear on the tea-caddy

[1]Lot 104.   [2]Used extensively on early Worcester wares and owning an oriental origin.

69

illustrated in Bemrose's *Longton Hall Porcelain* (Plate XXVI), and on the mug shown on Plate 21 (*d*). It would be easy to infer that, beginning in this bold manner, becoming smaller (Plate 10 (*e*)) and finally degenerating into small circles (Plate 19 (*g*)), such a border might possess limited dating value with which both potting and decoration would be seen to agree. Unfortunately there are many fallacies in trying to use borders in this way and caution is needed. A late type is No. 30 for which a date around 1780–95 seems safe.[1] Some of these borders appear to be confined to use on Liverpool wares and may therefore possess attributional value. Among such may be reckoned Nos. 4, 7, 8, 9, 12, 13, 16, 17, 22, 27, 28, bearing in mind that those copied from oriental sources (e.g., No. 7) were equally open to use elsewhere.

Blue as a ground colour receives its fullest expression as 'marbled blue', in which the colour is veined with gold so as to produce a marbled effect and used either as a complete ground or, more commonly, in the form of bands. Good examples of its use in the first named manner are to be found in a set of vases, one of which is pear shaped and the other two baluster shaped, at one time in the Clough collection, described and illustrated by Entwistle (*Entwistle MSS.*, 5/161). In each case, the reserves are painted with flowers on one side and Biblical subjects on the other, the flower painting being by the same hand and closely resembling that on the teapot shown on Plate 15 (*c*). Similarly decorated in every way is a pair of slender ewers with long narrow necks, curving lips and high loop handles, which are in the same collection; while yet another example is furnished by the bowl, ten inches in diameter, illustrated in Hobson's *Worcester Porcelain* and now in the Victoria and Albert Museum, presented by Mr C. W. Dyson Perrins. Figure subjects, probably also representing Biblical scenes, occupy the panels in this case, the painting long being suspected of being the work of Dr Wall himself. Specimens like this are rare, but vases, generally pear shaped and some seven or eight inches in height, are not infrequently met with and should be easily recognizable, apart from their marbling, by the streaky appearance of the ground colour which seems to be an invariable feature.

'Marbled blue' in the form of bands of colour is quite frequently encountered on a great variety of wares intended for domestic use, as well as on presumably ornamental pieces such as the bottle flask in the Victoria and Albert Museum, illustrated by W. B. Honey (*O.E.P., 1948 edition*, page 198). It was extensively used on teaware (Plate 21 (*c, e*)), particularly on ribbed patterns and also on some examples of the dome-lidded palm tree teapots, where it occurs as a band on the shoulder; and we find it on the necks of the two big jugs in the Schreiber Collection (Victoria and Albert Museum,

---

[1] See Plate 43 (*b, c, f*) for examples of its use.

Schr. 1.782 and 783). One of these is painted with a hare hunting scene which seems to be by the same hand as the painter of the bowl just described (the subject is known as a Liverpool print, Schr. II, 367), while the flower painting on the other resembles that on the bottle flask and on much other Liverpool ware.

Less commonly, blue grounds covered with an all-over diaper of gold trellis are met with, on which are reserved panels for the reception of fruit and flower painting. The decoration of certain bowls in this way is of a high order and calls to mind the work of the Giles atelier. At first glance they seem to have little in common with the wares just mentioned beyond their strong Liverpool potting characteristics. The streaky nature of the blue ground is, however, clearly visible beneath the richness of the close gold trellis, which, unlike most Liverpool gilding, is of excellent quality. One such bowl, presented to the Victoria and Albert Museum by Mr C. W. Dyson Perrins (C. 1155–1924) is painted in the manner of the 'sliced fruit' artist; two others which closely resemble it are featured here from the de Winton Collection in the National Museum of Wales, Cardiff (Plates 13 (a), 14 (a)), while a fourth, identical with the specimen on Plate 14 (a) is in the author's collection. Measuring about nine-and-a-half inches in diameter and painted inside with an orange and cut lemon, these bowls were evidently for use as punch bowls. They are admittedly good to look at, but it is doubtful if they are factory decorated and are thus no more credit to the Liverpool potters than are similarly decorated pieces to the Worcester factory. Perhaps one of the attractions of collecting 'Liverpool' lies in the fact that so little work of this kind seems to have been done.[1]

Plain blue grounds are rarely encountered, probably because the Liverpool potters never really mastered the technique. I have yet to come across a Liverpool example which is not streaky, which suggests that 'marbling' may have arisen with the idea of making what was an unavoidable defect less obvious. On the other hand, the possibility that such a defect might even be turned to advantage and given artistic value may underlie the blatant exaggeration of the brush work on the coffee cup (Plate 14 (d)) with a matching saucer of Worcester make. While the cup exhibits Liverpool potting features with a decidedly brown translucency, the saucer is typically Worcester with translucency of duck egg green, both being painted and gilded in the same way by the same hand. The explanation seems to be that the pieces were 'married' at the decorators' establishment to which each had been sent after receiving its

[1]These bowls, judged by their potting features and glaze, may reasonably be dated about 1770. They are scarce and it is curious that the hand of this painter is not more in evidence. Allowing for the effect of time on a painter's style, the somewhat similar decoration on the big Herculaneum bowl (circa 1800, Schr. II, 349, Plate 54) is the work of another artist.

own factory's treatment in underglaze blue. The streaky effect here is not unpleasing. Less can be said in favour of a plate with fan-shaped panels (Victoria and Albert Museum, *C.712/24*) in which the achievement is blotchy rather than streaky.

Specimens of Liverpool ware with powder blue grounds are but seldom met with, indeed, for long I thought they did not exist. Plate 31 (*j*) shows a cup of this type which possesses good Liverpool characters. Lowestoft is the factory with which confusion seems most likely to arise and great care may be necessary in distinguishing between them. The test for phosphate in this case cannot be expected to give much help.

Equally uncommon is 'scale-blue' in ground treatment. Plate 22 (*d*) shows the only example I have come across and here again the hard, unpleasing effect probably accounts for its scarcity. The labour involved must have been quite disproportionate to the result achieved. It will be noticed that the scale is overglaze, thus largely accounting for its hard look, but the flower painting is recognizable as Liverpool and the question of provenance is settled by potting characters. This particular cup and saucer are illustrated by Entwistle. It is well recognized that the great charm of Worcester 'scale-blue' lies in its soft indistinctness. That is where hard paste French copies fail so completely. There appears, however, to be no justification for supposing that the so-called 'Bodenham' service, with its clearly marked scale and grotesque oriental figures should be attributed to Liverpool rather than Worcester. An early date is given as the reason for the scale peculiarities in this case. On the other hand, the possibility that more Liverpool 'scale' was made than this solitary example would indicate and has been credited to other factories must be borne in mind, particularly in cases where undue prominence of the scale is a noteworthy feature and has apparently provided the sole grounds for excluding Worcester provenance.[1]

'Scale blue' at Worcester immediately suggests 'exotic birds'. A Liverpool variety of the species exists, but, as will have been gathered, it has no scale connections. Yet, in its plump rounded contours, it is quite characteristic. Literally backward-looking, crested and spotted, with yellow neck, green and blue wings, red body and rump under which its tail feathers are coiled in a becomingly coy manner,[2] it is a remarkable object, perhaps not surprisingly solitary in its habits. It is invariably found perched on red twiggy branches, which bear fleshy-looking, dark green fig-tree-like leaves (Plates 20 (*g*), 23 (*j*)) and is found on a variety of wares, restricted, as far as my observation goes, to those of the middle period. Its appearance on teaware in conjunction with

[1]It seems likely that underglaze 'scale' also exists.
[2]'Prawn-tailed' is the description usually given.

PLATE II

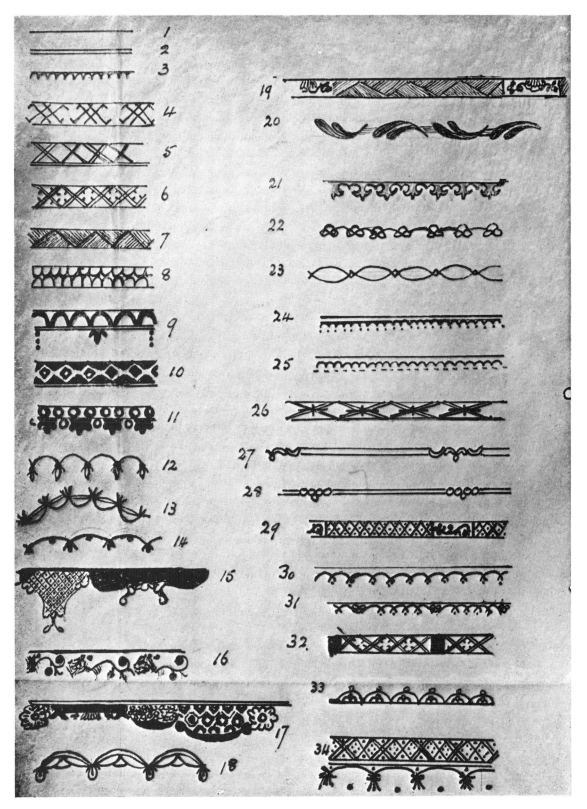

Some Liverpool borders, on the left in blue only; on the right in blue and red only

the so-called 'Barnes' border is not to be regarded as contradicting this statement.

Natural bird painting is rarely encountered on Liverpool porcelain, a fact which is perhaps remarkable, for we find it on earthenware, both saltglazed and tin enamelled, as the well-known wall pockets decorated with finch-like birds in moulded relief bear witness (type Garner, *English Delft-ware*, Plate 64 (*b*)). The semi-naturalistic bird painting on the cup and saucer shown on Plate 16 (*f*) should be compared with the Sadler-printed creamware plate of Wedgwood make (Schr. II.400). They clearly own a common origin and raise the possibility that the painter of one may be the engraver of the other. That, perhaps, is of less importance than the permissible inference that the decoration of both took place in Sadler's establishment, giving support to the belief that, at that comparatively early date, Sadler was not merely a pottery printer, but that before his retirement in 1770, he was the owner of a large pottery decorating business employing a number of hands.

One of the best-known designs using natural bird painting is shown on Plate 31 (*d*). It is mentioned here, although there is more than a suspicion of a printed outline in many places. Aquatic birds sometimes appear as subjects of decoration (Plate 20 (*c*), 40 (*e*)).

The bowl decorated in this way shows that pencilling, in which lines, as opposed to broad washes of colour, are employed, was occasionally used by the Liverpool potters. On this specimen, it forms but part of the decorative treatment and is therefore unlike those well-known pencilled-all-over designs which are usually regarded as Worcester's peculiar property. Whether any of these, with their obvious 'Bristol-Worcester' associations, should be shared with Liverpool, for reasons already given, must be decided by those who undertake the task of sorting out this tangle. Apart from this possibility, I do not know of any all-over pencilled Liverpool ware.

When gilding came into common use at Worcester with the appearance of a fully developed Worcester style — and indeed, sometimes formed the whole decoration — nothing of the kind took place at Liverpool during any stage of development. The teapot, already referred to, which is shown on Plate 6 (*j*), is therefore of more than usual interest, for practically the whole decoration is carried out in sepia and gold. Honey gilding has been used, and it has that rich and slightly dull look associated with the best work of Worcester and Sevres at that time. The craftsmanship here is good. There is no reason to think that this teapot is not Liverpool decorated and one wonders why work of this quality is so scarce. Was a whole service made? The teapot shown on Plate 6 (*c*) prompts similar thoughts. In this case, the artistry of the design is enhanced by the delicate transparency of the enamels, to which no photograph could do justice. My feeling is that these and similar pieces do not form part of services, as we understand the term, although two or three companion pieces may have been made at the time. Certainly they help us to form the opinion that the Liverpool potters were versatile, good craftsmen and willing to try their hands at anything.

Few better illustrations of this could be found than an example of the Liverpool version of the well-known design, the 'stag hunt'. Now whether this design is originally Chinese and reached this country in a 'Meissenised' form, or whether it is a German design subsequently modified by Chinese influence, does not concern us here. It appears to show two men planning a stag hunt in one scene and in the other, putting the plan into execution; and the Chinese original (?), which I illustrate, shows these scenes reserved in panels on a delicately diapered ground of scrollwork in white enamel, which closely resembles low relief (Plate 16 (*a*)). The reproduction of this, apart from the necessary technical skill, called for the exercise of oriental patience. Where others were content to frame the design in conventional moulding,[1] or leave the surround blank,[2] the decorator of this cup and saucer (Plate 16 (*a*)) was at great pains to imitate the Chinese appearance as closely as possible by the use of white enamel — with tolerable success, as a glance at the illustration will show. The labour involved in decorating just one cup and saucer in this way must have been considerable, yet in this case, it seems likely that a whole service was made.

Similar ideas of the 'worthwhileness' of good craftsmanship must underlie much of the work of these early potters. One often hears surprised comment at the display of patience which all pencilled decoration betokens. Why go to this trouble to produce an effect which is so much like good printing, with which it was contemporary? One must assume that if the result seems disproportionate to the labour involved, the reward, in which artistic merit plays but a part, must lie elsewhere. The mass production methods of later days had scarcely begun to make themselves felt.

This stag hunt design seems to have been used at Worcester and is one of those which has conferred a too ready acceptance of Worcester status on the ware it decorates. In this respect, it is typical of a number of such which have contributed to the Worcester-Liverpool tangle in the same way. In all these, the rendering of the particular design will show little variation and from the outset, distinction is made difficult for that reason, bearing in mind the many resemblances which also exist between the wares of the two factories. Pieces showing the 'stag hunt' pattern which may confidently be regarded as 'Liverpool' are 1, the service represented by the teapot and coffee cup (Plates

[1] e.g. at Worcester, where it is found in mirror shaped reserves on a pleat patterned moulding (F. Lloyd Collection, No. 133).
[2] As it appears on certain 'hump-handled' teapots.

74

6 (*b*), 16 (*b*))[1], of which the bases are shown on Plate 50 (*a*); 2, a coffee can having a flat unglazed base, also 'scratch-cross' marked (described but not illustrated); 3, the cup and saucer with diapered ground in white enamel just mentioned and any others showing similar treatment. In addition, the design is found on wares for which a Liverpool attribution is no more than a probability, namely, the class of teapot for which the name 'hump-handled' has been suggested[2] and teapots of the type shown in Schr.I.494. The latter, with its squat form, moulded panels and stumpy scrolled feet strongly suggests an origin from silver shape. Such teapots are almost opaque to light and, as far as my own personal observations extend (limited to some four examples), possess no Worcester characters.[3] The design had a long run in this country, ranging from about 1756–60 at Liverpool to as late as 1790 at Newhall.

BLUE-AND-WHITE DECORATED WARE

Blue-and-white wares were made throughout Liverpool's long china-making history. During the early years, those made under Podmore's influence may be expected to exhibit many of the features customarily regarded as pertaining to 'Bristol-Worcester'. Factory decorated, and in some cases showing the use of similar painter's marks, the sorting out of these will clearly be a matter of considerable difficulty and is a task awaiting future research. Examples are illustrated here which have been selected with care. Those shown on Plates 3 (*c, e, f, g, j*), 5 (*a*) should command general acceptance.

But leaving aside blue-painted wares of this class, one is faced with the fact that blue-and-white china is far from being well represented in the early years of manufacture. This is perhaps the more surprising when it is recalled that Reid & Co. (1756–61) never claimed during their five years of manufacturing activity to make or sell anything other than 'all kinds of blue-and-white china'. This firm is generally credited with most of those blue-painted coffee cans having flat unglazed bases, although, apart from the support given by the wording of the advertisement, the reason for this belief is not clear. Some of these, as we have just seen, were made by Chaffers & Co. Again, Reid's contemporary, Samuel Gilbody, almost certainly made this kind of ware, as doubtless also did William Ball but a few years later. What has happened to all this remains a mystery, even allowing for the fact that a great deal was exported to our American colonies. To Chaffers & Co. in addition to some coffee cans, may be attributed the blue-painted coffee pot (Plate 4 (*a*)) and possibly the mug (Plate 5 (*f*)).

But if the quantity of surviving early blue-painted ware is disappointing,

[1]The Liverpool potting features are given in the chapter describing 'Ware'.
[2]See under 'Ware'.
[3]The type is illustrated and discussed by C. W. D. Perrins, *Apollo*, March 1947, page 66.

some of its decoration, its oriental origins barely discernible, is well done and charming in effect. Nothing of its kind could be better than the teaware shown on Plate 11 (b), with its almost pencilled appearance, so delicate is the drawing. It is interesting to note that exactly the same design may be found in thickly-painted coarsened lines of blackish-blue on teaware which is less well potted and characterized by a peculiar greenish-yellow cast. This is clearly the work of another factory and almost certainly of later date. The colour of this glaze is unlike the range covered by the greens, blues and greys, their variations and combinations which go to make up the bulk of the Liverpool glaze effects known to the collector; and occurring as it does on a variety of wares of widely differing type, may possibly be the distinguishing mark of a separate group. Among examples illustrated here may be noted: 1 the teaware just described; 2 a blue-painted cylindrical mug (Plate 40 (d)); 3 a small moulded leaf dish, blue painted in the same inky colour (Plate 24 (f)); 4 a bowl painted in enamel colours (Plate 13 (e)); and 5, a small pear-shaped vase copied from a Chinese original, decorated underglaze with a floral tracery worked in fillets of light-coloured clay (Plate 13 (b)). None of these show Worcester influence and all may reasonably be dated between 1765 and 1775.

There is no scarcity of 'blue-and-white' of the middle and late periods if we take into account both painted and printed wares. Some of it was of poor quality, particularly the latter, but there is no doubt that the deterioration in ware of this type which set in after Chaffers' death was widespread and continued for some years. It can be explained, if not excused when it is remembered that such ware was in competition with cheaply produced mass-decorated creamware, then being both made in and imported into Liverpool in great quantity. Saltglaze was quickly ousted from popular favour and the cheaper kinds of chinaware were seriously threatened, as also was delftware. It was an unequal contest, ending as it inevitably must with the final triumph of creamware.

As befits cheaply made articles, most of these wares were printed. Of blue painted wares which may be assigned to this period, the best-known design perhaps is the Chinese river scene in which a sloping ramp leads to a centrally placed object looking like an enormous peg-top surmounted by a mast. The picture is completed by the usual hut and trees with twisted trunks and leafage represented by clusters of small circles (Plate 48 (a)). This was a popular design which was in use at other factories. At Liverpool it is one of those which may sometimes be found with additional colouring in red enamel (Plate 10 (d)).[1]

Of other blue-painted wares which may be attributed to the middle period, the most meritorious are those which show additional moulded ornament

[1]Occasionally Liverpool examples are found crescent-marked.

and are considered under that heading. The little vignettes, as they are generally described, which occupy the panels reserved on this type of ware, do
not call for special mention. Other examples of rather uninspired painting
are illustrated on Plates 49 (*g*), 48 (*b*), and from a purely decorative point of
view, the best are undoubtedly to be found on the few dinner plates which
have come down to us (Plate 47 (*c*)), for which a date in the late 1770's
would appear suitable.[1]

Blue printed wares may conveniently be considered here. It is not known
when underglaze blue printing was first practised in Liverpool, but there is
every reason for supposing that this closely followed its introduction at
Worcester, customarily regarded as taking place in 1769. Modern views would
antedate this by several years and I have seen Liverpool examples which would
seem to demand a much earlier date. The earlier wares were, of course,
overglaze printed, frequently in that blue to which the term 'sticky' has been
aptly applied, from its wet appearance — a deep rich colour badly used.
Many of the designs are quite characteristic and include a convolvulus with
very squiggly stalks, a moss rose which has been referred to as very mossy
(Plate 46 (*b*)), a conventional Michaelmas daisy (Plate 46 (*a*)), and one in
which fern fronds play a very prominent part (Plate 49 (*d*)). These are
probably factory decorated, but there is no clue to the factory of origin,
which one suspects, on admittedly no evidence, to have been James Pennington's. The matter is not an easy one on which to form an opinion. There is a
well-known design in which a central floral motif is surrounded by a 'pilgrim
shell' wreath (Plate 45 (*b*)). It is often found on reeded ware which has links
with Christian's factory which are hard to overlook (Plate 21 (*e*)), yet it is
found sharing a border with the group just mentioned.[2] This is one of those
patterns which sometimes receive additional treatment with enamel colours,
in this case with not very happy result (Plate 42 (*h*)). For representative
examples of all these, reference should be made to Plates 45, 46, 47, 48. A good
design in underglaze, well executed and pleasing to look at, features a landscape with trees and partridges (Plate 47 (*a*)).

In many ways the good quality of the late 'blue-and-white', most of which
was probably made by Seth Pennington, atones for the shortcomings of the
ware we have just been considering. The fashion for teaware of this type was
now on the wane and even in provincial centres like Liverpool there is not
much evidence of its manufacture in the last two decades of the century.
The large teapot (Plate 41 (*c*)), which has a capacity of about half a gallon,
was probably intended as a punch pot. There is in the Victoria and Albert

[1]Plate 47 (*c*) is painted, but seems to have a printed outline in places. It conforms to a well-
known pattern.
[2]See 'Borders', No. 12.

Museum a specimen of this size in saltglaze which is inscribed 'Punch'.[1]
This example is interesting on account of the manner of its underglaze blue
painted decoration, which depicts a group of persons seated around a table,
one of whom is pointing to a teapot obviously meant to represent the piece
decorated. That this is so is shown both by its size and by the unusual form
of bird knop on the cover which is faithfully drawn. Plate 40 (*f*) shows a
large pear-shaped vase, the cover of which carries an identical bird knop.[2]
The vase is blue-painted with a Chinese river scene in which a pagoda amid
trees and distant mountains are depicted, while in the foreground are three
figures, one of whom is seen to be carrying a large vase, again shaped like the
subject of the decoration. The scene is empanelled in a scroll framework,
surmounted with a well executed scale diaper on the shoulder of the piece,
the potting and decoration of which are of the highest order.[3]

Yet another example of this mannerism, in which the decoration is made
to include a picture of the object decorated, is provided by the Isabella ship
bowl in the Liverpool Museum (Plate 40 (*a*)). The inside is painted in blue
with a ship in full sail, the legend 'Success to the Isabella' and the date 1779.
The outside, also blue painted, shows two sailors, one of whom is holding a
bowl and between them is a large chest bearing the words 'Spanish Gold'.
Here then, are three specimens, reasonably the work of the same artist, who
clearly possessed considerable ability and was working in Liverpool about
1780; for if the date on the bowl commemorates launching, as seems most
likely, it could well have been made sometime afterwards. Two names at once
suggest themselves, Robert Pennington, born in 1763 and his younger brother
John, born a year or two later.[4] Now Robert's apprenticeship seems to have
taken place in Liverpool and terminated in 1784 when he went to London,
whereas it can be inferred that his brother's was served in Staffordshire and
that he did not come to Liverpool until 1784. In any case, John would have
been very young at the time and Robert seems, therefore, the more probable
choice.[5]

Bowls of this type had been made by the Liverpool potters, usually of
delftware, from early days. It is assumed that they were made for presentation
to commemorate the termination of a successful venture in whaling or
slave-trading and, in that way, are illustrative of the history of Liverpool as a
port in a direction now long forgotten. It may be so, but while such events

[1] Note the Leeds type of handle.
[2] Characterized by its unusually high pedestal.
[3] Mr Allman's collection.
[4] See short biographical notes on these two men.
[5] The recent discovery of the Bow 'John Bowcock' bowl, dated 1759, now in the British
Museum, shows that this mannerism is neither new nor confined to Liverpool.

would qualify for being recorded in this way many times during a vessel's career, launching would occur but once. These bowls are admittedly now very scarce, yet I believe no instance is known in which the same ship appears on two or more bowls, thus favouring the view that, dated or undated, launching was the event commemorated.[1]

A known painter of ship bowls at Seth Pennington's was John Robinson who migrated to Burslem. He was responsible for the famous delftware bowl $20\frac{1}{2}$ inches in diameter, inscribed 'Success to the Africa Trade', which he took with him to Burslem and presented to the Institute at Shelton, where, Mayer informs us in 1855, it still remained. The description which Mayer gives would infer that Robinson was responsible for the whole decoration, including that of the landscape, with horses and trees, etc, on the outside, as well as the ships on the inside. It is quite likely that in this and similar cases the ship painting was the specialized work of one man and the painting on the outside that of another. That would explain the obvious links between the Isabella bowl decoration and that of teapot and vase. A close comparison between many specimens of this class would no doubt help to clear up much that is obscure, but the difficulty that so many of the most important are in public collections and consequently immovable would have to be taken into account.

Porcelain examples, when the date permits, are generally credited to Seth Pennington, though the advertisement of his elder brother John, when he moved to new premises in Folly Lane in 1779, clearly shows that this honour may have to be shared. In addition to the Isabella, just mentioned, there fall to be recorded: the 'Polar Star' (n.d.),[2] the 'Will. R. Bibby',[3] 1783, the 'Molly' (n.d.)[4], all in Liverpool Museum and believed destroyed by enemy action in 1941; the 'Ralph Farrar'[5], also dated 1783, the 'Lord Grosvenor' (n.d.), the 'Swallow' (n.d.,) painted in polychrome, in the Victoria and Albert Museum, and no doubt many others in private hands. There are also bowls of this type bearing neither name nor date.

The vases, however, of this period may be reckoned its principal adornment. The majority of these were painted in blue underglaze, judging from the surviving specimens, but blue underglaze printing is found on many pottery examples which seem to date from the end of the century. Although

[1]In making this observation, the much more numerous delftware examples qualify to be taken into account.

[2]In *W.L.A.*, 22nd August 1777 we read of the arrival of the *Polar Star* with three fish (a whaler).

[3] and [4]both slave-traders.

[5]In the collection of Mr E. Allman of Bootle. Gatty (op. cit., page 45) records one in the possession (in 1882) of Mr Crompton of Bootle, with ship inside and the inscription. 'Success to the King Prusha'. Most of these bowls measured about $9\frac{1}{2}$ inches in diameter

Mayer does not mention the fact, Gatty's description of the set of 'chimney ornaments', which were given to Mayer by Seth Pennington's daughter, makes it quite clear that the decoration of these combined the use of under-glaze blue with flowers in enamel colours. This is so important in enabling us to identify similarly decorated pieces, that I give Gatty's words from his now scarce monograph. '101. Set of beakers and jars for the mantelpiece, in porcelain; painted with blue decoration under the glaze and with bunches of flowers of various colours over it. There are also traces of gilding. These were purchased by Mr Mayer from Miss Pennington, of Everton Terrace, in 1854, daughter of Pennington'. This helps to confirm the provenance of certain teaware of late date, not infrequently met with, to which this description would apply (Plate 42 (e)).[1]

---

[1]Further information about the vases of this period will be found under 'Ware'.

PLATE III

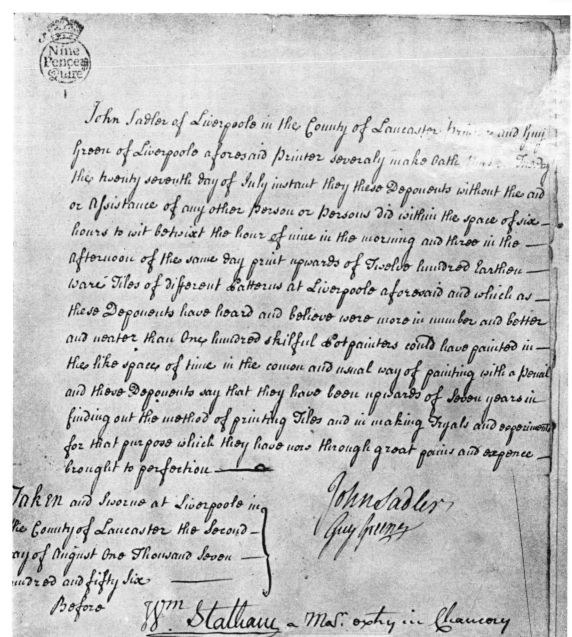

Sadler's tile printing experiment, 27th July 1756. The signed affidavit of
John Sadler and Guy Green

CHAPTER FIVE

PRINTED WARE

O N A CERTAIN DAY in July 1756, John Sadler, a Liverpool printer, claimed that he had found out, experimented upon for a number of years and finally perfected a method of decorating earthenware by means of printed designs. That, with the assistance of Guy Green, a former employee of Sadler's father who had helped in the researches, these two did, on the 27th day of July 1756 'print upwards of twelve hundred tiles of different patterns at Liverpool aforesaid, within the space of six hours'. This was a sworn statement and was supported by a certificate given by Alderman Thomas Shaw and Samuel Gilbody, both potters, stating that they had satisfied themselves of its truth.[1]

It had seemed as if the dust of controversy had long since blown from this once much discussed topic. The view finally accepted favoured the idea that the decoration of suitable articles by means of transfer prints took birth at Theodore Janssen's Enamel Works at York House, Battersea, where the engraver Ravenet, his pupil Hancock and the Irish engraver, John Brooks were working. It has long been known that the business partnership in this concern consisted of Janssen, Brooks and Henry Delamain 'the younger', the latter a practical potter who had recently left Dublin where for a short while he had been in business as a delftware manufacturer. On 1st November 1753, Delamain was petitioning the Irish House of Commons for financial assistance, on the grounds that his delftware industry was of some national importance and claiming that he was coal-firing his kilns, being the first person to do so.[2] Rather surprisingly also, he mentions at the same time, almost incidentally, that he 'had purchased the Art of Printing Earthenware with as much Beauty, Strong impression and Despatch as it can be done on paper'. The importance of the latter statement to the student of Liverpool ceramics needs no stressing, for it has always seemed possible that the credit for being the first person to print on *earthenware* might reasonably be accorded to Sadler on the evidence available. This could, indeed, still be so

[1]Plates III, IV.
[2]Journal of the House of Commons, Ireland, 1753, volume 5, page 17.

if Delamain bought the 'Art' from Sadler; and as Dudley Westropp makes this suggestion[1], the known facts and their possible bearing on this interesting subject may be reconsidered.

Although Westropp's paper on 'Pottery Manufacture in Ireland' was published in *Proceedings of the Royal Irish Academy* in 1913, it seems to have received little recognition in this country until commented upon by Mr Bernard Rackham nearly twenty years later.[2] The conclusion then reached[3] was that Delamain must have bought from John Brooks, the Irish engraver, who had left Dublin about 1746 and settled in London. Brooks, while not himself an important engraver,[4] had some distinguished pupils; and Mr A. J. Toppin thinks there is reason to believe that he was the inventor of the process of 'printing on enamels, a process that eventually became of great importance to the Ceramic Industry in England'. Mr Cyril Cook,[5] following the lead of two brief eighteenth-century accounts of the life of John Brooks, thinks also that the credit for the invention of the new decorative process belongs to Brooks and that with its adoption, 'Janssen, Delamain and Brooks were the pioneers in its exploitation on a commercial scale'.

Clearly, Delamain is likely to have been in possession of his knowledge on this matter, however obtained, for some months before his claim to it could have been made in these circumstances; and the further likelihood that the opening of the York House Enamel Works in the summer of 1753 was related to this knowledge is a reasonable assumption. From that point onward doubts arise. If the 'Art' related to printing earthenware, why were the first attempts made on enamel? If Delamain bought from Brooks, how was this comparatively obscure engraver enabled to carry out experiments in pottery printing to a degree which could have resulted in a saleable discovery, a difficulty which presumably would be hardly less in the case of enamel printing? And why, having succeeded in doing this, was it necessary to sell the secret to a man with whom he was about to enter into partnership?

These are difficult questions to answer. Mr Cyril Cook has suggested[6] that the reference to 'Earthenware' in Delamain's petition may mean that Brooks' invention was related in the first place to printing this type of ware; and that the establishment at York House was set up with the object of decorating Dutch tiles, of which there is mention in the public notices appearing in June 1756, when the stock of the factory was advertised for sale.

[1]*Pottery Manufacture in Ireland*, 1913.
[2]*Porcelain as a Sidelight on Battersea Enamels*, Trans. E.P.C., No. IV, 1932 (supplementary note, page 73)   [3]Inferentially and not necessarily Mr Rackham.
[4]Toppin, Trans. E.P.C. 1932, page 61, *Artists at the Battersea Factory.*
[5]*Apollo*, May 1952, page 149, *John Brooks and his Engravings on Battersea Enamels.*
[6]*Apollo* May 1952, loc. cit.

PLATE IV

WE Alderman Thomas Shaw and Samuel Gilbody both of Liverpoole in the County of Lancaster Claypotters whose names are hereunto subscribed do hereby humbly certifye that we are well assured that John Sadler and Guy Greene Did at Liverpoole aforesaid on Tuesday the twenty seventh day of July now last past within the Space of six hours print upwards of One Thousand two hundred Earthen Ware Tiles of different Colours and patterns which is upon a moderate computation more than One hundred good workmen could have done of the same patterns in the same space of time by the usual way of painting with pencils That we have since burnt the above Tiles and that they are considerably neater than any we have seen pencilled and may be sold at little more than half the price We are also assured the said John Sadler and Guy Greene have been several years in bringing this Art of printing on Earthenware to perfection and we never heard it was done by any person or persons but themselves We are also assured that as the Dutch who import large Quantities of Tile into England, Ireland &c may by this Improvement be considerably undersold it cannot fail to be of great Advantage to the Nation and to the Town of Liverpoole in particular where the Earthen ware manufacture is more Extensively carried on than in any other Town in the Kingdom. for which Reasons we hope and do not doubt the above persons will be indulged in their request for a patent to secure to them the profits that may arise from the above useful and advantageous Improvements

Thos. Shaw

Samuel Gilbody

Sadler's tile printing experiment, 27th July 1756. The signed certificate by Alderman Shaw and Samuel Gilbody

There does not seem to be anything to support this ingenious suggestion, which is difficult to reconcile with at least one fact of outstanding importance. If we turn to the wording of the certificate given by Alderman Shaw and Samuel Gilbody referring to Sadler's experimental printing of tiles in July 1756, we read,[1] 'We are also assured that the said John Sadler and Guy Green have been several years in bringing the art of printing on earthenware to perfection and we never heard that it was done by any other person or persons but themselves. We are also assured that as the Dutch (who import large quantities of tiles into England, Ireland, etc.,) may by this improvement be considerably undersold . . . ' It is inconceivable that, had an earlier printing of tiles by others taken place, the Liverpool tile makers could have been so completely ignorant of the fact as this would indicate. News may not have travelled fast in those days, yet the Liverpool potters advertised their wares in the London papers and well knew what was going on there.[2] Turner[3] has something pertinent to say about this certificate. He states 'So far as we know, earthenware had not previously been printed on. But we do know that both enamel and porcelain have been decorated with transfer prints at Battersea and for Bow. Messrs Shaw and Gilbody may not have known the latter fact. They may have known and still be within legal limits in making their certification'.

Turning to Mr Dudley Westropp's suggestion that Delamain bought from Sadler at a time when Sadler was trying to make up his mind whether to apply for a patent, it may be surmized that, although in his affidavit he claimed to have been working on the discovery 'upwards of seven years', it is doubtful whether he would have had more to sell by the middle of 1753 than had John Brooks. The real objection to this possibility must lie in the fact that, had Sadler sold his secret in this way, it would have been impossible for him to have considered applying for a patent in respect of the same invention three years later. There is not the slightest doubt that he did consider doing so, for the document was addressed to Charles Pole, the local Member for Parliament and duly witnessed.[4] The application was not proceeded with for reasons which will be discussed. As a barrier to any previous sale, it is absolute.

Neither John Brooks nor John Sadler therefore commend themselves as

---

[1]Plate IV.
[2]John Eccles & Co. of the Park Lane Pothouse, Liverpoole, were advertising in the *General Evening Post*, 22nd July, 1756. (*Apollo*, February 1955, page 50).
[3]*Transfer Printing on Enamels, Porcelain, Pottery*, 1907, page 8.
[4]Reproduced in Plate V, q.v. One of the documents which Mayer obtained from Miss Sadler (see Mayer's *History*). These have unaccountably been lost, but good photographs are in my possession.

persons from whom Delamain could have purchased his 'Art' and one has to look elsewhere. Michael Hanbury, a copperplate printer and engraver of Skinners Row, Dublin, exhibited specimens of printing on *pottery* to the Dublin Society in 1758.[1] This is described as 'a new invention for ornamenting with great despatch, china and earthenware, etc., from copper-plate engraving on the unburnt glaze'. He received an award of twenty guineas. This was two years after Sadler's experiment on tiles and long after ceramic printing is said to have been employed at Bow and many other centres. Now, Henry Delamain had died in January 1757 and his Will, proved in London and discovered at Somerset House by Mr A. J. Toppin,[2] contains no reference to any interest he may have had (in the way of rights or otherwise) in pottery printing. It is, therefore, possible that his original purchase may have been from Hanbury, who, prevented by this sale from otherwise benefiting from his discovery during Delamain's lifetime, was able to exploit it later after the Battersea failure. Hanbury is mentioned as a copperplate engraver and printer in George's Lane and Skinners Row, Dublin, between 1748 and 1755, so that this possibility is not ruled out. He died in 1762.

Links between the Battersea manufacture and Ireland were strengthened when W. B. Honey drew attention to the printed and over-painted decoration on some Limerick delftware plates dated 1761 and to its resemblance to Battersea work.[3] He describes them as having 'a soft purple-brown overglaze line' and continues, 'it is tempting to conjecture that the Limerick engraving was the work of one of Delamain's associates. It is unrecorded and unlikely that Brooks ever returned to Ireland after the closing of the Battersea factory, but a possible engraver is Michael Hanbury of Dublin.' This lends support to the idea that, in spite of the lapse of time, Hanbury may also have had a hand in the original discovery.

Henry Delamain was well-known in Liverpool, so well in fact that when he petitioned the English Parliament for a subsidy to enable him to develop his coal-firing discovery on the grounds of its national importance, he was able to write to his wife from Liverpool in December 1753 and say that the Mayor, Corporation and all the potters would sign the petition on his behalf.[4] As this took place a month after he had made his earthenware printing claim, if any exchange of ideas took place between Delamain and Sadler at that time, its direction was more likely to be from Delamain to Sadler than the other way round. But with this, as with most discoveries, it is probable that the ideas which lead up to them are taking form in the minds of many

[1] *Guide to Irish Pottery*, M. S. Dudley Westropp, page 14.
[2] Trans. E.C.C., volume 8, 1942, page 158, *The Will of Henry Delamain the Dublin Potter*.
[3] Trans. E.C.C., 1942, page 155, *Limerick Delftware*.
[4] Dudley Westropp, op. cit., page 14.

men who are abreast of the times and to no one person can be awarded the credit of discovery when it finally comes. The scanty and rather conflicting information we possess indicates that the basic idea of applying a printed decoration to enamels and ceramic wares emanated from Dublin, whence it spread to other parts of Ireland, to Liverpool, and to London and in so doing received its full development.

This historical background of pottery printing is of more than passing interest to the student of Liverpool wares. The technique of the Limerick plates just referred to, with their soft purple-brown line is comparatively rare on eighteenth-century wares.[1] It can hardly be a coincidence that it is found occasionally on some early Liverpool porcelain, producing an effect which resembles that of the Liverpool 'polychrome' print although distinct from it.[2] All this fits in well with the fact that Liverpool was on the direct route between Dublin and London, its potters well acquainted with Delamain and prepared to do much to help him in his schemes. That their help was not called upon is another story. This type of printing and the wares on which it is found will receive consideration later.

While the evidence in favour of Sadler's claim to be the first person to print on tiles may be allowed — and his claim really amounts to nothing more — it is therefore much less certain that the credit for printing the first lead-glazed earthenware should go to him also. One must remember that, at the date we are considering, the development of creamware was in its infancy and that the ordinary lead-glazed earthenware of the time was mainly unsuitable for this purpose.[3] In February 1757, Thomas Lawrenson, a Liverpool engraver, announced in the public press the forthcoming appearance of a pamphlet which, among other things, was going to discuss 'the new and curious Art of printing or rather re-printing from Copper-plate, Prints upon Porcelain, Enamel and Earthenwares, as lately practiced at Chelsea, Birmingham'. Many have searched for this pamphlet without success and presumably it was never published. The wording of this announcement is interesting and will be considered further when the few facts known about this engraver are recorded.[4] Here it may be said that it affords no evidence that printing on earthenware, meaning the lead-glazed variety, had successfully been attempted at this date, since neither of the localities mentioned were associated with ceramic printing in any form, or with the manufacture of earthenware.

[1]W. B. Honey, ibid.   [2]Plate 34 (*a*, *b*)
[3]The creamware would be dark in colour or colour-glazed in Whieldon fashion and other lead-glazed ware would be made from dark coloured clays. No printing on saltglaze took place until many years later (see Sadler's letter of 30th November 1764, Appendix IVA (18).
[4] See biography Lawrenson.

On the other hand, there is no mention of Liverpool. It cannot be doubted that Lawrenson knew of Sadler and Green's experimental printing, which must have received the widest publicity and had occurred but a few months previously. A possible explanation is that Sadler, at this date, was not using copper-plates but woodcuts.[1]

Much discussion has centred round the back-dating of Sadler's experiments. According to the affidavit, Sadler and Green had been upward of seven years in finding out and perfecting the method.[2] The Certificate mentions 'several years'. In 1799, a Mr Moss, writing in the *Liverpool Guide*, stated that 'Copper-plate printing upon china and earthenware originated here in 1752'.[3]

We have seen there is every reason to suppose that something of this matter must have been known to Sadler at least as early as the date of Delamain's visit in 1753 and it is likely that he had carried out some experiments on a small scale. It seems equally certain that he could not have done much, for he had no kiln of his own and the borrowing of one by a printer could not have been kept secret. When Alderman Shaw stated that he had never heard of this process being done by anyone else, it may still have been his kiln which had been used for any experimental work which had taken place, as it probably was on the day of the demonstration. We can doubt the strict accuracy of the claim, as Turner says,[4] without assuming to doubt either the affidavit or the certificate. He goes on to say that the outstanding matter of importance is the fact that twelve hundred tiles were printed on a certain day and with that we can agree.

The third document demanding attention in this matter is the application for a patent addressed to Charles Pole Esq., the local Member for Parliament.[5] This step must have received the serious consideration of Sadler and Green at the time and it may have been decided not to proceed in the matter, partly because it came to be realized on enquiry that, at this date, Sadler could claim no more than that he had adapted an older discovery which had already been put to practical use; and partly because it was thought that by working the process secretly and relying thereby on making discovery as difficult as possible, their interests would be better served than by relying on the doubtful protection afforded by the patent laws.

THE FIRST FIVE YEARS

At this time, the Dutch were sending into this country large quantities of hand-painted tiles; and it is clear from the wording of the certificate that

[1]Few English pottery prints from woodcuts have yet been identified.
[2]The Sadler documents, Plate III.
[3]Mayer, op. cit., page 56, also quoted by Turner, *Transfer Printing*, page 12.
[4]Op. cit., pages 15, 46.   [5]Plate V.

PLATE V

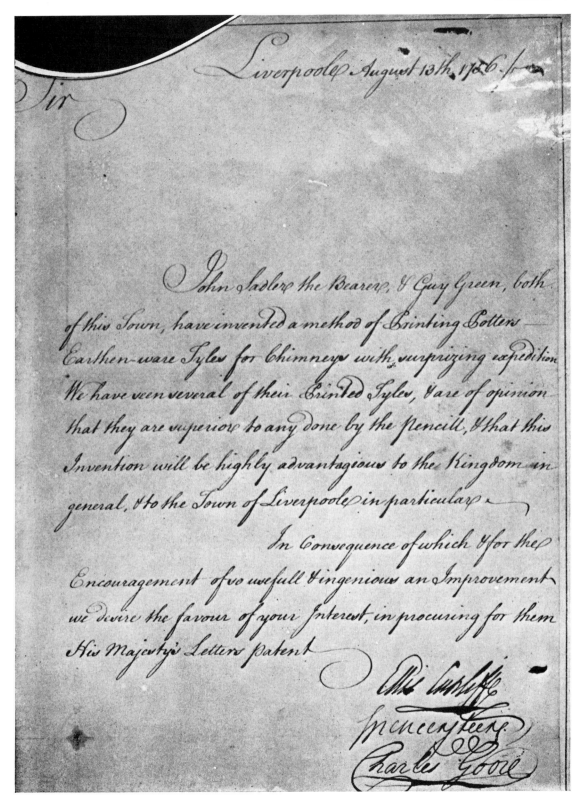

Sadler's tile printing experiment, 27th July 1756. The petition for a patent, not presented

Sadler, by taking full advantage of the rapidity and cheapness of his new method of decoration, intended to lose no time in under-selling them. It is therefore likely that his immediate preoccupation would be with tiles, which he bought from every maker in the town.

Firing at first must have been done in a borrowed kiln, but with the rapid development which now began to take place, it would not be long before Sadler had a muffle of his own. This must have been installed long before he entered into any agreement with Wedgwood for printing creamware. As soon as that event took place (1761), we are in possession of good information concerning the development of pottery printing in Liverpool, the Sadler-Wedgwood correspondence being of the greatest value in this respect. Before that date there is a gap in our knowledge which is hard to fill. What exactly apart from tile-printing did Sadler do in the five years which elapsed between the date of his experiment in 1756 and the beginning of his association with Wedgwood in 1761?

It is unlikely that he printed much domestic earthenware before this event. As far as I know, no examples to which a pre-1761 date may confidently be given are known, for, as already stated, the earthenware of the day with the possible exception of saltglaze, was mainly unsuitable to receive printed decoration. In December 1761, Sadler sent to Wedgwood a 'China pint Tythe pig' and 'a K. Pruss. enam. blank', presumably as samples of what he was doing (but he charged for them). At the same time, he sent a 'mid-size printed T-pot' and from the fact that it was invoiced at one-third the price of the others, it must have been earthenware. This seems good evidence that he was printing domestic earthenware at that date, but that his china printing was better developed and a more important branch of his activities.

While the year 1761 thus marks the earliest recorded date of Liverpool china printing, it had been done much earlier, not only by the printer Sadler but by the Liverpool china makers, of whom three were in active production between 1756 and 1761. Popular enthusiasm for the leaders of the Allies in the Seven Years War (1756–63), both military and political, was the occasion for the appearance of a quantity of ware decorated with portraits in their honour. These were black on-glaze prints, at first entirely confined to use on chinaware, on which they undoubtedly represent the earliest achievement at Liverpool. With Frederick the Great heading the list, this gallery included Pitt, Wolfe, Prince Ferdinand and, later, George III and Queen Charlotte. No Liverpool portrait of George II is known on porcelain, but an enamel example existed in the destroyed collection of the Liverpool Museum (No. 3102). One of the rarest is the portrait of Prince Frederick, which is probably Sadler printed.[1]

---

[1]This portrait has since been identified by Dr B. Watney as that of the Young Pretender.

The flanking prints here are floral sprays tied with a ribbon, identical with those found on other Sadler signed mugs of the series, a fact which, generally speaking, might justify the conclusion that all pieces so printed represented the work of one and the same engraver.

With the signing of peace in 1763, there was probably an increased demand for mugs of this type which may have lasted to the end of the year; and time limited in this way, these portraits possess a certain dating value. Unfortunately, they give little help in distinguishing between the wares of the different factories, for Sadler's practice of buying from all and sundry would clearly prevent it. This will be referred to again when we come to consider the manner in which Sadler conducted his business. It is hard to avoid the impression from the number of Sadler-signed examples which have survived that most of this ware was Sadler-printed.

Frederick suddenly rose to great popularity at the end of 1757, due seemingly to his victory over the French and Empire troops at Rosbach. His portrait on Hancock's Worcester mug appeared in December of that year and the Liverpool potters, if not pioneers in this, quickly followed suit. Many portraits of Frederick on Liverpool wares must date from about this time. Chaffers, by reason of the greater size and importance of his manufacture and the completeness of its decorating department in Podmore's hands must be reckoned an early competitor in this field. The jug (Plate 35 (b)), which was given to Mayer by Charles Chandos Pole, a descendant of the Pole who fought the 1761 Election and the mug (Plate 35 (c)) are both decorated with prints of Frederick in Court dress and are examples of this factory's work,[1] although it is unlikely that either were printed there. A jug of similar shape and size, which was formerly in the Liverpool Museum, carried a portrait of George III signed by the Liverpool engraver Billinge, but here, the central position of his signature may be taken as good evidence of Chaffers' factory printing.

Samuel Gilbody ordered from Jeremiah Evans, the Liverpool engraver, an engraving of Frederick in Court dress and, a fortunate circumstance, he had his name engraved on the plate, showing that he required it for his own use. From this we could learn something of the ware he made and that he made use of printed decoration. Unfortunately the mug carrying this print — the only example known — and bearing the signatures 'Gilbody maker', 'Evans Sct', was destroyed by enemy action in 1941, when the treasures of Liverpool Museum were lost. Good photographs remain in which the signatures are clearly legible (Plate 35 (a)). No printed ware attributable to Reid & Co. has been identified.

To these three Liverpool-printed versions of Frederick in Court dress

[1] Said to be adapted from a painting by Pesne and engraved by J. G. Wille.

must be added a fourth which occurs on a Wedgwood creamware teapot, reasonably identified as Billinge's work from his characteristic flanking scrolls. No Worcester example of this print is known, but yet another version exists on a Bow teapot (Schr.I.110), similar in every respect. A different copper plate seems to have been used in every one of these five examples.

Gilbody's first public announcement of himself as a china maker appeared in February 1758 when his Evans-engraved portrait of Frederick was probably to be seen on the ware then offered for sale. It is unlikely that Sadler, whose business instinct rarely seems to have been at fault, was left behind in this matter. Competing keenly in a market in which he had already done pioneer work, in which he was very interested and intended to make his own speciality, he could not neglect a situation where public fervour and private profit could be so closely linked to his advantage. Evans engraved and signed a portrait of Frederick in armour for Sadler's own use. This is after the painting by Pesne, Houston's engraving of which was also used by Hancock on the well-known Worcester mug dated 1757. Pieces which carry this Evans-signed print are, 1 a bell-shaped mug in Mr Allman's collection; 2 a cylindrical mug, formerly in the Dykes collection; 3 a cylindrical mug, illustrated and described by Frank Tilley (*Antique Collector*, June 1954, page 123).[1] A mug similar to the last, also bearing this print, but having had Evans' name removed by Sadler, is seen on Plate 39 (*f*). There is no reliable clue to the maker of mugs of this type.

In many ways Liverpool was particularly well placed for the developments now taking place, being already the seat of many flourishing craft industries in which the use of kindred arts could be readily diverted to new service. In addition to ordinary pottery making in all its branches, pipe-making was carried on[2] and there was an extensive manufacture of glassware of every kind, useful as well as ornamental. The latter included engraved and cut glass, stained glass, opaque white glass (at Warrington) and glass decorated by a method of printing in colour.[3] But Liverpool as an important centre of a watchmaking industry is of particular interest. There is little difference between an enamelled dial or watch-back and copper similarly enamelled which is intended for fashioning into a medallion or trinket box after receiving a printed decoration; and R. J. Charleston tells us[4] that the enamel used in this way was in all essential respects identical in composition with that used

[1] Now in Mr Allman's collection.

[2] Pipeclay was imported from North Devon and used both in pipe making and in making saltglazed ware. 'Shall make enquiry of the pipeclay you are short of. More likely to be sold to some of our pipemakers than to the china works' (Green to Wedgwood, 1771).

[3] Henry Baker, q.v. In the Liverpool Sept-centenary Exhibition, 1907, 'two squares of glass with purple prints of classical scenes, signed ' "Baker, f. Liverp." '.

[4] 'English XVIIIth century opaque white glass', R. J. Charleston, *Antiques*, December 1954, page 488.

in the manufacture of opaque white glass. Among the watch engravers, too, there were doubtless many who were willing to learn to adapt their methods to suit the new demand for pottery print engravings. No more than average competence would be required. And so the conditions in Liverpool at this time were entirely favourable to the rapid development of transfer printing on pottery, porcelain and enamels, now linked together more closely because of the new method of decoration which they shared.

Enamels call for no more than a passing reference. The extent of the development of such an industry in Liverpool is unknown. The present trend of informed opinion favours a Staffordshire origin for much work of this type formerly attributed to Battersea, although clearly there is no technical difficulty in accepting all the scarce Sadler-printed examples which have survived as of Liverpool manufacture, as undoubtedly they were. The information we possess seems to show that, as far as Sadler was concerned, enamel printing covered a very short space of time, probably not more than the two years from 1758 to 1760. Of the medallions, Liverpool Museum possessed four, *viz:* the Bucks Society's arms, George II, Frederick the Great in Court dress but without a hat, and William Pitt. A fifth, the Freemasons badge, is in the Victoria and Albert Museum, where also may be seen another, printed with a Pillement subject (Schr. III.405) which occurs in identical form on a Liverpool tile. One of the most interesting of the Liverpool enamels takes the form of a snuff-box, Sadler-printed and signed, exhibiting a Calendar for the year 1759 with Dominical Letter tables. This was advertised for sale in the *Liverpool Chronicle* on 8th December 1758 at Parker's toy shop.[1]

Here it may be remarked that Sadler's description of himself as an enameller has nothing to do with enamels of this type. When he gave up printing his newspaper *The Liverpool Chronicle* in 1757, he gave as the reason that he 'was engaged in the Enamelling of Tiles', meaning that he was engaged in printing them. No other means of decoration was then open to him. 'Jet enamelling' was the term frequently given to pottery printing in black in those days, as may be seen from the description of one of the lots in a sale of Worcester porcelain in December 1769: 'A beautiful bowl with fox chase jet enamelled and a large jug'.[2] No mystery therefore attaches to the contracted form of the word enameller, as 'Enl' or 'Enaml', which sometimes appears after Sadler's signature.[3]

The explanation of the description 'Enamel blank' which Sadler applied to one of his samples sent to Wedgwood, presents greater difficulty. No prints of the type referred to exist in outline, i.e., in a form such as would be

[1]Sadler subsequently married Parker's daughter.
[2]Nightingale, quoted in Schr. I. 675.
[3]For the use of enamelling in this sense. See letter, Appendix VI A (*i*).

suitable for subsequent completion by colouring. It may be thought that standards governing the correct use of words in those days were not high. One recalls the legend 'Rhodes pinxit' beneath the decoration of one of a pair of leaf-shaped dishes in the Schreiber collection (Schr. I.466), a decoration which, but for a narrow green edge, is entirely printed.[1] Yet Sadler was an educated man, knowing well how to use words, as his letters to Wedgwood clearly show. The reference might be to a print without any inscription, a sort of proof before letters, were it not for the fact that this is the state in which most pottery prints are found. A more plausible explanation is the suggestion made by Mr H. R. M. King that 'blank' is a misreading for 'black'.

THE ASSOCIATION WITH WEDGWOOD

With the development of printed decoration at Liverpool taking place in this manner, we arrive at the time at the close of 1761, when Sadler entered into arrangements with Wedgwood to print his newly perfected creamware. We do not know when he took Green into partnership, but it has been supposed that this took place about the same time. Wedgwood's first invoice, which covered the period 23rd September 1761 to 7th November 1763, was addressed to 'Sadler & Green'. Clearly, this provides no proof of partnership until the later date, yet there is little doubt that the two men had worked in close association ever since the date of the experimental printing seven years earlier. During this interval much had been accomplished under Sadler's guidance and many difficulties had been overcome. But the association now formed with Wedgwood put an end to all uncertainty. It was a decisive event in Sadler's life, a business association which was destined to last more than thirty years. Pottery printer in its widest sense Sadler remained, but there is no doubt that henceforth, earthenware printing became his chief preoccupation.

Sadler's method of doing business was simple and seems to have varied little up to the date of his retirement in 1770. He bought wares 'in the white' from any potter who would sell to him, printed them with or without additional colouring, from copper plates bought from free-lance engravers and sold them at his own prices at his shop in Harrington Street. Before long he undoubtedly had engravers in whole time employment, Jeremiah Evans among them and possibly Billinge also. We may have a reference to this when, on 13th August 1763, he wrote to Wedgwood 'we having the engraver under our eye' and a little further on 'we have three engravers at work

---

[1]No china painter of this name is known. Reference may be to the David Rhodes who 'enamelled' for Wedgwood. No definite connection has been proved. See Appendix IV A (23), Green to Wedgwood; and Appendix VI A (6), J.W. to Cox.

(or should be) in London and two here'. For some time, Evans and perhaps one other engraver would be able to deal with the situation at Liverpool, but even at this early date we get an insight into the way this pottery printing business was growing, due in great part to Sadler's association with Wedgwood.

With Wedgwood, Sadler at first seems to have followed his usual custom, buying the undecorated ware from him and selling it back when 'processed'. This evidently proved unsatisfactory to both men and arrangements were made whereby business was done on the basis of a contra-account, Sadler never entering into ownership of the ware but making a charge for printing and taking payment partly in cash and partly in undecorated ware. The adjustment was not always to Sadler's liking and we find him on one occasion complaining 'We have above £100 worth of your ware in the white now by us, instead of which we expected cash'. Plain speaking, but Sadler was never afraid of speaking his mind and Wedgwood, the greatest potting figure of his day, thought no less of him for doing so. It is of some importance to realize that Sadler at no time made similar arrangements for decorating any other potter's ware. 'You may rest assured we never printed a piece for any person but yourself' he wrote to Wedgwood on 11th October 1763 and we can accept that statement.

The correspondence between these two men has been carefully preserved by Messrs Wedgwood;[1] and although it does not, except in a few instances, directly concern the student of Liverpool porcelain, the few extracts which have been given may be sufficient to show the valuable contribution it can make to our knowledge on many matters of cognate importance. From it we can learn some of the sources from which these pottery printers derived their prints, the manner of reproducing them, the date, manner and colour of the issue, the date when a colour was first used and the prices charged. We learn also of their competitors and, in some cases, what they thought of them;[2] of the difficulties they had to contend with; and above all, we are able to form an accurate idea of the truly enormous output of printed wares which was so rapidly reached. Thus, from a weekly turnover during the first two years of about £8 per week — and a glance at the charges for printing will show that even this represents several hundred pieces — it rose to £48 per week at the time of Sadler's retirement in 1770.[3] It was in this year that Green placed an order with Wedgwood for 1,764 pieces which had to reach Liverpool, receive printed decoration there and be ready for dispatch to America *within*

---

[1]Extracts from a few letters are given in Appendix IV A.
[2]Appendix IV A (25) and (26).
[3]A letter of 23rd February 1764 gives some idea of printing charges at that date: bowls and ewers, 4s. dozen, teapots 5s. 6d. dozen, teacups, saucers and coffee cups, 3s. dozen. These prices would average sixty pieces per £1 and indicate an output of about 150,000 pieces a year.

fourteen days. Quick work in an age of horse-drawn carts and rutted roads, which must betoken the ability to handle business on a big scale.[1]

SIGNED WARES

It is difficult to form a reliable opinion on the relative proportions of factory-printed and Sadler-printed china during the early years. One unavoidably gets the impression that the latter predominated, but, as far as my own observation extends, Sadler's signature is never found joined with that of his partner Green. From an examination of a number of signed pieces, certain conclusions may be advanced.

It might be safe to assume that all the signed pieces were printed in pre-partnership days and that, unless the plates happened to be worn out, they would continue in use if required during the partnership with the signature removed. There would be no difficulty in doing that, for, as Sadler says in his *Note Book*, what you do not wish to appear can be removed from the inked plate with a pencil and spirit of turpentine. Even the pair of cylindrical mugs in the Victoria and Albert Museum, bearing red-printed Sadler-signed portraits of George III and Queen Charlotte, comparatively late in date as they appear to be, provide no obstacle to this view.[2] Signed wares of any kind to which a date later than 1763 may reasonably be allotted are uncommon by any standards.[3] Many reasons for this may exist, but where Sadler is concerned there is little doubt that he liked no name to appear but his own, even to the exclusion of his partner. A complete blank was preferable to a shared honour. This would explain why, with very few exceptions, no engraver's name is found on Sadler-signed prints — or on others printed by him. The exceptions are the three early prints of Frederick in armour which have already been mentioned.

Sadler's signature took many forms. From my observation, it is always associated with the word 'Liverpool', either in full or in contracted form. It appears sometimes as 'Sadler', with or without his initial 'I', but never as 'John Sadler'; and sometimes it is followed by the contraction for enameller. Any of these variants may follow one of three arrangements. These are: 1 Central (Plate 38 (*a*)); 2 Name on left, 'Liverpool' on right, the 'Bucks' print, when signed, usually taking this form (Plate 37 (*c*)); 3 Everything on the left, the right side being blank except in those rare examples in which Evans' name appears in the blank space. From the last arrangement, as an identical print is known in both states, i.e., with and without Evans'

[1]Canal not in use, see Appendix IVᴀ (26).

[2]Probably dated 1763 and printed in celebration of the peace treaty. There is a similar pair in the British Museum.

[3]Green's signature alone is occasionally found, as on Wedgwood's Wesley-portrait teapots almost certainly indicating a date later than 1770.

name, it is a fair inference that in all cases in which the right side is blank, the asymmetrical arrangement is accounted for by supposing that the blank space originally lodged the engraver's name.[1]

The implication of this is that the engraver's name appeared at Sadler's discretion. In this, Sadler would appear to have been but following established custom, for Holdship did the same thing at Worcester and afterwards at Derby. It is not difficult to see that it could be argued that an engraving ordered and paid for, whether as a special item or as part of a contract, clearly became the property of the buyer to use as he pleased. If the engraver put his name on it, removal in the manner already indicated was easy enough if the publisher did not wish it to appear.

CLASSIFICATION OF LIVERPOOL PRINTS

Liverpool prints fall into three groups. The first of these, comprising the majority, are completed line engravings. These are mainly in black on-glaze, but prints in light sepia (Plate 38 (c)), brick red (Plate 38 (e)) ,dark brown (Plate 39 (b)), and purple (Plate 38 (d)) are all quite commonly met with. While all these are complete in themselves and are intended to be reproduced exactly as they are, those in black and purple are frequently found colour-washed, or even touched with enamel colours. Plate 37 (d) shows the Liverpool print of Boucher's *La Terre* in uncoloured state and Plate 37 (e), a version which has been colour-washed and enamel coloured.

A distinctive type of purple print is found on ware which closely resembles that usually associated with the 'red cow' print already described (page 39). Purple printed ware of this character is generally regarded as Worcester although I do not think the printing is attributed to Hancock, whose work it does not particularly resemble. The colour is itself a difficulty, for purple was not one of the early colours. Sadler apparently did not use it until 1764[2] and it is difficult to believe Worcester was making ware of this type at that date. The date assigned to the examples in the Schreiber Collection is 1765.

Prints of this type are more often found additionally coloured than otherwise, mainly washed, with but a touch of enamel. The use of a characteristic blue for sky or water (equally unsuitable for either) and of a purple-red for the clothing of figures is quite distinctive. These two colours are found similarly associated on a great assortment of wares, printed and otherwise, many of which can be shown to have Liverpool attachments. When not over-coloured, these purple prints form an attractive class. The subjects

[1]See page 89. The Evans-signed example illustrated in the *Antique Collector* is now in Mr Allman's collection.
[2]Letter, Appendix IV A (16). It is reasonable to assume that, being solely engaged in pottery printing, Sadler would not be behind his competitors in these matters.

usually depict classical ruins amid foliage, with water and figures in the foreground (Plate 36 (*a*)).

That frequently very charming type of black print for which the name 'smoky primitive' has appropriately been suggested (I think by W. B. Honey) should be considered here. Many well qualified to express an opinion have found difficulty in regarding these as Hancock's work, being quite unlike anything we can attribute to him before he went to Worcester, or, with reasonable probability, after he went there.[1] If the ware so decorated is 'Worcester', there remains the difficulty of accounting for the printing of such a quantity before December 1757, when the dated King of Prussia mug appeared. Something less than a whole year is available for this task, including all the preparations necessary at Worcester before the new process could be put into use. No doubt other possibilities could be suggested which would enable this class to be regarded as Hancock-printed, without providing any completely satisfactory solution to the problem.[2] On the other hand, it is fairly easy to account for it as Liverpool-printed. In the first place, time is wholly on the side of the Liverpool engraver, who is unconfined by any standard of achievement in 1757. Secondly, it is agreed that the general effect of these prints is such as would be produced by over-inking, by which is meant that too much ink has been allowed to adhere to the transfer paper. Without going into technical details of the different ways in which this might be brought about, it is a fact that other Liverpool ceramic prints exhibit exactly the same feature. A reference to Plates 37 (*a*), 38 (*b*) should make this clear. Moreover, our forbears may have been right and it does no harm to remind ourselves that sauceboats carrying prints of this type were generally regarded as 'Liverpool' fifty and more years ago, when a number of them appear as such in the Catalogue of the British Museum.[3] The matter is referred to again from a potting aspect, in discussing the origin of the 'scratch-cross' group with which these sauceboats show relationship. The agreement between potting and printing which is here disclosed gives further support to the view that 'smoky primitive' printing owns a Liverpool origin.

There are one or two well-known examples of this type of printing which have been 'embellished' by the addition of enamel colouring, e.g., the sauceboat which carries prints of a squirrel and a pheasant on the outside and of a

[1]The difficulty created by the print of the 'longtailed macaw' is discussed on pages 102 et seq.
[2]e.g. that Hancock engraved them while at Battersea, where he did not use them, but sent them to Worcester for use there, although as far as we know, he had no interest in the place at that time.
[3]Two double-handled sauce boats, Nos. X6, X7; two single-handled sauceboats, Nos. X8 and X9, all in British Museum Catalogue; and two single-handled sauceboats, similar to the last in Schr. collection (I, 463).

milking scene within (Schr. I.463, uncoloured, and Victoria and Albert Museum, *1213/24*, coloured). From a purely decorative point of view, as might be expected with such heavily inked lines, the result can only be described as a complete failure, indeed, it would be difficult to find a worse piece of clobber than this particular sauceboat presents. That may account for the fact that little work of this kind seems to have been done. It certainly serves to emphasize its unsuitability as decoration at a factory like Battersea, where, fortunately perhaps, its occurrence is unknown.[1]

Apart from the over-inked appearance of these prints, their outstanding features are: 1 their perspective, distances being very cleverly and delicately suggested (Plates 34 (*d*), 34 (*g*)); and 2, the curious raised appearance of many (but not of all) which can be easily felt by the finger, but which often contrives to convey the effect of engraving. In some cases, the effect may be that of pencilled decoration and instances may be recalled where printing of this type has been mistaken for it.

It would seem that the raised effect has nothing to do with the nature of the ware, or with the quality of its surface in respect of its fitness or otherwise to receive printed decoration. This is shown by the fact that these 'raised' prints occur alike on soft-paste porcelain of eggshell thinness (Plate 34 (*e*)),[2] on the more heavily potted wares of 'scratch-cross' type, (Plate 34 (*c*, *g*)), on Bristol hard paste porcelain and, more rarely, on creamware.[3] It is confirmed by finding 'raised' printing and normal printing on the same piece of ware, or perhaps one should say on the same article.[4] This might be thought to indicate that the effect must be the result of the engraver's technique, were it not for the fact that all 'smoky primitives' are not raised in this manner. Not only do some not exhibit the feature, but one can even find examples of the same subject on the same type of ware, one of which is quite raised and the other not at all so. Thus, on thickly potted ware, the 'Kingfisher and ducks' print, occurring on the inside of double-handled sauceboats, is found in both states,[5] while the print known as 'La Cascade' provides a

---

[1]And consequently giving no support to the suggestion that it could be Hancock's work.

[2]These very thinly potted pieces all show eversion of the rims, of oriental origin and common to many Worcester and Liverpool copies. But these tea bowls exhibit a feature which is uncommon on Worcester wares of any period, namely a very small and a very undercut footring (Plate 34 (*e*)). Disregarding any help from the character of the printing, as something in dispute, this print is reversed, a common feature of much Liverpool ceramic printing, but a rarity at Worcester, if indeed it ever occurs.

[3]Knowles Boney, 'A Ceramic Conundrum', *Apollo*, January 1955, page 15.

[4]Ibid. The Boucher print and another on the body of the vase are 'raised'; the Hancock butterfly prints on its cover are not.

[5]From copper-plates showing very slight differences only. The Worcester plate (Victoria and Albert Museum Schr. I. 612) with print in Hancock's style is a different design.

good instance of the same thing on very thin porcelain. There may not be much difference in appearance between examples in each state; and a possible explanation is that, while the characteristic line of all prints of this class may be admitted as a distinguishing feature, the final effect is something to which the pottery printer has also contributed.

This could happen in different ways, notably by the type of ink and by the firing temperature used. A raised effect seems to be entirely confined to black printed pieces.[1] It is true that printing of this kind is rarely found in other colours and consequently opportunities for comparison seldom present themselves. I have seen 'La Cascade' in a light purple-brown line in which the effect, so far from being raised, is that of an underglaze print. This must be the result of fusion of ink with glaze and accounted for partly by the kiln temperature used and partly by the nature of the ink. It is well known that Worcester lilac-coloured prints sometimes deceive the eye by their underglaze appearance, probably for the same reason.

It is worth noting that close examination of these 'Cascade' prints on tea bowls of this type shows that, although closely resembling one another, many plates seem to have been in use. The differences are slight, though fundamental. It is unlikely that this has any bearing on this aspect of the problem which these prints present. The subject was popular and no doubt many plates would be required.[2]

The second group of Liverpool prints embraces those in which the printing is partly or wholly in outline only. These are always intended for enamel colouring and are not found in an uncoloured state. The outstanding example of the group — a small one — is the 'red cow' print (Plate 32), to which reference has been made in describing the type of ware on which it may be found. It was a popular subject and many plates showing minor differences were obviously in use. The differences, however, which strike the eye do so by reason of the colour treatment, of which there are two versions. In one, the hindmost cow is black (cross hatching), the ground is colour washed in wavy bands of blue and pink (occasionally chocolate-brown) and there is a red sun: in the other, both cows are red (no cross hatching), ground colour is completely absent and there is no sun. The latter seems to be far less commonly found and is restricted to creamy ware with the pale green translucency.[3]

The outline is not dead black, but a dark brownish-black; the enamels are bright and, to some extent, distinctive. This print, unlike those of the

---

[1]In fact, it is most marked on those which are blackest and the epithet 'sooty' has been applied to them for that reason.

[2]Further information on the subject of this print will be found under 'Reversed prints'.

[3]The value of such an assertion must always be limited by limited opportunity for study, in this case possibly about one hundred pieces.

'smoky primitive' group, has never been claimed as Hancock's work, although the ware carrying it is generally regarded as Worcester. The dissimilarity from Hancock's engraving is remarked upon by Mr F. A. Barrett[1] and one might say that for years this print has been a cuckoo in the nest to Worcester collectors, something quite unexplained, but which none were willing to disown. That it has good Liverpool attachments, which are in keeping with the claims already advanced in respect of the great bulk of the ware on which it is found, can be shown in the following way.

1   The Liverpool covered cup (Plate 32 (d)) carries an outline print in dark brown which shows exactly the same technique and is from the same source. Cups of this shape may also rarely be found with the 'red cow' print.

2   This design is reproduced, line for line and similarly enamelled, on a pair of bottle flasks (Plate 32 (b, c)).

3   Flasks of this type, shortly to be discussed, form a well-defined group, some of which are painted, e.g. the well-known 'Acrobats' flask (Plate 32 (e)), while others are printed with added colour, in the manner of this pair showing the Liverpool links we have just noted. These links are strengthened by an example from the Schreiber Collection (Schr. I.470), which exhibits Liverpool printing of another kind. From the *Catalogue*, we learn that this flask is of the same form as that carrying the 'Acrobats' (Schr. I.459), while its printing is similar to that seen on a Liverpool plate in the Collection (I.469) which is additionally polychrome printed (Plate 33 (a)).

4   Some bowls with the 'red cow' print will be found carrying companion prints of subjects not in use on Worcester wares.[2]

5   When the subject known as 'La Terre' is found as a companion print (Plate 37 (e)), it takes the form in which it is seen on the Liverpool cup and saucer shown on Plate 37 (d).

6   These companion prints are mainly colour washed with the spare use of enamel, the technique being similar to that used on the 'purple ruins' group, but less often seen on Worcester wares.

In some few examples of the 'red cow' print, the ground wash of blue and pink is replaced by one of bluish-green and chocolate-brown. These colours, of exactly the same shade and used in the same way are found as ground treatment in the *painted* chinoiserie of the Liverpool bowl depicted on Plate 10 (c). The use of such a rare combination of colours in this situation could not be accidental and must indicate identity of origin.[3]

[1] *Worcester Porcelain*, page 8.
[2] It is rare to find prints from different sources on the same article but the possibility cannot be completely ruled out.
[3] In making this comparison, the 'red cow' print is also on a bowl and the potting characteristics of the two bowls are identical. See Plate 29 (a) for a third example of this printing.

The use of enamel on these prints is chiefly reserved for the clothing of the figures. Part of the design — the herdsman, cattle, foliage and rocks — occurs on a delftware plate in the Victoria and Albert Museum. In is initialled $_M{}^E{}_B$ on the back, with the date 1760 underneath. An exactly similar plate is in the British Museum, both being presented by William Edkins, grandson of Michael Edkins, a Bristol painter of delftware. William vouched for them as the work of his grandfather, an attribution which receives some support from the initials, which are credibly those of Michael and Betty, his wife, but perhaps more support from the fact that the family possessed half-a-dozen plates similarly marked. Mr R. J. Charleston of the Victoria and Albert Museum, to whom we owe much of our knowledge of Michael Edkins, thinks the attestation is correct.[1]

It is quite possible that these plates did assist the attribution to the Worcester factory of ware decorated with the complete print. This would at least fit in with the belief, long current, that the hand of Michael Edkins, as a supposed painter of Bristol opaque glass, could be traced on much porcelain of early Bristol or early Worcester origin, with some of which the 'red cow' ware seemed to be allied. Mr Charleston's researches have clearly shown the impossibility of this,[2] for, born in 1734, Edkins was still a journeyman delft decorator in 1760, or thereabouts. That date completely disposes of him as a possible decorator for the early soft paste Bristol works, or indeed for any Worcester porcelain of pre-1760 date. Regarding the bottle flasks, it can be said that they qualify for inclusion with wares which show late type decoration (printing) on early type ware.[3] The printing itself has been seen to possess Liverpool links and these pieces therefore have good claim to be regarded as of Liverpool origin. The painted examples call for separate consideration. While 'Acrobats' is probably the work of a saltglaze decorator,[4] other examples show the hand of the 'fine-brush' painter. Proof that the latter is Podmore's work is lacking, but such an assumption would well accord with our knowledge.

A third type of Liverpool printing is that to which the term 'polychrome' has been applied. Its particular interest to Liverpool collectors lies in the fact that it does not seem to have been used elsewhere. Its recognition is comparatively recent, the first recorded contribution to the subject being by the late Dr Newman Nield in a short paper, based on three examples, which he read before the Ceramic Circle in 1935.[5] The attention focused on it in this way has resulted in many others being brought to light; and while it is uncommon, it is by no means as rare as was at first thought.

[1]*Michael Edkins and the problem of English Enamelled glass* in Trans. Soc. Glass Technology, 1954, volume 38, page 3.   [2]Ibid.   [3]The date generally given is 1755 or earlier.
[4]'English eighteenth-century opaque white glass', R. J. Charleston in *Antiques*, Dec. 1954, page 490.   [5]Newman Nield, Trans. E.C.C., No. 3, 1935, page 71.

The printing of the different colours was evidently done in one operation. The colours used were confined to a pinkish-red, a nondescript brown, yellow, and sometimes, a little green. The amount of the design which is actually printed is variable. Here and there it may be little more than outline only, the effect being made up by overpainting and the use of a little enamel. The subjects are usually flowers in the form of sprigs and small posies (Plate 32 (*b, d, g*)). More rarely do we find a landscape and figures as on the teapot illustrated in Dr Newman Nield's paper (Plate XXXI and Victoria and Albert Museum, *C.6 and A/1935*).

Whether it is to be regarded as a great technical achievement is open to doubt. As long as each colour was reserved to its own area of the copper plate, no great difficulty should have presented itself; and the reason why comparatively little appears to have been done — and why it does not seem to have been attempted elsewhere — was probably because, as decoration, its artistic content cannot be reckoned very high. Probably the most remarkable thing about it is its very distinctive character, for which it is hard to find an explanation. As we proceed to examine the development of the ordinary type of ceramic printing which, so far, has claimed our attention, it will become evident that the conditions in which this took place were such as would be likely to deprive it of much attributional value. Here we have a type of printing which is sufficiently distinctive to be easily recognizable and the possibility therefore that it may carry attributional value requires careful consideration.

My personal knowledge of the matter is the result of an examination of no more than some twenty to twenty-five examples. As one would expect, such information as we possess points to Sadler and Green as the printers. From Sadler's *Note Book* comes the following entry (undated): 'Printing different colours on one plate. Ink the plate with the proper colours in the proper places with a pencil or bit of stick, then let it dry awhile and scrape it off with a knife'. The reference seems clear enough and the only point that arises is whether Richard Abbey, who must have become acquainted with the method during the time of his apprenticeship (1767–73), made use of it when he left and set up in business on his own account. His advertisement on this occasion tells us that he printed all sorts of Queens' ware in variety of colour,[1] but porcelain is not even mentioned. As a competitor in this matter he may therefore safely be disregarded. This would fit in with the ware itself, most of which seems to demand a date before rather than after 1770 and leaves with Sadler or with the partnership the credit for this interesting development.

[1] *W.L.A.*, 17th December 1773. Multicoloured printed creamware, later to become so popular, must have been coming into use at this time, but there is no printing on creamware known to me which resembles this printed porcelain.

Dr Newman Nield, in the paper to which I have referred, writes, 'Though the pieces have not been chemically examined and none of them has the characteristic cross and incision under the base, they appear to belong to the soapstone group which has come to be known as "scratch-cross". This certainly applies to one of the three illustrated by him, a mug, which, apart from its Liverpool handle, is reminiscent of the bell-shaped mugs of that group (Victoria and Albert Museum, *C.4 and A.1935*). It thus provides a potting link between the group and Liverpool wares.[1]

For the marking to which he refers, we must consult a pair of polychrome printed Liverpool plates in the Schreiber Collection (Schr. I.469), one of which carries an incised stroke in the paste but no cross. These plates are decorated with a centrally-placed coloured print having a brown outline (Plate 33 (*a*)) depicting a landscape and figures, surrounding which are numerous florets printed in polychrome. One or two of the latter happen to be identical with some on the vase among Dr Nield's pieces and on a similar vase in my own possession (Plate 33 (*e*)). The central print on this plate has already received notice for the help it can give in establishing the Liverpool origin of the bottle flasks.

There is considerable uniformity in the potting features of all these polychrome printed pieces. The great majority are conspicuously grey in appearance and, although not heavily potted, show but moderate translucency of a straw colour. Occasionally the surface colour is decidedly green, as in the case of the bowl (Plate 33 (*e*)), and here, certain imperfections in the paste combined with a yellowish-green translucency indicate a different article and probably a different factory of origin. Such differences are to be expected — indeed, they might well be more marked — for when wares are alike they are more likely to have been printed at the factory of origin than when they show diversity, in which case Sadler as the 'outside decorator' is more likely to be responsible. Here, for the moment, the actual factory (or factories) is of less concern than the undoubted fact that all the examples so far examined of the type of decoration now being considered must be regarded as of Liverpool origin.

The validity of deductions drawn from the relatively small number of examples available for study may be questioned. But it is a reasonable working hypothesis that we have here a cohesive group possessing good Liverpool potting characteristics, which are combined with a distinctive type of decoration, the like of which is not found on wares which can with certainty be attributed to any other factory. In such circumstances, printed decoration of this type may be considered to possess good Liverpool attributional values.

Polychrome printing with slightly different features is occasionally encoun-

[1]Resembling the mug of Plate 26 (*c*) but for the latter's back-turned handle.

tered. In this variety, the forms employed are less standardized and it has a more finished appearance, although the technique seems to be precisely the same and there is no reason to doubt its Liverpool origin. A good example is provided by a sauce boat in the British Museum, moulded and coloured in relief with the addition of polychrome flower printing (Plate 33 (*h*)). In this case, the potting features give good support to a Liverpool attribution. This assistance is lacking in the case of the big 'Britannia', whose flowered robe also frequently shows printing of this type. But the pedestals of these figures, the provenance of which is still conjectural, may show prints with brown overtones 'in the Battersea manner' (Schr. I.436), yet which it would be difficult to reconcile with a Battersea date and for which a Liverpool origin may yet be found acceptable.[1]

This leads to the reasonable proposition that all the printing on any given piece of ware must be the work of the same atelier.[2] When two types are present, one of which is Liverpool work (e.g. polychrome), the other must also own a Liverpool origin; and it follows that when the latter is distinctive in type, it will carry attributional value when found as the sole decoration. The bottle flask just discussed in its relationship with the pair of Schreber plates illustrates this point and the Britannia may provide another example.

Before leaving the subject of the polychrome print, perhaps the most difficult thing to explain is why one finds so little ware of similar type decorated in other ways. An exception is provided by the bowl (Plate 33 (*e*)) already mentioned, both the paste and glaze of which are readily identifiable in the painted cup shown on Plate 14 (*b*) and in the coffee pot (Plate 34 (*a, b*)) the printed decoration of which somewhat resembles the effect of polychrome. The distinguishing features here are: 1 the very green appearance; 2 the greenish-yellow translucency; 3 the presence of small depressions here and there in the paste, frequently but not always circular, glaze-filled and a millimetre or two in size.

A type of print which seems to provide links with the early Irish developments, referred to at the beginning of this section, has been reserved for special mention. It is a line engraving in one colour only, a brownish-purple, in which the outline and a limited amount of the subject is delineated, leaving considerable scope for added washes of suitable colour. On the coffee pot illustrated here, the general effect is pleasing, if a little lacking in sufficient colour contrast and is decidedly unusual (Plate 34 (*a, b*)). The relationship of the technique employed to that of the printed and painted Limerick armorial delftware plates, described by Honey as 'having a soft purple-brown

[1] See page 57.
[2] But see page 88. The argument applies with less force to engraving, for we know that Hancock's plates were sometimes disposed of.

overglaze line' (*Trans. E.C.C., 1942,* page 155) seems to be close, for the softness of the line is one of the most striking features of these prints.

Additional interest attaches to this coffee pot by reason of the subject of its printed decoration. This version of the 'long tailed macaw' print resembles a drawing numbered 4 in a small booklet of six prints published by Sayer, more closely than any other known to occur on printed wares. In this, the bird remains perched on the moulded edge of its parapet, whereas in every other known example on porcelain, it appears on a branch (Plate 34 (*c*)). Further, this coffee pot bird is much better drawn in its contours, providing a closer copy of the book drawing in this respect than do those found on the 'Scratch-cross' mugs which provide the other examples of its use. All six engravings in this book have been thought to be Hancock's work, together with their 'raised' or 'smoky primitive' counterparts on porcelain when so found.[1] Such an assumption, however, would require us to believe that, in this case, when Hancock wanted to use his book engraving on porcelain, he not only deliberately altered it in a material respect but re-engraved it badly,[2] leaving it for some obscure Liverpool engraver to reproduce more faithfully and with better draughtsmanship. The importance of this newly-discovered coffee pot is evident. Our concern is less with the book engraving than with the authorship of its ceramic versions, of which two are now known to exist. The discovery of the coffee pot must make it clear that neither can be attributable to Hancock; and, by extension, it follows that no printing of the distinctive type found on these mugs can also be so attributable. This is in accord with other known facts about this printing and with the views expressed from a potting point of view about the provenance of the later examples of the 'scratch-cross' group carrying printing of this type.

TRENDS IN DEVELOPMENT

Viewing the work of Sadler's 'Printed Ware Manufactory' separately and as a whole, the printing of tiles and creamware must have been overwhelmingly predominant, with china printing taking second place and confined mainly to the period of the Seven Years War. The reasons for this are clear. In the first place, Sadler's Wedgwood commitments after the war was over made great inroads on his time, as a glance at the correspondence between the two men will show; and when these had been met, tile printing remained to claim his attention. Secondly, china printing in such circumstances did not pay. The all-conquering creamware was winning this battle too. A clean-looking creamware printed 'pint' would sell for not much more than one-

---

[1]C. Cook, *The Life and Work of Robert Hancock*, 1948, Item 119.
[2]Compare the drawing on Plate 34 (*a*) with that on Plate 34 (*c*).

fourth the cost of a china example which was quite possibly less well made and certainly no more durable. Very quickly creamware captured the markets.

Considerations of this nature naturally governed the industry in Liverpool as a whole, for what was unprofitable to Sadler was likely to prove so eventually to the china makers themselves. Blue-printed ware apart, there is little evidence of china printing in Liverpool after 1775.

It clearly emerges from any study of Sadler's printed wares that the colouring of prints in different ways must have formed part of the print decorator's art from early beginnings and continued.[1] As the vogue for black-printed porcelain declined, its place was taken by creamware, in many instances similarly coloured. Circumstances determined that the colouring of prints, when it was intended they should be so treated, must have been in the hands of the printer, in order to avoid selling an unfinished article. In this way, the 'Printed Ware Manufactory' grew by easy stages into a decorating establishment where pot-painters were employed and where any form of decoration falling within the decorator's art could be applied. In later years this side of the business had grown to an extent that made necessary the opening of a separate china painters' shop at No. 39 Harrington Street. It is unlikely, although the suggestion has been made, that either Sadler or Green had any skill as pot-painters, or attempted work of that nature, but confined themselves to the printing side of the business which so rapidly reached such large dimensions.

THE SOURCES OF THE PRINTS

Cyril Cook, in the *Life and Work of Robert Hancock* has given us a good list of the sources from which the Worcester engravers obtained their designs and reference should be made to this standard work for information on the subject. The same sources were, of course, open to the Liverpool engravers. Many of the small albums of prints published by Robert Sayer, map and print seller at the 'Golden Buck', opposite Fetter Lane, Fleet Street, London, were on sale in Liverpool, where they could be obtained from the booksellers John Sibbald and Robert Fleetwood. One of these albums, *The Draughtsman's Assistant*, contained a number of prints in common use by the Liverpool pottery printers among them one forming the subject of the hare hunting scene on the big Schreiber jug (Schr. I.782). Another of Sayer's publications, *Portraits of the English Stage in the days of Garrick*, was used for the decoration of a set of Liverpool tiles; while yet another, a small booklet of six prints of birds, possibly from drawings by Charles Fenn, the bird and flower painter, includes that of the long-tailed macaw to which reference has already been made.

[1]Wedgwood's letter, Appendix VI c (5).

Less well known, perhaps, but serving the same purpose we find *Drawings in the Chinese, Gothic and Modern Taste for any Manufactory business and Engravings of any kind in Architecture, Ornaments, Landscapes, Heraldry, etc.*, This modest compendium was published by Mr Darley Edwards in the Strand, London, and sold in Liverpool at the office of Williamson's *Advertiser*. Thus there is no lack of evidence of the interest of the town in publications of this class.

The good engravers would, when required, engrave their own designs. From one of Sadler's letters we learn of Mr Sam Wale, 'a good natured man of great merit'.[1] He seems to have been Sadler's principal designer in London and on one occasion is recommended to Wedgwood as possibly obliging enough to sketch a pattern for him to his liking. Quite often, however, such men would engrave the paintings and drawings of others, but disdained mere copying which they might refuse to undertake as beneath their notice.

Sadler, with his business instinct, had his own views about this. 'The top draughtsmen', he writes, 'will not copy anything that is published, unless particularly insisted on. Whether they think it betrays a want of invention, or that they could not charge so much for a copy as an original, I know not, but suspect the latter' (S. to W., 29th April 1763). This could imply that good original engraving was done at Liverpool, but that more was done by the cheaper and possibly more expeditious method of copying prints already published. It is open to doubt whether Sadler's methods of reproduction were used at Worcester. From what follows later, it will become apparent that 'reversed' prints are among the inescapable results of one method used in reproduction and that 'reversed' Worcester prints, while apparently they do rarely occur, are certainly the exception rather than the rule. Surprisingly enough, in some cases these can be found bearing Hancock's signature, in spite of the fact that we have a right to expect that this denotes original work to a degree incompatible with mere copying. The explanation of this is conjectural.

When Sadler wrote on 2nd July 1763, 'We are going on very rapidly, having an extraordinary draughtsman who has done us many subjects and just suits us', the reference is surely to someone working in Liverpool. The name of Jeremiah Evans suggests itself, for he was a good draughtsman and at this time probably in Sadler's permanent employment. The date corresponds with the appearance of that excellently engraved pair of red printed, Sadler-signed portraits of George III and Queen Charlotte,[2] but these are more likely to be the work of Billinge.

There can be little doubt, however, that the bulk of the plates used by

[1] Appendix IV A (7).
[2] On tankards in British Museum.

Sadler in this early essay in mass production was the work of hack engravers who copied everything they could get hold of. It cannot be too strongly stressed that, once a subject had been engraved, there was no copyright in the print, which became anybody's property to use as he liked. So great was the demand for prints at this time that no published design escaped this form of piracy if it provided suitable decoration for the potter. In this connection, the oft-quoted description by Miss Meteyard of Wedgwood searching the print shops of London will be recalled. Even the Member for Liverpool, Sir William Meredith, was pressed into this service[1]; and when we read in one of Sadler's letters (already quoted) of the five engravers who were working for him so busily that 'we shall wear out all our plates if we live', it is clear that these engravers were busy copying the prints that Wedgwood and his friends were searching the printshops of London to find. Any lingering doubt on this matter should be removed by Sadler's remark in a letter dated 29th April 1763, where he says 'Prints will be of more service to us than any subjects we can get designed on purpose . . .'. Prints were his raw material.

While the source of many prints, with their various permutations, has been traced, that of many still remains obscure. Among these must be reckoned the most famous of all, the 'Tea Party'. Watteau has been held responsible for the design, of which there are several versions, each of which is found with minor variations. Two common Liverpool versions are shown on Plates 38 (d), 39 (d). The latter is found 'reversed', both as a Liverpool print and as Worcester, this being shown by the page pouring tea from a kettle held in his left hand. The use of separate chairs instead of a garden seat provides yet another version in use at both factories.

Because no copyright in any published design was recognized, every conceivable liberty was taken with it with impunity. Portions were altered from caprice or for no obvious reason at all, or omitted altogether so as to make the print fit a smaller object.[2] A common mutilation took the form of omitting a tree, because its height or overhang was inconvenient. A more entertaining liberty was taken by the Liverpool engraver of the subject called by Cyril Cook 'Lovers and dovecot' (Cook, op cit., Item 62). In this the dovecot has been replaced — and apparently its atmosphere too — by an irate woman appearing from behind a bush with a baby in her arms (Plate 39 (a)).

Apart from such wholesale alterations, or different versions of a subject which are easily recognizable at a glance, there is a much larger group, so large, in fact, that hardly any can be excluded from its ambit, in which slight differences only can be detected on close and careful examination. These may be sufficient to show that different copper plates are involved and it follows that the possibility that we may be looking at the work of different engravers

[1]Appendix VI c (6).   [2]This was done at every factory.

or the product of a different factory must be borne in mind. For this reason, the attributional value which prints should be considered to bestow on the porcelain they decorate cannot be highly rated. The provenance of any piece is primarily settled by considerations of paste and glaze. The matter might not unfairly be stated that, while identity of subject has not the slightest value in this respect complete identity of impression has value only when certain conditions are satisfied. This arises from the fact that copper plates could be and sometimes were disposed of when no longer required.[1] Even a signature loses its force in such circumstances and, as will shortly appear, it was not always removed. Good reasons existed for allowing it to remain, for a well-known name would clearly possess a sale value for the new owner.

Illustrating these points, it is of interest to note that, in the Museum of the Worcester Royal Porcelain Company are a number of copper plates of subjects well known as pottery prints, which, with four exceptions, have no 'line for line' representation among the Museum's printed pieces. The number of these plates may be around two dozen. Of these, those which with certainty find such representation are: Queen Charlotte, Shakespeare, Fishing group (signed by Ross) and a group of Masonic accessories.[2] On the other hand, there is a copper plate, the subject of which shows a lady walking with a child in a garden, while on the left, a man carrying a stick approaches. As a Liverpool print of the middle period and one used later at the Herculaneum factory, it is well known. But as far as I have been able to find out, no example on Worcester porcelain is known and its presence therefore in this collection is unexplained.

A copper plate of the 'Tea Party' signed by Hancock was found at Coalport by Jewitt in 1862 among a number of others, which included one engraved with Holdship's rebus and the word 'Derby'. Many suggestions have been advanced to account for their presence, unnecessarily it would seem, for it could be explained easily in ways which would not involve any discovery of importance. Above all, it does not afford proof that either of them was ever used at Caughley, Coalport's predecessor, and it seems to be generally agreed that the mere presence of such collections of copper plates proves nothing that would not be equally obvious without them.

REVERSED PRINTS

Many prints on pottery, porcelain and enamels may be found in two states, one of which is the reverse of the other, or the reverse of a book illustration

---

[1] Cyril Cook, op. cit., page 69.
[2] I am indebted for this information to Mr Cyril Shingler of the Worcester Royal Porcelain Company.

from which it derives. In the former case, the original will be denoted by right-handed action, when figures form part of the subject; in the latter and in the absence of any such indication, the paper print will usually be the original, although exceptions to this may occur.

The causes of reversal are not the same in every case. It will obviously occur when a copper plate which has been made for use on paper is subsequently used on ware or enamel, for a print will appear on pottery exactly as it is engraved owing to the intermediate reversal which takes place on paper. Many publishers would doubtless be glad to get rid of their old plates when it was decided that they were of no further use; and in the case of Hancock, in his double role of book illustrator and pottery printer, there may have been a prior understanding to that effect. In the great majority of cases, reversal did not matter and most of the instances in which it is found on 'Battersea' enamels or Bow porcelain are probably accounted for in this way. It was rarely accidental, due to the failure of the engraver to realize that a plate made for use on paper *must* produce a reversed print if used on pottery or enamel.[1]

Instances of its occurrence on Liverpool wares are common and here, although in some cases the cause will be as just stated, for the majority we must find another explanation. In this, we are assisted by Sadler's apparently insatiable demand for prints, which it will be remembered, 'will be of more service to us than any subjects we can get designed on purpose'; and in some way, these must provide the key to this problem.

Two methods of reproducing from prints offer themselves, neither of which presents great difficulty. In one, a tracing is taken and one or other side of the paper is rubbed with chalk. The chalked side is then placed on the prepared copper plate and the lines traced with a fine point,[2]

The other method is, perhaps, even easier. By placing the print face downwards on the prepared plate, a clear impression can be obtained by gentle rubbing down with a burnisher.[3] The difference in result might be summed up by saying the second method yields greater accuracy, but a reversed print is unavoidable, whereas the first is much less accurate but reversal is avoidable at will, according to the side of the tracing which has been chalked. Both these methods, particularly the latter, might prove more laborious than simple straightforward copying, which, while calling for

---

[1] See letter (Appendix VIA (*i*)) from Wedgwood to his brother John. In this case Wedgwood seems to have been to blame for the mistake, for which a too literal interpretation of his instructions was responsible.

[2] I am indebted to Mr C. Shingler of the Worcester Royal Porcelain Company for this information.

[3] For this information I am indebted to Mr George Vokes of the firm of engravers of that name in Wardour Street, London.

greater skill in draughtsmanship, was clearly open to any competent engraver whose aim was not line for line reproduction.[1] In this case, the result would only show reversal if a mirror image was used to provide the material for copy.

Of these four ways in which reversed prints might be accounted for, it may be said that, whereas the first is more likely to be the cause in those rare cases in which they are found on Worcester wares, the second and third commend themselves in attempting to explain the much more numerous Liverpool examples, while the use of the fourth is speculative. The fact that most of these Liverpool reversed prints have no line for line right-handed representation on pottery or porcelain need cause no surprise when their origin from paper prints is recalled. While in most cases these may have been destroyed, it must be clear that very little, if any, reproduction could have taken place from prints on pottery or porcelain by these methods.

The subject is an interesting one and worth more consideration than has been given to it in the past. When in addition we remember Sadler's remark that what is unwanted can easily be removed from the inked plate by the use of a little turpentine,[2] some of the vagaries of eighteenth-century pottery prints begin to disappear.

Some, perhaps, but by no means all. It can hardly be doubted that whenever 'right' and 'left' prints of the same subject are found, whether on paper or on pottery, the right-handed version represents the original state and the other is a copy which, in some way, is the result of the means of reproduction used. Because the incidence of reversed prints at Liverpool is so much higher than at Worcester where they scarcely seem to be known, a *prima facie* reason exists for regarding any early left-handed print as of Liverpool origin. Such an assumption is clearly unaffected by the provenance of any right-handed version of the subject on porcelain or pottery which may exist.

With this in mind, the subject known as 'La Cascade' presents considerable interest. The only right-handed versions of this print which have so far been identified on porcelain are of Liverpool origin. Reference should be made to the cup and saucer (Schr. I.787) and to the Liverpool mug with round loop handle and flat unglazed base shown on Plate 39 (*g*). Left-handed versions are more commonly met with, but a Liverpool origin for many of these receives support on grounds other than mere left-handedness. Some belong to the 'smoky primitives' and as such may be found on cups and saucers of egg-shell fineness, good copies of the oriental in every respect but one, namely the presence of a markedly undercut footring (Plate 34 (*e*)). Precisely similarly

[1] The skill required in each case might not be very different.
[2] Sadler's Note Book (unnumbered pages).

potted ware may be found decorated with another print of this class, the 'Flute lesson' (Plate 34 (*f*)). This print, unlike the former, is also met with on thick and very opaque ware which is clearly of 'scratch-cross' type (Plate 34 (*g*)), providing another Liverpool link; and it may be added that the date around 1760 which is generally assigned to these 'La Cascade' prints of this type is conformable with this view.

Completely different in character are left-handed versions of the same subject in reddish-brown or brown within a painted border of feathery scrolls. This border is well known on Liverpool printed wares and is quite characteristic (Plate 38 (*d*) and Plate II No. 20 borders). One would not expect to find the same border in use at Worcester and, as far as I can ascertain, no instance of its use on an undoubted piece of Worcester has been recorded.[1] The case for Liverpool looks complete until we have to find an explanation for Hancock's signature N O T reversed, occurring on one of these reversed prints. One such, black printed, is recorded by Cyril Cook, the border in this case being the thin black line favoured at Worcester.[2] Another example printed in sepia was in the Dykes Collection.[3] One must assume that the signature in both these cases formed part of the original plate as it left the engraver's hands, in the absence of any evidence to the contrary. And there we must leave the matter.

No reference to the subject of reversed prints would be complete without mentioning the Liverpool tile print which depicts Trajan's column and the ruins of the temple of Castor and Pollux. This is red printed, but the subject is found in black overglaze on two large dishes in the Schreiber Collection, attributed to Worcester (Schr. I.633 and 643); and on these it appears the other way round. The engraving of all three prints is good and it would be difficult to affirm which represents the original state, were it not for the deduction which a knowledge of Sadler's methods would seem to justify.

This leads to the meaning which should properly attach to the use of the word 'copy' in this connection. The claim is still heard, though less frequently than it used to be, that Liverpool prints are just copies of Worcester's, usually badly executed. That is likely to mislead unless interpreted in the light of what has been said concerning the manner in which so much of this printing seems to have been done. Equally clearly, without some basis of agreement in terminology, attempted comparisons are wasted time. While

[1]Apart from the single black line, borders were little used on Worcester printed wares.
[2]Op. cit., Item 19 (ii).
[3]Exhibited City of Manchester Art Gallery, 1924, No. 95. A note on another cup and saucer having this print (No. 94) states, 'The paste and general style of these pieces suggests the work of a contemporary Liverpool factory decorated with prints by Sadler and Green.

therefore what follows is necessarily imperfect, it may assist in a better understanding of the difficulties involved.

LIVERPOOL CERAMIC PRINTS IN PERSPECTIVE

Risking repetition, it cannot be stressed too strongly that the Liverpool pottery printers copied everything printable they could find. The printing department of the Worcester Porcelain Company was doing the same thing, but to a less extent because their need was proportionately much less. Hancock rarely, if ever, engraved his own designs, but always those of others, as also mainly did the Liverpool engravers,[1] using other methods, possibly less skilful but more adapted to the requirements of mass production. It should therefore be perfectly clear that the many resemblances which can be seen to exist between the prints of the two factories are the result of the fact that both borrowed from the same sources, while the differences are partly the result of the different methods employed. We can readily agree that there was no Liverpool engraver whose work compares in technical excellence with that of Robert Hancock, who must be held responsible for all the engraving in the first decade of pottery printing at Worcester and for much subsequently until he left in 1774. But it will be remembered that when he arrived in Worcester, he already had considerable pottery printing experience,[2] whereas both Jeremiah Evans and Thomas Billinge at the corresponding date had yet to gain theirs. Both these men were doing ordinary copper-plate engraving at Liverpool until at least a year after the date of Sadler's tile printing experiment in 1756 and therefore had to learn to adapt their methods to pottery print engraving. The improvement in Evans' case can be seen from a comparison of his signed 'Frederick in armour' mug, to which may be assigned a date early in 1758, with his later work as exemplified by the 'Bucks Society' and, probably, the 'Tithe Pig'. These are both good prints. Among others equally good must be reckoned the pair of red-printed Sadler-signed portraits of George III and his Queen found on tankards, one pair of which is in the British Museum and another, similar, in the Victoria and Albert Museum, Kensington. They are probably attributable to Billinge.[3]

Prints of this quality fall little, if at all, below Worcester standards and many other Liverpool-printed pieces illustrated in these pages serve to show the high standard which was soon reached. The Liverpool version of 'L'Amour' (Plate 39 (e)) is so good, that in the hands of a past owner it had, perhaps not

[1]Samuel Wale, who worked for Sadler in London, certainly engraved his own designs.
[2]It is now generally believed that he came to Worcester from Battersea — or possibly Bow — where he may have worked for a short time after the factory at York House closed.
[3]The flanking scrolls more resemble his work than that of Evans.

surprisingly, acquired Worcester status, with correspondingly enhanced value and benefit to him. It is not difficult to see that in these and similar instances, if we were dependent on the print alone for evidences of authorship, there would be nothing to prevent a Worcester attribution, indeed, one could go further and say that such a mistake would be inevitable. In the case of the Royal portraits, it is fortunate that they are Sadler-signed, because the potting characteristics of these mugs render them indistinguishable from ordinary Worcester wares.[1] In the case of the other print, its origin is proclaimed with equal certainty by the uncompromisingly Liverpool features of the jug. These and similar pieces therefore represent potential losses to Liverpool which are only prevented from becoming effectual by the merest chance. It is doubly unfortunate that losses so incurred affect only the best prints, with consequent impoverishment of the remainder from which the quality of Liverpool prints stand to be judged; and this may be expected to continue until prints are kept in their proper perspective in making attributions and until the characteristics of Liverpool porcelain become better known.

This brings us down to fundamentals in any attempt to compare the pottery prints of these two centres of the art. Some basis of agreement on what we decide to call 'Liverpool or 'Worcester' is necessary before any comparison is possible. It is not difficult to see that the decorative value and charm of the 'primitives' would be sufficient to raise the general level of ceramic printing anywhere and cause a swing in favour of any atelier fortunate enough to establish ownership. Something similar could be said of certain other groups for example those known as 'purple ruins' and the smaller 'red cow' group, for both of which considerations in favour of a Liverpool origin have been advanced. The further possibility that yet others await redistribution cannot be ruled out. Until a fair measure of agreement on such matters is reached, the issue is best avoided.

On the evidence considered, we might be justified in maintaining that the best Liverpool prints are good, but that their quality is diluted by avoidable loss and obscured by an unavoidable mass of hack engraving made necessary by Sadler's methods.

[1]Many conflicting opinions have been expressed on the provenance of these mugs at different times. While it is unlikely that the W.P.C. would send ware to Sadler for printing, Sadler may have bought 'in the white', as was his custom.

CHAPTER SIX

SHORT BIOGRAPHICAL NOTES

THE LIVERPOOL PORCELAIN MAKERS OF THE EIGHTEENTH CENTURY

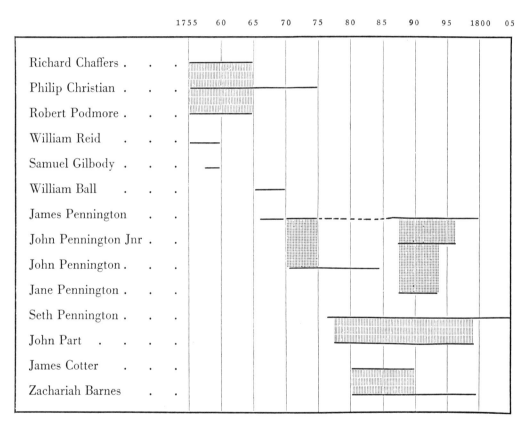

The line-shaded areas denote the existence of a partnership.

The dotted areas indicate a close business relationship in which there is no proof of partnership.

The dotted line marks the period of James Pennington's presumed absence from Liverpool.

The partnership between Christian and his son, Philip, is not shown; nor is that of Seth Pennington with 'Edwards'.

The dates in some cases are approximate only, being dependent on directory entries, bankruptcy notices, etc.

RICHARD CHAFFERS

Richard Chaffers is said to have been born in Mersey Street, Liverpool, the son of a shipwright.[1] The date of his birth is usually given as 1731, a date which has to be reconciled with the recorded facts that he died in 1765 leaving twelve children, one of whom (Elizabeth) was old enough to marry in 1770.[2] John Rosson, son of Elizabeth and grandson of Chaffers, writing in 1854, states that he was forty years of age at his death, which would put the date of birth at 1725.[3] While there is no reason to suppose that this is anything more than a conjectural assertion, it is probably near the truth, for it fits in with much that we know from other sources.

His name first appears in a list of about a dozen apprentices in the Town Records in 1743. Whether this was the date of enrolment, as seems likely, is not stated, but in any case it rules out 1731 as the date of birth. There is no mention of the name of his master, nor is there any confirmation from other sources of the oft-repeated statement that he served his time with Alderman Thomas Shaw, one of the town's leading potters and shortly afterwards its Mayor.

Chaffers seems to have started in business in premises which occupied part of the present site of the western end of the Museum.[4] This property, the first building on the left as you ascended Shaw's Brow (now William Brown Street), had previously been a pottery[5] worked by John and Samuel Livesley, who mortgaged it in 1747 to 'Richard Chaffers and Co.' who apparently entered into occupation at that time and became the Livesley's tenants. That much is clear, from which it follows that Richard Chaffers must have been at least twenty-one years of age at that date and was then in business as a potter on his own account. He was probably financed by his father, but there is no indication of the identity of the 'Co.' If it was Philip Christian, there is no other reference to him as a partner until the date of the Podmore agreement in 1755.

It is of some interest that the exact position of this pottery is readily identifiable from its established relationship to 'Mr Parker's pump', which stood on the site of the 'Angel' inn. There was a well here which enabled Parker to offer water 'from his pump next Chaffers' China pothouse' (*W.L.A., 15/11/1758*) and the site of this well was discovered on this very spot during excavations for the Museum extension. Chaffers' mill for grinding colours was one of three which stood on land to the east of Limekiln Lane, whereon

---

[1]Mayer., op. cit., page 24. The source of this is unknown, but there is no reason to doubt its accuracy.   [2]M. Andrew Rosson, auctioneer.

[3]Letter to *Liverpool Mercury*, Appendix II.   [4]1747.

[5]Gatty, in the *Liverpool Potteries* (page 15), tells us that from Municipal plans and Deeds we learn that this pottery had a frontage of 90 feet.

now stands Lime Street station. It was the most southerly of the three and occupied the angle between the present Skelhorne Street and Lime Street, at a distance of about twenty-five yards from the corner.

Chaffers was made a Freeman in 1754 and the following year the journey to Cornwall in search of a supply of soaprock took place. The story of this as it originally appeared can be read in Appendix II; and its credibility is discussed in that part of the book which deals with our sources of information. By the summer of 1756, Chaffers was back in Liverpool, having completed his arrangements for a supply of the mineral. Not long afterwards the first shipload arrived at Liverpool 'amidst the cheers of the assembled spectators',[1] but it was not until December of that year that the announcement appeared 'The porcelain or china ware made by Messrs Richard Chaffers & Co. is sold nowhere in the town but at their Manufactory on Shaw's Brow. Considerable abatement for exportation and to all wholesale dealers. All the ware is proved with boiling water before it is exposed for sale'.[2] The advertisement appeared for the last time in 1758.

The year 1761 in Liverpool was marked by a keenly contested Parliamentary election, in which Richard Chaffers took a great interest.[3] He was a scrutineer, together with Alderman Clegg, James Clegg, and John Livesley (a potter), and evidently made himself responsible for organizing the potters' vote, as a result of which Sir William Meredith was returned. This was the occasion when we learn that 'one hundred-and-two potters voted for Sir William, all of whom gave plumpers which carried the Election'. Plumper was the word in common use for voter, but here it may refer to a saltglazed mug of the well-known Liverpool bell-shape, a surviving example of which, inscribed 'Ser William a Plumper' was presented to Joseph Mayer by a Miss S. M. Ffarington and formed part of the Mayer bequest to Liverpool Museum. The mug was presumably given to the voters as 'advice'. Unfortunately this, the only known example, was destroyed by enemy action in 1941, but by the greatest good fortune, a porcelain mug of Chaffers' make (Plate 2(a)) came to light recently which had been issued after the Election and was evidently intended to commemorate it, for it bears the inscription 'Success to Sir William's Plumpers 982'.

Apart from a few meagre facts, we really know very little about this early potter. John Rosson, repeating at the end of a long life what he remembers hearing from his mother, tells us that he was a 'man of full and sanguine habit' and that he lost his life in performing a kindness to his old associate,

[1] Jewitt, *Ceramic Art of Great Britain.*
[2] *W.L.A.*, 10th December, 1756.
[3] April–May, 1761. See Sadler's *Poll and Squib* book containing a collection of letters, pamphlets, lampoons, etc, referring to it.

Podmore, who was lying dangerously ill of a fever. This is repeated by Mayer and we can accept it unquestioningly, but Podmore did not die, as the narrative goes on to imply, for the church registers provide good evidence to the contrary by recording the baptisms of further children.[1] The disease was probably typhus, endemic in this country in the eighteenth century, particularly in seaport towns.

We can readily believe that Chaffers was a good master and a likeable character. From the little we know, we get an impression of resourcefulness, untiring energy and great courage in everything he did. That he was a good potter must be admitted, although John Rosson's account of Wedgwood's praises in this connection will be accepted with reserve. He died on 8th December 1765 and an obituary notice published by the *Advertiser* seems worth recording. 'On Wednesday was interred at the old Church in this town the remains of Mr. Richard Chaffers, the most eminent facturer in this country, a gentleman universally esteemed by the traders in general and all his acquaintance. He has left a disconsolate widow and twelve children'.

The names of only two apprentices are known with certainty, namely John Harrison, indentured 30th October 1760 and Peter Clarkson under date 14th February 1761, although there must have been many others.[2] Harrison may have been the son of Lawrence Harrison (1723–94), a maker of delftware whose name appears on a bowl in the Greg Collection dated 1748;[3] but while Clarkson's name is met with again in connection with the baptism of a daughter (1769), neither of these men is known later as a maker of porcelain in the town. John Rosson's letter tells us that Richard Caddick, who subsequently achieved considerable local fame as a portrait painter, was employed in his early years at Chaffers' works. There is no trace of his name as an apprentice decorator. Mayer states[4] that there is a portrait of Chaffers by Caddick, an unconfirmed statement which probably alludes to the portrait by Chubbard, formerly in the Liverpool Museum and destroyed by enemy action.

It is a somewhat curious fact that, although Chaffers seems to have left twelve children and the registers disclose the burial of two more in 1754, no entries referring to births or baptisms of any of these can be traced. Any proof that later Directory entries of the name refer to members of this

[1] See under Podmore.
[2] There is some confusion in John Harrison's dates. Toppin gives 10th October 1750 as date of apprenticeship (Trans. E.P.C., 1929, page 44), and points out the impossibility of this if Chaffers was born in 1731, but all the data we possess rule out 1731 as the date of birth. Ent. MSS. I/53 give the 1760 date, source not stated.
[3] Equally, if Harrison's indenture date was 1750, he could not have been a son of Lawrence H.
[4] Op. cit., page 28.

116

family will therefore depend on the circumstantial evidence, if any, which may be provided by domicile, etc, and in a certain few instances, that is forthcoming. Johnson Chaffers, who is described as a surgeon and given an address at 12 Shaw's Brow in the 1790 Directory, is probably a son. Similarly, we can attach Captain James Chaffers for a like reason. His address is the same as that of Chaffers' widow, Ann, who was still living in Dale Street in 1790, in the house built by her father-in-law. She died some time between then and 1805 and was buried in Saint Nicholas' Church.[1] Richard, a cooper, who was living in Chapel Street in 1790, may reasonably be the one commemorated on the well-known blue-painted 'pepper-box' inscribed with his name and dated 1769.

Chaffers' daughter Elizabeth, who married Andrew Rosson in 1770, has received mention, while of Benjamin, a grocer living in Dale Street in 1790 there is no further information. There is mention in the Town Records of one, Anthony Blundell Chaffers, as a son of Richard Chaffers, and it is just possible that here we may have a clue to the identity of 'Huniball Chaffers', who, although mentioned as one of Chaffers' executors, has never yet been traced.[2] The fact that Chaffers' mine foreman in Cornwall, Gauregan Teppit, actually addressed a letter to someone in Liverpool of that or similar name, who clearly was exercising the authority of an Executor, is sufficient proof that such a person existed.[3] Teppit was not a very educated man and 'Huniball' is sufficiently like 'Blundell' to offer a reasonable solution of this mystery.

The Teppit letters seems to indicate that one, Edward Chaffers, also a son, was another executor. It is not impossible for Chaffers to have had sons old enough at the time of his death, assuming that took place at the age of 40, to have acted as his executors, but it is improbable; and there we must leave the matter. The identity of Edward Chaffers is separately discussed.

Whether, as Mayer states with the support of John Rosson, Chaffers was a maker of delftware in his early years, is true or not, it is certain that Chaffers & Co. made both china and earthenware during the life of the partnership. The latter included both saltglaze and ware of Whieldon and Astbury type. Regarding the saltglaze, the evidence for this statement will be found in the two 'Plumper' mugs, one in porcelain, the other in saltglaze just mentioned.[4]

[1] Ent. MSS. I/53.
[2] M. & M., edition 1874, page 735.
[3] Ibid. On 29th January 1766. Huniball Chaffers paid the amount then outstanding. See under 'Edward Chaffers'.
[4] Bulletin of the Liverpool Museums and Arts Committee, April–June 1954, *The Liverpool Plumper Mug*, Knowles Boney. It is generally conceded that proof of the manufacture of saltglaze 'carries' wares of the other types mentioned; and we have the evidence of the tortoiseshell ware given to Mayer by Christian's granddaughter Mrs Rockliffe (Mayer, op. cit., page 37).

These can only have been made at the same factory, taking all the circum-stances of the election into account, and the porcelain example is clearly of Chaffers' make. But there are other instances in which a porcelain article will be found to have a saltglaze counterpart, or exhibit links with saltglazed articles which might be thought to indicate a common origin; and although Chaffers & Co. did not necessarily make them all, they may conveniently receive consideration here.

A good example is provided by the porcelain sauce boat carrying a moulded design of 'Liver', fruiting vine and masks (Plate 41 (d)), all the elements of which are found singly or jointly on moulded sauce boats in saltglaze. We can point to the porcelain saucer (Plate 18 (e)), the matching tea bowl of which has been replaced for the purpose of the illustration, by what is almost a replica in saltglaze. There is the 'Worcester' wall pocket (Schr. I.473), with its moulded design of cattle and buildings and its counterpart in saltglaze in the same collection (Schr. II1.69)[1]; and that pair of sauce boats, formerly in the Wallace Elliot collection, with a moulded pattern of roses in relief, one in porcelain, the other in saltglaze. In the last instance, it is true that 'silver shape' could provide the explanation, though hardly so in the case of the wallpocket; and the possibility that this kind of dualism may be evidence of a Liverpool origin is rendered more likely when the closeness of the link between Worcester and Liverpool porcelain is borne in mind.

Considering the porcelain alone which was produced by this combine and in the absence of information provided by a controlled series of analyses of the various types of ware, certain conclusions appear to be justified from which the following groups emerge.

1   The 'John Fell' jug group (Plate 1 (c, d)). This jug is dated 1762 and is one of a fairly large class.[2] The inscription reads 'A free gift to John Fell China house joyner 1762'. John Fell's Will was proved at Chester in 1771 and in it he bequeathed his house on the south side of Cable Street, Liverpool. The jug is therefore a document for this class. Another well-known and very similar jug is painted in colours with scenes from a potter's workshop and inscribed 'Multorum manibus grande levatur onus' and bears Thomas Spencer's name (Plate 1 (a), Hanley Museum). Thomas Spencer was a Liver-pool potter who married Elizabeth Gibson at St. Peter's Church, Liverpool, in September 1764. Printed examples also occur, that shown on Plate 35 (b) being given to Mayer by Charles Chandos Pole, a descendant of the Pole who fought the 1761 election. Both these jugs, therefore, are also documents.

[1] Different moulds, same motif. The motif is known on a Staffordshire teapot (Schr. II, 291) for which there is a 'block' and on another example in the Earle collection.
[2] Described in *Apollo*, March 1951, by Collington Bishop and now in Bootle Museum. Chaffers & Co. had a monopoly of china making between 1761–5.

2   The 'Plumper' mug group. This mug must have been made immediately the election results were known (May 1761), for on it is recorded the number of votes polled by Sir William. It can therefore be dated with as much certainty as if it actually bore a date and thus represents one of the earliest of our documents.

3   The group of which the 'lady and parrot' mug (Plate 9 (c)) is the type piece. The document for this is discussed on page 62.

4   A fairly large class, mainly but not entirely teaware, which is characterized by its very green appearance and a type of English flower painting in which a cabbage rose and a spray of orange-coloured flowers are prominent features (Plate 4 (b, c, d)). There is good sanction for this attribution which is entirely acceptable apart from the support given by the almost identical colour of the 'Plumper' mug.

5   Many flat-based coffee cans of which the bottom edge is chamfered (Plate 8 (c)) and a certain number of larger mugs showing the same peculiarity. These are tied to group (3).

With less certainty, but with good reason, we may further attribute 6. A proportion of the 'scratch-cross' group, probably most of it, the choice being governed as far as possible by dating considerations.

7   A considerable quantity of ware in which Worcester features can be observed, but which, for a variety of reasons, may appear to possess greater claim to be regarded as 'Liverpool' products. Many types will be represented and each will receive consideration in the appropriate place, but in each case if the claim be allowed, Chaffers & Co. are the presumptive makers.

8   Isolated pieces, such as the 'Liver' decorated sauce boat (Plate 41 (d)), of which a counterpart exists in saltglaze or other type of earthenware.

This leaves unaccounted for a large quantity of ware for which there are unsufficient criteria for any label except 'Liverpool'. Where we can be certain of so little, it is probably safe to assume that the big Chaffers' partnership made most of the china in Liverpool between 1755 and 1765 and that this will include the whole of that which can be shown, or presumed, to possess a soaprock content, because they alone had a supply of this mineral. It is equally certain that they made ware which did not contain this ingredient, possibly because there were times when insufficient supplies were available.

PHILIP CHRISTIAN

The date of Philip Christian's birth in unknown and, as in the case of so many Liverpool potters, our information about him has to be pieced together from the usual miscellany of sources, the newspapers, directory entries, parish registers, etc. Even so, the record is scanty and no Liverpool potter has left such a tradition with so little documentary support, He was not a

119

Freeman and therefore had no vote and apart from matters of potting interest, he seems to have taken little part in the town's affairs.

He came from a prominent Isle of Man family of Norse descent. The name occurs in the annals of seventeenth-century Liverpool, for in 1661, we find Thomas Christian among those making 'a full and voluntary payment to King Charles II towards the supply of His Majesty's pressing occasions'. The name is repeated, probably denoting the same personage, in the Liverpool Roll of 'The Association of 1696', but there is no further mention of it until 1734, when John and Thomas Christian, Freemen, appear in the Voters' List.

Neither of these men was a potter. We first meet with the name Philip Christian in the parish registers in 1741 and the reference may be to potter Philip. It must, however, be remembered that until the discovery and publication of the Agreement with Chaffers, showing that Christian had been associated with the manufacture of porcelain in Liverpool from its earliest beginnings, he has always been thought of as the *successor* of Chaffers, although as a maker of earthenware throughout his whole career. In this agreement, which is dated 14th June 1755, he is described as Philip Christian of Liverpoole, potter. No further mention of his name occurs until, in the Teppit letters,[1] he is referred to as one of Chaffers' executors (January and February 1766). In the latter year, his name appears as a potter with an address in Lord Street in the first issue of the Liverpool Directory showing that he was there during Chaffers' lifetime in 1765. At this date, the houses were not numbered, but identity with the Lord Street pothouse at once suggests itself, there being no other pottery in the street. This was the oldest established pothouse in Liverpool and was situated at the corner of Lord Street and Frog Lane (Whitechapel).[2] It was not in Christian's ownership in 1758,[3] although its kilns were then in use and a release in 1774 shows that by that time it had ceased to be a pottery. Tradition places Christian's pottery on Shaw's Brow on the site of part of the present Walker Art Gallery; and it was presumably here that he was carrying on his manufacture at the date of his entry into partnership with Chaffers. It is, therefore, possible that the Directory reference is not to the Lord Street pothouse but to a retail shop for the disposal of, Christian's own earthenware, which he was making and marketing, in part independently of Chaffers & Co. In that case, the partnership might sell Christian's earthenware under licence with advantage to the partners, while Christian's position as an independent maker of earthenware at this time would be safeguarded.

[1] Appendix III b and *Marks and Monograms*, p. 735.
[2] It extended from Lord Street to Button Street (see plan of Liverpool potworks, L.). Kiln wasters were found by Entwistle on this site in 1920, during the laying of an electric cable.
[3] *W.L.A.*, 21/4/58).

120

This fits in well with the little we know of this man. It is significant that tradition has never linked his name with that of Chaffers during the partnership years, nor must we lose sight of the fact that he never had anything to do with the soaprock licence, which was drawn entirely in Chaffers' name.[1] All this seems to indicate that his rôle in the partnership was confined to that of a subscriber of capital.

Soon after Chaffers' death, a new company was formed to take over the assets and the lease of the Shaw's Brow premises under the title 'Philip Christian & Co'. The identity of the 'Co.' was long a matter of speculation. As the result of re-editing a letter written by Wedgwood, in which the words 'Mrs. Chaffers' partner had previously been read as 'Messrs Chaffers' partner', the mystery has been solved in favour of Chaffers' widow.[2] The name of the business was changed to 'Philip Christian & Son' about 1772, appearing as such in the 1774 Directory, the son being another Philip.

From now on, as might be expected, it is difficult to distinguish between the activities of father and son, as the latter became increasingly interested in the business and involved in its affairs. According to Entwistle, Philip junior was responsible for the sale of the lease of the soaprock mine to the Worcester Company in 1775 for £500 and he is also credited with the negotiations in the matter of the colour mill in the following year. Both father and son were members of the Mock Corporation of Sefton, a body whose activities seem to have been mainly social; and both signed the 'Loyal Petition to the King' organized by the Liverpool merchants in 1775 protesting against the War against the North American colonists. Incidentally, this petition contained the names of no fewer than thirteen Liverpool potters.

For many years before this event took place, the Liverpool potters had been feeling the effects of foreign competition and Christian had been trying to enlist the support of Wedgwood and the Staffordshire potters in favour of a bill to make foreign china dutiable. The Worcester Company had written to Wedgwood with the same object. But although the Liverpool potters were supported in this matter by their member, Sir William Meredith, Wedgwood would have nothing to do with it. The man whose creamware was soon to be found on the tables of every hostelry between London and St. Petersburg knew he had nothing to fear. His sensible retort was that our potters should meet the competition by making something as good. The year was 1767.[3]

Some time between 1774 and 1777, the firm left the old premises at No. 12 Shaw's Brow. In 1777, the Directory entry appears as 'Philip Christian & Son

---

[1]*Marks and Monograms,* edition 1874, page 735.
[2]Appendix VI c (2).
[3]Appendix VI c (2).

Merchants, Folly Lane'. It is a somewhat curious fact that many Liverpool potters appear to have suffered this change from potter to merchant about this time and one wonders what significance, if any, attaches to it. In Christian's case, it probably indicated neither that he was engaging in business on a bigger scale, nor that he had turned middleman and was selling another's goods, but that, getting near the age of retirement, it sounded more respectable.

This address and description is maintained in the Directory for 1781, at which date the old premises are shown to be in the occupation of Messrs Pennington and Part, China Manufacturers. These changes are probably not unrelated to the disposal of the lease of the soaprock mine in 1775 and taken together, these events seem to show that this China Manufactory came to an end in that year under the old management.

As already stated, the earthenware business with which Philip Christian's name is traditionally associated seems to have been carried on at a large potworks at the top of Shaw's Brow. Actually, the frontage of this was on a short strip of road between the top of the Brow and the beginning of Folly Lane (now Islington) called Islington Terrace. According to Gatty (op. cit., page 17), it was a long narrow pottery with a frontage to Shaw's Brow of about fifty yards, but extending back about two hundred yards across the north side of the present Hunter Street. In a drawing made by W. G. Herdman in 1845, which depicts Shaw's Brow as seen from the corner of Lime Street and London Road, a mill is shown on what would appear to have been part of the site of this pottery (Herdman, *Pictorial Relics of Liverpool*, volume 2, Plate XXXVII). Mayer (op. cit., page 36) tells us that Christian's pottery was on the site of Islington Terrace (see plan of the Liverpool potteries) and some confirmation of this is afforded by Entwistle's statement that Christian owned a property on Folly Lane as early as 1765, although the authority for this is not given (*Entwistle MSS., I/59*) and reference to a potworks may not be intended. This district is full of associations with the name of Christian, but the conclusion that in every case the reference is to potter Christian may be open to doubt. As early as 1745, a Mrs Christian is mentioned among the subscribers (£10) to the New Infirmary building fund, among a long list of persons who had sponsored the project (Baines, *History of the Commerce and Town of Liverpool*, 1852, page 413). This is an interesting list, for, as Baines says, it must represent the names of those who were the principal inhabitants of Liverpool at that time. The lady in question was probably not related to our potter, but was the wife of a Mr Christian, who, according to Herdman, was the donor of some excellent leaden statues which for long adorned the lawn in front of the Infirmary and must, therefore, have been very close to Islington Terrace and Philip Christian's potworks. But Herdman

122

was probably in error in stating that the house of this Mr Christian stood on the corner of Christian Street and the east corner of Islington, this being an assumption because of the identity of name with that of the potter, to whom tradition accords the building of this house many years later at a time when the locality had acquired strong potter-Christian associations. At this date, the whole of this district, now covered by Hunter Street, the lower end of Islington and the south end of Christian Street was occupied by a popular public garden and place of amusement. In it was Gibson's Coffee House and the 'Folly', an eight-storied tower with a gazebo, from which a good view of the Welsh mountains could be obtained. About 1785, the Folly Gardens were closed and the tower and coffee house were pulled down, the materials being bought by Christian (almost certainly Philip junior) and used to build the house at the corner of the street which later was to be called after him.

Philip Christian's will was made in March 1785 and proved at Chester in August of that year. He therefore died between these two dates.

The names of some of Christian's apprentices are known. Most notable among them is that of Robert Wilcox.[1] Others receiving mention are Robert Lane (1767), William Aspinall and John Podmore (1774), but whether the latter, whose name is duly recorded in the Freemen's Committee Book, is to be regarded as the son of Robert Podmore, as has been stated, is open to doubt.

Christian undoubtedly continued to use soaprock to some extent, for the mine lease was not sold until 1775, and we have no means of knowing how much he abandoned it in favour of bone ash; and, remembering that the three brothers Pennington and William Ball were all making chinaware during the greater part of the time we are considering — and copying one another's methods as much as possible — it is not surprising that the means we have of identifying anything that Christian made, with reasonable certainty, are small. A possible exception may be made in the case of ware showing unmistakable signs of saltglaze influence, some examples of which are illustrated here. In practice, however, this is not very helpful, unless, as sometimes does happen, such close resemblances in potting and decoration can be seen to exist as could only be accounted for satisfactorily by supposing a common factory of origin.[2]

Much discussion has centred round the formulae given in Sadler's *Note Book*. Among these is one to which reference is frequently made (quoted by

---

[1] Appendix VI B, Extracts from Wedgwood's letters — 'Served his time with Christian and then went to Reid until they failed — '. Literally, that can only mean that he was apprenticed to Christian as a maker of earthenware, in pre-partnership days.

[2] To think otherwise would be to assume that Philip Christian was the only Liverpool maker of saltglaze.

Mayer) called 'Christian's China Body' and it might be thought that it would be helpful in identifying his ware. The fact is that expert potters to whom the matter has been referred can make nothing of it and the same applies to the formula for 'Glaze'. The reason in each case is that there is an unknown item which makes the whole thing valueless and no information is therefore possible from this source.[1] Nor can we turn to Mayer himself for help in this matter, for he obtained no porcelain of reputed Christian's make from any of the potter's descendants. He did, however, obtain some half-dozen pieces of pottery from Christian's grand-daughter, Mrs Rockliffe of Edge Hill, Liverpool. These were of tortoiseshell or Whieldon type and eventually formed part of the Mayer bequest to Liverpool Museum (Catalogue Nos. 2334–8).

ROBERT PODMORE

Our scanty knowledge about Robert Podmore while in the service of the Worcester Porcelain Company has already been recorded in describing the circumstances in which he left Worcester and came to Liverpool in 1755. In that account, the Worcester spelling of the name 'Podmore' was followed, although as will be seen, the spelling 'Padmore' appears in the Liverpool Agreement. The possibility that the different spelling may have been intentionally used as some sort of disguise in order to evade the penalty to which he may have rendered himself liable, can be dismissed. A more likely explanation is to be found in the greater carelessness in name spelling which prevailed in those days. Even so, we are faced with the fact that the Liverpool parish registers clearly show that, at this date, there were two potters in Liverpool, one Robert Podmore, the other Richard Padmore, living near each other, both married and both bringing up families at the same time. The records of these men are quite distinct throughout; and although there is little to lead one to think that they may have been related, that possibility cannot be entirely ruled out.[2]

The first entry is in 1756 and concerns Robert Podmore (death of son Robert, October 1756). He was then living in the Haymarket and we find two more entries referring to Robert at the same address before the first mention of Richard Padmore occurs in 1759 (baptism of daughter Fanny). His address is also given as the Haymarket on this occasion and it is therefore a fortunate occurrence in helping to avoid confusion that, in the same year, Robert

---

[1]For a letter on this subject see Ent. MSS. 10/155.
[2]I am indebted to Mr Cyril Shingler of the Worcester Royal Porcelain Company for the information that, although in the original Partnership Deed of the Company, Podmore's name is always clearly engrossed as 'Podmore', his first name appears as Richard in the copy of Clause 22. This could be entirely fortuitous. On the other hand, it could be a mistake arising from the fact that both men were in the employment of the Company at that time.

Podmore's daughter Ann was baptized from an address in Shaw's Brow. It may be that this change of address, which was probably to premises at or adjoining Chaffers' works, was connected with the arrival of Richard in Liverpool and affords grounds for thinking that these two men were related. It clearly establishes their separate identity, while these entries as a whole completely accord with the view that Robert Padmore, described in the Liverpool Agreement as of Worcester and said to be knowing and expert in making a certain kind of china, can hardly be other than Robert Podmore lately employed by the Worcester Company because of that knowledge.

In this way, the entries in the parish registers continue over the years. We are dealing with a time when the birth rate was high and the death rate almost equally so. Infant mortality, viewed from any standard, was appalling. Richard's wife died in 1762 and in the following year he married Mary Burgess, a widow, by whom he had several more children. Shortly after, he moved to Crosshall Street where he seems to have resided many years, the last entry occurring in 1783.

Robert did not die in the epidemic which caused Chaffers' death in 1765, as Rosson states in his letter,[1] but continued to prosper, with the recording of the births of four more children. He moved to Preston Street about the time of Chaffers' death and the last entry relating to him occurs in 1776. According to Entwistle, he was buried in St. Nicholas' Church (? date), but I am unable to confirm that statement. Neither of these men was a Freeman and therefore their names do not occur in Voting Lists, but it is difficult to understand why there is no mention of them in any issue of the Liverpool Directory, in which the name is met with but twice. In 1790, John Podmore, potter, is shown as living at 8 Shawhill Street and in 1796, presumably the same person is described as a Customs officer living at the same address. It is likely that this is the John Podmore who is named in the Freeman's Committee Book in 1774 as apprenticed to Philip Christian & Son and who was made a Freeman in 1780, but he is unlikely to have been John, son of Richard, whose baptism is recorded at St. Peter's Church in 1764. The identity of Edward Padmore buried at St. Peter's Church on October 16th 1765 is unknown.

The name is met with in the Midland counties, but is not known in Bristol with either form of spelling. It is of some interest to note that a William Podmore was among those who signed the Roll of 'The Association of 1696 in Liverpool', writing his name and not making a 'mark'.

SAMUEL GILBODY

There is little information about this Liverpool potter. He was the son of Samuel Gilbody, a clay potter who is first mentioned in the Town Records in

[1]Appendix II, page 198.

1705 and who died in 1752. From the fact that this man was made an Overseer of the Poor in 1725, he was probably of some importance. His pottery was on the north side of Shaw's Brow, identifiable with the one which later was worked by his son; and he had a retail shop 'for the sale of white earthenware' at the bottom of Dale Street (Downdscroft).[1] He married twice.

The dates of birth and death of Samuel Gilbody junior are unknown, nor do we know whether he was a son of the first or the second marriage. The latter took place in 1731 and young Samuel seems to have been old enough to take over the Shaw's Brow pottery on his father's death in 1752. This was immediately to the east of and adjoining Chaffers' works and included a mill for grinding colours 'which was usually occupied with the pothouse'. According to Gatty[2] this pottery had a frontage of nearly one hundred feet. In addition, Gilbody had a retail shop on the other side of the street.

In the certificate which, in company with Alderman Thomas Shaw, he signed in 1756 concerning Sadler's tile printing experiment, he describes himself as a clay potter; and it was not until some eighteen months later that he began to advertise in the local papers as a 'china facturer', with china ware of all sorts for sale.[3] This advertisement appeared for about six months. The only piece of ware which could be identified with certainty as having been made by him — a mug inscribed 'Gilbody maker' — was destroyed in 1941 by enemy action (Plate 35 (a)).

The wording of his advertisement is interesting. It will be observed that it contains no mention of anything other than china ware of all sorts from which it seems a fair inference, that, at this date, he had abandoned the manufacture of earthenware entirely. We might also be entitled to conclude that, by early 1758, his manufacture of china had passed the experimental stage and was on a scale sufficiently large to require a separate retail establishment for marketing. That is an important deduction, for it marks him with an output which places a complexion on his activities very different from that which is gained by the contemplation of one solitary, albeit well-authenticated example of his work, which has been lost.

From Gilbody's association with Alderman Shaw, a former Mayor of the town, we may think he was a man of some standing among the townsfolk and counted for something in the little band of experimenters in the new found art. Unfortunately financial failure overtook him, as it did so many more of these pioneers. Heavy kiln losses and insufficient capital was the usual story.

[1] He appears in the 1734 Voters List as a potter.
[2] Op. cit., page 16.
[3] *W.L.A.*, 13th February 1758, 'To the Publick, S. Gilbody, China Facturer, at his warehouse on the south side of Shaw's Brow is now selling wholesale and retail at the lowest prices China ware of all sorts, equal for service and beauty to any made in England — '.

In June 1761, a notice appeared referring to his bankruptcy and announcing the sale of premises and stock by assignees, but it seems likely that some attempt at carrying on business in her own name was made by his wife, Hannah, for six months later, a bankruptcy order against her as a 'clay potter' also appeared in the *London Gazette* (9th January 1762).

REID & CO.

Although Richard Chaffers began his preparations for making chinaware at least as early as 1755, the credit for being the first in the field with a marketable product must go to Reid & Co. On 19th November 1756 the following appeared in the *Liverpool Advertiser:* 'Liverpool China Manufactory. Messrs Reid & Co. proprietors of the china manufactory, have opened their warehouse in Castle Street and sell all kinds of blue and white china ware, not inferior to any make in England, both wholesale and retail'. Chaffers' first advertisement did not appear until three weeks later.

The announcement just quoted had been preceded by an advertisement for apprentices (24th September) which read 'any young persons with capacities for drawing and painting may meet with suitable encouragement by applying to the proprietors'. Two more similarly-worded notices appeared in 1758. In 1760, the firm was still in need of apprentices, which they seem to have had difficulty in obtaining. The names of none are known to us.

Reid's pottery was situated on the south side of Brownlow Hill, to which it had a frontage of about sixty yards; and it extended back to what is now Pleasant Street about the same distance.[1] The site was therefore a rectangle of about three-quarters of an acre. The land was on lease from the Corporation to William Reid, who built the new potworks at what must have been a considerable outlay. At this date, the locality was completely rural and well outside the boundaries of urban growth. Close by on Mount Pleasant a little to the south was the 'Old Bowling Green' a tavern kept by William Roscoe, brother of James Roscoe the potter of Shaw's Brow and father of William, who was born here in 1753. Shortly afterwards Roscoe moved to a house a little lower down; and from many sources we learn that young William, as a small boy, was a frequent visitor to Reid's china works, which adjoined his father's garden. It was here that he received his first lessons in painting from pot-painters who were employed there, with one of whom, Hugh Milligan, he became very friendly.

William Reid's father was a merchant and Reid himself a house painter. It was, therefore, presumably the 'Co.' that provided the technical details involved in manufacture, though we have no certain information on this point. Success could hardly have been expected without the services of experienced

[1]Gatty, op. cit., page 20.

potters and perhaps this aspect of the matter was better looked after than appearances might suggest, for this was one of the Liverpool potteries in which Josiah Wedgwood had an interest. The volume of business seemed to have reached considerable proportions and continued for some six years before failure finally occurred, the reasons for which are by no means clear. Wedgwood's interest in the bankruptcy proceedings then became obvious, but it is unlikely that he financed the venture from the start, for he was then in partnership with Whieldon and but twenty-five years of age at the time. The sudden appearance of William Reid, a house painter, among the experimenters in china making must always be regarded as one of the mysteries of the industry in Liverpool.

For our information concerning the type of ware made, we have to rely on the advertisement just given and on the description of the goods offered when the bankrupt stock was sold. This referred to 'best blue-and-white cups and saucers at 3/- per set; best second ditto at 2/- per set; enamelled coffee cups from 2/- per dozen'. The last named may indicate that some enamelled ware was produced, but its cheapness, even at sale prices, makes it more likely that the reference is to printed decoration which it will be remembered was referred to as 'enamelling' in the language of the day. Conjecturally, the coffee can printed in black over-glaze with the design known as 'La Cascade', and which has no Chaffers' features (Plate 39 (*g*)) may represent this group.[1] It is currently believed that much of the ware of this factory was exported to the American colonies.

Reid's bankruptcy was announced in 1761. In June of that year a reference to 'the late partnership' reveals that a Mr McNeale had been one of the partners. The administrators of this debtor's affairs issued another notice in September, in which a selling-off of teaware at the factory was advertised, followed by an annoucement of the sale of the premises and the remainder of the stock in January 1762. It would seem that the Castle Street retail shop had already been given up, for the stock was sold at Mr Reid's shop in Harrington Street, a property which may have belonged to William Reid's father.

Wedgwood's interest was probably a mortgage and an announcement made in December 1761 seems to indicate that he and a Mr Dobson, a Liverpool merchant, were the assignees. This read 'To be sold by public auction on the 5th January next at 6 o'clock. All these new erected buildings now used as a China Manufactory, with the Colour mill and premises appurtenant thereto, situated on Brownlow Hill, near Liverpool and lately occupied by Reid & Co. of Liverpool, held by lease under the Corporation of Liverpool. Any person desirous to view the premises may apply to Mr Wedgwood at Burslem in Staffordshire, or to Mr John Dobson in Liverpool'.

[1]Evidence of date later received now makes this unlikely.

The indebtedness to local tradespeople was small, amounting to no more than about £25 and the chief creditors were Wedgwood and Dobson. Many years afterwards slanderous statements were made by a Mr Boyer to the effect that Wedgwood owed his rise and fortune in the world to selling this bankrupt's estate and keeping the money. Wedgwood issued a statement of account and was able to show that the charge was without foundation; but Reid's failure was severe and he never recovered from it.[1] He was still working as a housepainter at the address in Harrington Street thirty years later.

WILLIAM BALL

William Ball had a pottery in Ranelagh Street, where he is shown as a china maker[2] in the Liverpool Directory for 1766. For how long before that date he had worked there we do not know. There is no earlier issue of the Directory, he did not advertise and, not being a Freeman, his name does not appear in the town records or in the voter's lists. Sadler, in his *Note Book* refers to 'Ball's best white glaze' and was evidently in the way of doing business with a man of this name for, on 10th June 1763, he wrote to Wedgwood, 'Mr Ball tells me the pint mugs will take sixpence each in powder gold to gild them on the edge'.[3] This reads more like the activity of a decorator than of a potter and the reader must decide whether the reference is to the same man. That there was a pothouse in Ranelagh Street as far back as 1758 is shown by the fact that the birth of a child to the clerk of the pothouse in Ranelagh Street was registered in St. Peter's parish church in that year.[4] There is no evidence of any other pottery in this street at any time, nor of any other potter and solid grounds therefore exist for identifying William Ball with the tenancy as early as that date.

He receives mention again in the 1767 Directory and in 1769, but not in 1772. At some time, therefore, between these dates he disappeared from the scene and, unless the entry in the 1796 Directory which reads 'William Ball, gent', with an address at 9 Garden Street, Wapping, is accepted as a reference to him, we do not hear of him again. Thus the length of his china-making life in Liverpool, of which we have absolute proof, is limited to three or four years, but it may have been — and almost certainly was — considerably longer.

In common with other Liverpool china-makers, it is most likely that he had previously made some kind of earthenware. Attempts have been made to identify him with a William Ball, potter, of Limehouse, who may have been working at the little known factory there which failed in 1748.[5] This man and his wife Mary, had a daughter Elizabeth who was baptized at the parish

[1]Letter from Wedgwood on the matter, Appendix VI c (1).
[2]Gatty, op. cit., page 11.   [3]Appendix IV a (10).
[4]Recorded by E. S. Price, *Sadler, a Liverpool Pottery Printer.*
[5]Toppin, Trans. E.P.C., 1931, page 70.

church in 1747, but there the record ceases.[1] It was thought that he might have gone to Staffordshire from Limehouse, or possibly to Liverpool. There were many potters of this name in and around Burslem at this time and a little later, but none on investigation could be shown to have had any connection with Limehouse; nor did anything emerge which might enable one to link William Ball of Limehouse or any of the many Staffordshire potters of the same name with our Liverpool china-maker of the 1760's.

These negative results sound unimpressive, but they conceal much hard work on the part of those concerned. Some idea of the difficulties encountered may be gathered from the fact that there were two sets of Burslem families, both headed by a William and Mary Ball and both almost certainly having families at the same time; while the prevalence of the name in the area is further shown by the fact that one 'William Ball' died there in 1760, and yet another such in 1763.

Beyond a bare statement that the china made by William Ball was almost certainly non-steatitic, we know nothing about this potter's productions. Nor have we reason to feel greater confidence when called upon to speculate about his earthenware. In the Schreiber Collection is the well-known salt-glazed mug bearing the incised inscription 'William Ball' and the date 1747 (Schr. II.79). Was it made at Limehouse, at Liverpool or in Staffordshire? Inscriptions of this nature, as is well known, seldom record the name of the maker but that of the recipient of the piece and there is no reason for supposing otherwise in this instance. Any resemblance therefore between the word 'William' of this mug with that of the 'William' of the 'Ser William a plumper' classic, must be more likely to link it with the Chaffers combine than otherwise, for there can be no reasonable doubt that the 'Plumper mug' is a product of that manufacture. One might also reflect that, had William Ball been potting in Liverpool as long as the date 1747 would make possible, he would have left a deeper mark on the pages of Liverpool's history.

As a coincidence and nothing more, it is perhaps worth recording that such a mark was indeed left by another of the same name. It so happens that Liverpool's oldest document is a 'Grant by Anabilia, daughter of William Balle of Lyverpol to Alan Walsemon for eleven years, of one burgage[2] 'except half garden, in Lyverpol'. The date of this is 1293.

EDWARD CHAFFERS

The authority for stating that Edward Chaffers was one of Richard Chaffers' executors is the author of *Marks and Monograms*. It derives from the letters

[1]Mrs MacAlister, Trans. E.C.C., 1933, page 47.
[2]Burgage. A strip of land, rental value one shilling, allotted by King John to new settlers. It will be recalled that the King came to Liverpool and granted the town its first Charter in 1207.

130

which were written after Chaffers' death by Teppit, the foreman of the Cornish soaprock mine. Together with one 'Huniball Chaffers' he is described in these as a son, but the reason for this is not stated.[1] Any difficulty in supposing that Richard Chaffers could have had one son old enough to act as his executor would clearly be much increased by having to suppose that he could have had another possessing the necessary qualification. Edward Chaffers, however, was not a son, but probably either a brother or a cousin and he is almost certainly the person of that name who is described in the 1766 Directory as a merchant living in John Street.

Between 1769 and 1772, he moved to St. Paul's Square. There is no trace of any other person of the same name in Liverpool at this time,[2] or later.

Shortly before 1768, we find him with an interest in a mug works on the south side of Shaw's Brow, near the Old Infirmary. These works had been owned by Woods & Co., who made 'sugar moulds, drips, chimney moulds, large jars for water, crucibles, melting pots, etc.'. Among the products turned out were black mugs,[3] and it is interesting to note that Sadler, in his *Note Book*, refers to the proper use of manganese in making a good black and praises the method used by 'Edward', whose black was much 'blacker and smoother than his own'.

About the year 1768, it would appear that the mug works on the south side of Folly Lane (see plan), then in the occupation of Jonas Bold & Co., were taken over by Edward Chaffers, who left the Shaw's Brow premises, which were closed. The amalgamated business was then carried on in Folly Lane where it was still trading in 1772, but by 1774 Edward had evidently left, for business was resumed under the old name of Jonas Bold & Co.

Edward Chaffers must have been a man of substance and of some importance. As a senior churchwarden and overseer of the poor, we learn that he was made responsible for the distribution of £600 advanced by Liverpool Corporation for public relief. Elected a member of the Liverpool Chamber of Commerce in 1774, he continued to live in St. Paul's Square, described as a merchant, until 1810, when he went to live at Everton. The entries then cease. His eldest daughter, Ellen, married William Cross of Red Scar, near Preston, whose third son, Richard Assheton Cross (Lord Cross) became the possessor of the documents referred to elsewhere in this book.

[1] M. & M., edition 1874, page 735.
[2] It is stated in Entwistle MSS. 1/54 that a person named Edward Chaffers died on 9th December 1805 and was buried in St. Nicholas Church. A search of the registers has failed to confirm this.
[3] *W.L.A.*, 18th June 1756. Some of the black ware customarily attributed to Staffordshire and Jackfield was undoubtedly made in Liverpool. Much was exported to Ireland (see Dudley Westropp, *Guide to Irish Pottery and Porcelain*.)

THE PENNINGTON FAMILY

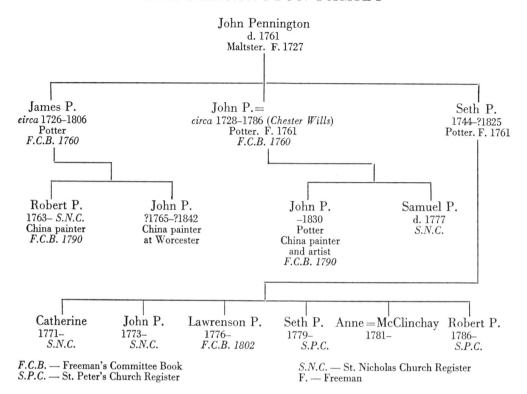

F.C.B. — Freeman's Committee Book   S.N.C. — St. Nicholas Church Register
S.P.C. — St. Peter's Church Register   F. — Freeman

John Pennington was a maltster of Liverpool, who married about the year 1725 and had three sons, James, John and Seth. All became potters and these men and many of their descendants made notable contributions to the pottery industry of Liverpool. John the maltster died in 1761, but before the turn of the century, the Pennington family included among its members at least three more who were called John, all of whom had pottery associations in one way or another, in Liverpool. The task of sorting these men out and preserving their separate identities is one of some difficulty; and although great care has been exercised, it is possible that in some cases the conclusions reached may be incorrect. A glance at the Pennington pedigree should help the reader.

JAMES PENNINGTON

James Pennington was born about 1726, but the first mention of his name is in 1760 in the Freemen's Committee Book, as a potter with an address in Dig Lane.[1] In the following year he was made a Freeman and his name occurs in the voter's list of the 1761 Parliamentary Election. Two years later he was

[1]The long interval between birth and registration is unexplained.

living in St. Peter's Street,[1] but it is not until 1769 that there is any connection of his name with a pottery, when we find him at 'the china works' in Park Lane.

The only site of a pottery in Park Lane which has been identified was on the right-hand side going south, at the far end and close to the Blundells Street turning. It had a frontage of some sixty feet and a depth of about two hundred feet.[2] A mill for grinding colours stood to the westward. The map of 1769 shows the site as then occupied by a pottery, on land whereon is now the Wapping railway goods station and yard.

From an advertisement by him announcing the sale of 'a large quantity of china ware' at the lowest fixed prices in July 1769,[3] it is likely that James Pennington had been making china here since Thwaites and Wilcock, makers of earthenware, had given up these potworks two years earlier.[4] He was still there in 1772,[5] but about this date he must have moved to Copperas Hill, where to took over a small potworks previously occupied by Thomas Mears.[6] According to Gatty[7] this was situated on the south side, on a site now marked by the Ainsworth Street turning. He was evidently working this pottery in 1774[8] but he could not have remained much longer, for in December 1775 arrangements for a re-lease were in progress, with no mention of James Pennington's name.[9] Now the records show that his brother John was also at these potworks in 1772[10] and remained there until 1779[11] and from that fact it is likely that they were in partnership. The disappearance of James from the scene at this time may reasonably be linked with the story of the family quarrel, said to have been caused by James divulging the secret of the famous Pennington blue when in his cups.

There is no reason to doubt the truth of this story, which goes on to relate that James migrated to Staffordshire with all his family. This undoubtedly took place. His name continued to appear in the list of voters, being recorded in the Poll Books of 1780, 1790, 1802 and 1806, but this does not prove residence in Liverpool at the corresponding date, for many an absent potter returned habitually in order to do this. That he did eventually return is clear, both from a *Directory* entry in 1794[12] and by the transfer to him of two apprentices by his nephew — another John — in the year 1796.[13]

It is stated by Mayer — and generally believed — that James' quarrel about the secret of the blue colour was with Seth.[14] This is most unlikely. Seth must

[1]Baptismal Register, St. Nicholas Church.   [2]Gatty, op. cit., page 22.
[3]G.G.A., 28th July 1769.   [4]*W.L.A.*, 8th May 1767.
[5]Dir.   [6]Dir.   [7]Op. cit., page 20.   [8]Dir.
[9]Gatty, op. cit., page 20.   [10]St. Nicholas Church Register.
[11]See under John P.
[12]*Universal British Directory*, Liverpool section.   [13]F.C.B.   [14]Op. cit., page 35.

have been fifteen or sixteen years younger and it is more likely to have been with John, with whom the records show that James had always been closely associated and with whom he was actually working a pottery about the time the breach took place. John's death, which occurred in 1786, made James' return to Liverpool possible; and this event seems to have taken place soon afterwards.

In 1787, Richard Gerrard took a lease of these china works 'and two gardens'.[1] Gerrard was not a potter but a Dock Commissioner[2] and it may be assumed that he took over the property as an investment. There is little doubt that the pottery was worked from now on by John's widow, Jane Pennington, her son John and the returned exile James.

Jane Pennington figures in the 1790 Directory as a potter, with an address at Springfields, Folly Lane. This was close to the potworks; and when James voted in 1790 from this address, it is likely that he did so as a resident and not as an absentee voter. He was actually living there in 1794, according to a Directory entry,[3] in which year Jane Pennington retired from business, for a winding up notice reads 'All persons having any demands against Mrs Jane Pennington of Liverpool, china manufacturer, etc., . . . '[4] It will be noticed there is no mention of a partnership and it is unlikely that one ever existed. She died in 1797.

The intrusion of Thomas Wolfe into the affairs of this pottery now calls for mention. Thomas Wolfe, member of an old established firm of potters making creamware at Stoke, had for many years sold his earthenware from a Liverpool dockside warehouse.[5] For a time he traded as 'Wolfe & Co.', the 'Co.' being John Davenport, but the partnership was dissolved in September 1794.[6] In 1795, he bought this pottery, as is clearly shown by a plan in Mayer's possession marked 'Mr Wolfe's house and china works in Folly Lane, planned on assignment, 2nd October 1795, that part under the Corporation planned on lease, 22nd February 1790'.[7] James Pennington, with nephew John, was still there, but the following year John evidently gave up, for we learn that two of his apprentices, John Evans and James Turner, completed their indentures by assignment to James Pennington.[8] John, who always seems to have been more interested in decorating the ware than in making it, is shown at an address in Islington (Folly Lane) in 1802[9] and again four years

[1]Gatty, op. cit., page 18.   [2]Dir. 1790.
[3]*Universal British Directory*, Liverpool section.   [4]G.G.A., 30th October 1794.
[5]From about 1785. He advertised that he kept 500 crates ready packed in his warehouse at Liverpool Dock, suitable for the West India or American markets 'at a day's notice'. (G.G.A., 23/5/98).
[6]G.G.A., 25th September, 1794.
[7]Gatty, op. cit., page 19.   [8]F.C.B.   [9]P.B.

later in Cheapside,[1] but in 1807, described as an artist, he was living at Everton.[2]. Here he apparently remained until 1830, after which date the record ceases.

James must have remained in the business until the close of the century when again we find the pottery up for sale. From a plan dated May 1801, when it was styled the Islington China Manufactory[3] we learn that it had been modernized 'with slip house, printing and gold rooms' and probably in recent use. A previous announcement refers to 'All that new erected China Works with Steam Engine . . .'.[4]

In the Directory for 1796, Thomas Wolfe is called a china manufacturer but there can be little doubt that this is a misunderstanding connected with the fact that he had just become the proprietor of the Folly Lane China works; and the same issue shows him as the occupier of a Staffordshire warehouse at the Old Dock. There is not the slightest reason to suppose that he ever made any china himself, although it is quite clear that china production was actively going on at these works at this time. That James Pennington was responsible for this gains support from the fact, already mentioned, that he took over two apprentices in 1796 and from the circumstance mentioned by Gatty[5] that one of Eye's undated plans is inscribed 'Works in Folly Lane, Shaw,[6] afterwards Pennington and Wolfe'. It is, of course, quite possible that some of Wolfe's Staffordshire earthenware was also marketed here.

The last reference to James Pennington is in 1806 and shows him at the same address in Cheapside as his nephew John. Cheapside was a continuation of Dig Lane, which it may have absorbed; and it is probably not a coincidence that the first reference to him shows him to be living in Dig Lane in 1760. He must have been about eighty years of age at his death.

It is difficult to form an idea of the value of his contribution to Liverpool porcelain, for we are unable to identify anything that he made. There is no reason to suppose that it was outstanding.

JOHN PENNINGTON

John Pennington was the second son of John the maltster. We first hear of him in 1759, in Cheapside[7] as a potter. In the following year his name occurs in the Freemen's Committee Book and in this same year he was made a Freeman. In 1762 and 1763, he was living in Dig Lane[8] almost certainly with

---

[1]P.B.　　　　　[2]Dir.　　　　　　　　[3]Gatty, op. cit., page 19.
[4]G.G.A., 22nd May 1800.
[5]Op. cit., page 18.　　　　[6]Reference to Ald. Thos. Shaw, who was the lessee in 1743.
[7]St. Nicholas Church.　　　[8]Ibid.

his brother James. We find him at Mount Pleasant in 1769[1] and in 1771 at Brownlow Hill.[2] During these years there is no mention of his name in connection with any pottery undertaking and it is probable that he was a journeyman until about 1768. In December 1775, he issued an announcement referring to malicious damage which had been done to a colour mixing mill in his possession 'near the road leading to Low Hill'. In this, he describes himself as a china manufacturer, as at that date he undoubtedly was, but he makes the interesting disclosure at the end that a similar thing had occurred at this mill some six or seven years previously. The wording indicates that he was also the owner on the first occasion — and therefore running a potworks at the time — but it does not follow that he was then making china. It is a reasonable inference that he was making it in 1772 at Copperas Hill[3] where he was probably in partnership with his brother James, who had just commenced production there.[4] There is continued proof of his presence at Copperas Hill throughout the 1770's and it must have been here that the rupture with James took place over the matter of the colour secret.[5] In 1775, there was a re-lease[6] of these premises to John, now the sole proprietor.

That this is correct is shown by the fact that in June 1776, we find him advertising in his own name for a journeyman turner in the china business at this address.[7] He evidently prospered here, but the works proving too small for his expanding business, he moved to a more commodious pottery in Folly Lane[8] in 1779. The announcement issued on this occasion is the only clue we possess to the type of ware made.[9] The most important item refers to the 'likeness of vessels taken and painted in the most correct and masterly manner', followed by a reference to merchants and captains of ships. From this we must assume that some of the bowls and jugs decorated in this way were turned out by this factory.

There were two potteries in Folly Lane. Pennington's was on the north side about midway between Soho Street and St. Annes Street, on the site of an old mug works owned thirty years earlier by Thomas Shaw.[10] At that date, it included a house and garden which seem to have been transferred with the pottery; and it is likely that John went to live there because he sold his residence, number two, the Haymarket, in December of the same year.[11]

For a description of this pottery, we have to rely on a document which

[1]Ibid.   [2]Ibid.   [3]Ibid.   [4] and [5] See under James.
[6]Gatty, op. cit., page 20.   [7]G.G.A., 7th June 1776.   [8]Ibid, 25th June,1779.
[9]Given in full at end.
[10]Gatty, op. cit., page 18. See plan of potteries.
[11]W.L.A. 17th December 1779, Lot 2, stated to be 'now in the occupation of John Pennington'.

PLATE VI

The last remnant of the Liverpool potteries: Seth Pennington's oven as it appeared in the 1850's

PLATE VII

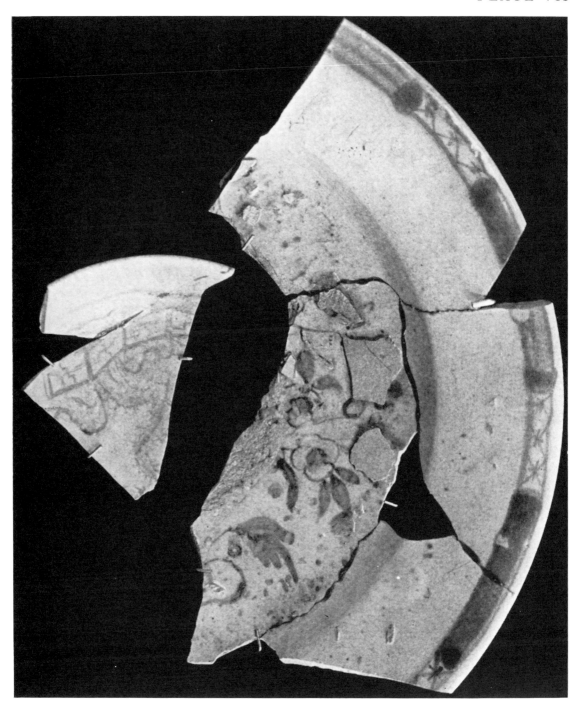

Fragments of tin-glazed porcelain unearthed by Peter Entwistle at
Trueman Street in 1916

renewed the lease to Richard Gerrard Esq., in 1787, when it is described as being rectangular in shape, with frontage and back of 147 yards and sides of 25 yards. This included the house and garden and therefore there is no indication of the actual size of the pottery.

Ill-health seems to have troubled John Pennington and the china-making life of this man of which we have definite proof must have been less than twenty years. On 10th March 1784, his wife Jane was advertising the pottery for sale. In this she was unsuccessful, for the advertisement was repeated on June 2nd and again on September 8th, when the tell-tale words 'lately used as a manufacture of china' were added. Production had then evidently ceased. John Pennington died in October 1786 at the age of 58 years and his Will was proved at Chester. He was therefore born in 1728.

The names of two apprentices have been traced, namely, William Wright, who was entered in 1780 and later went to Staffordshire, where we find him at Hanley Green in 1806; and Joseph Cartlidge, who was apprenticed in 1782. The Cartlidges were a family of potters, originally carrying on business at Sutton, Lancashire, and trading under the name of Stephen Cartlidge & Co. The possibility that they may have made porcelain later at Prescot cannot be entirely dismissed.

Of John Pennington's married life nothing is known. Two sons are mentioned but he probably had others, for there is no record of birth or baptism of any. John, who may have been the elder, first receives mention in 1790 in the Freemen's Committee Book and became both potter and china-painter. The little known about him will be found mentioned in connection with his association with his uncle James. The other, Samuel, died in 1777.

Some idea of the type of ware made by this man is obtained from the announcement he issued in 1779 on moving to Folly Lane and I therefore give it in full:

'John Pennington, China Manufacturer, begs to inform his friends and the public that he has removed from his late factory at Copperas Hill to one perfectly commodious situate in that part of Folly Lane called CHELSEA, where he now carries on business in the most extensive manner and makes cheap, elegant and serviceable china ware, which are for brilliancy of colour equal to any in Great Britain. Gentlemen who desire to have any particular device, coat of Arms, crest, cypher, etc., may have them neatly done according to direction. Also drafts or the likeness of vessels taken and painted in the most correct and masterly manner . . . . . Merchants, captains of ships and shop-keepers who purchase wholesale will have large and profitable allowances made to them.'

This is the only reference I have come across which states that any part of

Folly Lane was called Chelsea. As the site had quite recently been in use as an earthenware mug works, it is probably of Pennington's fancy and not particularly appropriate.

How long this pottery remained closed after John Pennington's death is not known, but it is possible that re-opening under the new Pennington set-up did not take place until 1787, when, as we have seen, Richard Gerrard acquired the lease. What is known of its later life will be found discussed under 'James Pennington'.

SETH PENNINGTON

Seth Pennington, youngest of the brothers, was born in 1744 and was therefore sixteen years younger than John. From the fact that his third child was called Lawrenson, he may have married a daughter of Thomas Lawrenson, the Liverpool engraver (d. 1769). There is a record of six children born between 1771 and 1786, four of whom were boys, but Lawrenson, who became a pot painter, was the only one to develop any connection with the pottery industry.

Nothing is known of his early years and the first mention he receives is on being made a Freeman in 1767. In 1771,[1] he was living in Crosshall Street, shortly afterwards moving to Charles Street, where his second child John was born.[2] At this date, he was probably a journeyman earthenware potter, but it cannot have been long before he turned his attention to making china, an event which it is reasonable to suppose had occured before he took over Christian's china works at No. 12 Shaw's Brow. There is no record of this important event, indeed, there is no document connecting Seth with this property until July 1785[3] when, described as a china works and dwelling house, it was assigned to 'Messrs Part and Pennington'. But this partnership is shown to have been carrying on business at this address in 1781[4] and must have been in existence at least as early as 1778, when, in that year, it is cited as party to the indentures of William Mercer.[5] Christian, it has been shown, left these works at some date between 1774 and 1777, probably in 1775, and, although there is no Directory assistance for 1777, it is likely that Seth may have taken over when Christian left.

This was not a favourable time for embarking on a new trade venture. It will be remembered that, in this year, began the war with the American colonists, an event which rapidly brought about a decline in trade which particularly affected the pottery industry. Further, at this date, the signs of decline in this industry had already been in evidence too long to attract fresh capital outlay unless success seemed reasonably certain. The facts are

[1]St. Nicholas Church.   [2]Ibid.   [3]Gatty, op. cit., page 16.
[4]Dir.   [5]Town records.

best explained by supposing that, from being a journeyman in Christian's employment, Seth became a salaried manager in 1775 before acquiring ownership of the works, which may not have taken place until two or three years later when John Part was taken into partnership.

Seth lived for some time at No. 46 Shaw's Brow, which he sold in 1784.[1] perhaps in anticipation of taking over the house which went with No. 12 and the potworks in the following year.[2] A little later, he may have been in some financial difficulty, for in 1788 he mortgaged the pottery for £500.[3] But everything points to the fact that, having got over the difficulties of the early years, this partnership prospered exceedingly, turning out a large quantity of pottery and porcelain of good quality and in great variety. Seth reputedly shared the family secret of the famous Pennington blue and it is not therefore surprising that so many examples of his work are predominantly blue-decorated. While it is likely that his reputation in this respect is based partly on the attribution to him of ware which could equally well have been made by either of his brothers,[4] there remains sufficient evidence to show what a first-rate potter he undoubtedly was. He alone seems to have been responsible for the vases and 'chimney ornaments' of the type featured on Plates 40 (e), 41 (b).[5]

In 1799, the partnership with John Part was dissolved and the pottery was advertised for sale after the longest run under unbroken management shown by any of the Liverpool potworks.[6] Manufacture, however, did not cease and Seth Pennington remained to carry on with a new partner, the style of the firm becoming Pennington and Edwards, with an address at No. 8 Shaw's Brow.[7] This change almost certainly indicated nothing more than re-numbering; and when dissolution finally came in 1805 or 1806,[8] there also came to an end fifty years of seemingly continuous endeavour in the manufacture of porcelain at these works! So ended also its manufacture in Liverpool[9] where, fittingly, at the same potworks almost exactly fifty years earlier, it had its beginnings.

[1] *W.L.A.*, 19th February 1784.
[2] Gatty, op. cit., page 16.
[3] Ibid, loc. cit.
[4] See under 'John Pennington'.
[5] John's advertisement contains no mention of vases and it will be remembered that vases of this type were given to Mayer by Pennington's daughter.
[6] Billinge's *Advertiser*, 12th August, 1799.
[7] Dir., 1803.
[8] Dir., 1806.
[9] The productions of the Herculaneum factory are excluded, because they are not indigenous, but represent Staffordshire and the work of Staffordshire potters. They lack the characteristics which own a Liverpool background.

The names of the following apprentices are recorded, namely William Mercer, Thomas Gerard, Jeremiah Swan, James Case and John Jones. William Mercer, who was born in 1764 and indentured in 1778, was made a Freeman in 1796. He subsequently migrated to Burslem, where he lived from 1806 to 1821 and was among that number of Liverpool Freemen who made a practice of returning to record their vote. The plate bearing his name (Plate 43 (c)) may have been made to celebrate his marriage in 1792. It was almost certainly made at Seth's factory and is therefore a guide to the type of ware of the period.

Both Jeremiah Swan and John Jones were entered in 1784. While Swan also went to Staffordshire later — he is known to have been in Stoke from 1806–16 — John Jones may perhaps be identified with a potter of that name who later worked at the Herculaneum factory.[1] Thomas Gerard was apprenticed in 1790 and subsequently went to Lane Delf; while James Case, who was entered in 1796, is said to have been working at Hanley Green in 1812 and may have been the father of Thomas Case who, in company with James Mort, was the lessee of the Herculaneum Pottery in 1833.

Seth Pennington must have owned — and probably at different dates, lived in — many houses on Shaw's Brow, according to Directory entries. In this connections, Nos. 31, 34, 36 and 46 all receive mention, but it seems possible that renumbering of the houses offers an explanation of these apparently frequent changes of residence. Mayer even tells us that his private residence was No. 79 'now Dick's Temperance Coffee House' and that he also had a town house in Button Street, then a fashionable neighbourhood. His name is found in the Poll Books in 1784, 1790, 1802, 1806, 1812, 1816, 1818, 1820 and 1821.

Seth went into retirement in the then fashionable suburb of Everton, where he apparently lived for many years. A glance at the Pennington pedigree will show that he had a son who was also called Seth, who was born in 1779 and consequently it is possible that some of the entries in both Poll Book and Directory may refer to him, although there is otherwise no proof of the existence of such a person during this time. If we accept the last appearance of the name in the Directory (in 1825) with its description 'gentleman, 5 Everton Terrace' as referring to potter Seth, he would be eighty-one years of age at the time.

Seth Pennington's was one of the last of the old pottery ovens — probably the last — to be demolished. There is a Herdman drawing of this oven made in 1830, which is illustrated in *Pictorial Relics of Ancient Liverpool*.[2] We are

---

[1]But hardly with a potter of that name whom the Directory for 1790 records as living at 15 Cook Street.

[2]Also described and illustrated by Mayer in the *History*. See Plate VI.

told that it stood on part of the site of the present Free Library and was still standing when Mayer presented his *History* to the Historical Society in 1855, at which time it was in the occupation of a firm of chemists and used for grinding emery. It was pulled down when the whole of the Shaw's Brow district, occupied by the potteries for so many years, was cleared for building the Museum, Public Library and Art Gallery which now adorn the site.

JOHN PART

There is no record of the date when John Part and Seth Pennington entered into partnership. That this took place before 1778 seems likely from the fact that William Mercer was apprenticed to the partners in that year; and as dissolution did not occur until 1799, the association must have lasted at least twenty-one years.

The first reference to John Part is in 1770. Wedgwood had evidently written to John Dunbibin, the Liverpool delft potter,[1] about the possibility of securing Part's services, for in June of that year, we have a letter from Dunbibin replying that he had read Wedgwood's letter to him 'and I imagine he'll agree with you, for his pay is but low here, but am informed he has sent you his proposals'. Whether, following this, he went to Etruria is not recorded. It seems probable that Part had been in Dunbibin's employment before the latter's bankruptcy in 1768, but Wedgwood's approach could be as easily accounted for by reason of a close acquaintanceship with Dunbibin, which undoubtedly existed.[2]

We find his name in the parish registers in 1780 and 1781 — in the latter year he was clerk to St. George's Church — and again in 1786 (St. Peter's) when he was living in Cumberland Street. Gore's Directory for 1790 and 1796 describes him as a china manufacturer, with an address at 12 Richmond Street. In 1802 he was living in Islington. He was a Freeman, for his name appears in the voter's lists in 1794 and in 1806, the latter date being the last reference to him. He was then living at Everton, presumably in retirement.

ROBERT PENNINGTON

Eldest son of James Pennington, was born in 1763. There is no record of him until 1784, when, described as an enameller of earthenware living in Soho, London, and 'late of Liverpool', he entered into an agreement with Wedgwood to decorate creamware at Wedgwood's London establishment in

---

[1]Dunbibin's advertisement in 1761 refers to delftware, gally tile and white stoneware (Patrick Hill pottery). At the date of his bankruptcy with John Lathom, his pottery was on Shaw's Brow.

[2]Dunbibin knew Wedgwood well enough to send his respects to Wedgwood's mother, brother and family when writing to him.

141

Greek Street, which was managed by Byerley.[1] His contract, which was probably typical of those prevailing at the time, was to work twelve hours a day, with one-and-a-half hours off for meals, at the current rates of journeyman pay. Its severity by our standards was reduced by a clause which permitted him to break it if he wished to return to Liverpool for 'family reasons'. The contract was for three years. Whether he completed his engagement is unknown.

The date of this would indicate that he went to London immediately his indentures were completed, as also 'late of Liverpool' would seem to imply and that the Greek Street job was his first as a journeyman. He is mentioned once again in the Liverpool Freeman's Committee Book in 1790, showing presumably that he had returned and he may reasonably be credited with some of the good decoration found on later Liverpool wares.

JOHN PENNINGTON JNR.

A younger son of James Pennington, of whom there is record neither of birth nor baptism. It is somewhat remarkable that, as in the case of his brother Robert, the first we hear of him is in connection with entering into an agreement with Wedgwood to work at his London establishment. This took place in July 1784, three months after Robert had been engaged; and from the fact that his father was a party to the agreement, we know that he was a minor at the time and therefore a younger son. Young John was to be taught 'the art and mystery of engraving in Aquatint for the purpose of printing on china'. The contract was for three years.[2]

It is very doubtful if he remained as many months, for we find him exhibiting in September of the same year as a student, at the exhibition held in Liverpool by the 'Society for Promoting the Arts'.[3] But short though his stay with Wedgwood must have been, it had been long enough to prove his talent. On 12th May 1787, Wedgwood wrote to Boardman, his Liverpool agent, 'John Pennington, son of James Pennington, painted for me for some time in London, but the place did'nt suit his health. — I hear he has lately been painting pictures in Liverpool and that it doesnt answer his expectation. Offer him work with me'. He went the following week, but there is no mention of his name among a list of painters in Wedgwood's *Commonplace* book in December of that year. The length of his stay on this occasion is, therefore, guesswork and it is likely that he again returned to Liverpool.

In 1792, he went to Worcester and took employment with the Worcester Porcelain Company, remaining in their service some fifty years and achieving

[1]17th April 1784. It is preserved among the Records at Barlaston.
[2]Process introduced into England from France by Charles Greville who communicated it to Paul Sandby about 1770. See 'Burdett' (Biographical section).
[3]'Portrait of a Boy and a Dog'. Catalogue No. 59.

considerable distinction as a porcelain decorator.[1] We do not know whether he went from Liverpool or from Wedgwood's employment, although the latter is generally believed to have taken place; and while his career at Worcester does not concern us here, it is of some interest to speculate whether any of the good decoration found on Liverpool china of the 1780–90 period may not be his work.

In his agreement with Wedgwood, there is no mention of Liverpool, as there is in the case of his brother Robert. His father was then (1784) still presumably living in Staffordshire, his family with him; and this would favour a Staffordshire apprenticeship for John and rule out the possibility that he could have decorated Liverpool wares during this time. But he seems to have been living in Liverpool between 1784 and 1787 and during some part of the period between the latter date and 1792. He may, therefore, reasonably be held responsible for some of the good decoration encountered which covers this period.

ZACHARIAH BARNES

Zachariah Barnes was born in 1742, a native of Warrington and brother of Thomas Barnes, a doctor of divinity. For many years he carried on business in Liverpool as a corn merchant, with no interest in pottery of any kind. In 1768 we find him trading as a general merchant and importing fifty firkins of butter from an address in Whitechapel.

The year previously he had married Esther Livesley, presumed to be the daughter of John Livesley, a potter who died in 1769[2] and we do not find him mentioned as a potter or as having any interest in a potworks until 1783, when the following announcement appeared: 'For sale by Barnes and Cotter at the Haymarket Pothouse, delftware consisting of bowls of all sizes, plates, dishes, tureens, wash-hand basons and bottles, etc., suitable for the American markets on very reasonable terms. Who likewise manufacture English China of fine quality, with variety of patterns at the lowest prices'.

The entry of Zachariah Barnes into the ranks of the Liverpool potters when forty years of age has a simple explanation. John Livesley, son of old John and presumably Barnes' brother-in-law, had interests in several businesses in Liverpool — as a brick and general merchant with his brother Samuel, as

---

[1]Binns (*Century of Potting in the City of Worcester*, 1865) states that he was the chief artist and heraldic painter. The Duke of Clarence service with figure of Hope as the central motif, is said to have been his first work there. Hobson (W.P. page 137) gives details of his Worcester career.

[2]An old Liverpool family of potters who at one time owned Chaffers' potworks (q.v.). From the *Manchester Advertiser* of 15th August 1758: Total destruction by fire of John Livesley's black-ware pothouse near the dog kennels, Liverpool.

a potter with Jonathan Wainwright at the Richmond Row 'Mug Works'; and as a potter in partnership with James Cotter at the Haymarket pottery. In 1779 financial disaster overtook him and he made himself bankrupt with Barnes one of the assignees. Notices concerning the realization of portions of his assets appeared in the public Press on 15th October 1779, on 17th December 1779 and again on 6th April 1780. On this last occasion the Haymarket Pothouse was up for sale, together with a windmill used for grinding colours situated in Folly Lane at the top of Shaw's Brow. The arrangements which were made on this occasion evidently gave Barnes a controlling interest. James Cotter, member of an old established family of Liverpool potters and a practical potter himself, remained responsible for the processes of manufacture.

There was nothing unusual in such an arrangement, in fact, it was so common that Gregson tells us that every merchant of note in Liverpool had some interest in a pothouse.[1] But whereas in these cases, custom favoured anonymity, Barnes allowed his name to be substituted for that of his bankrupt predecessor in the name of the firm and in so doing — he became a potter. Whether he ever succeeded in acquiring any proficiency in the potter's art and if so, to what extent, is uncertain. Any attempt to answer such a question must be answered in the light of the knowledge that during the remainder of the life of this old-established potworks, Barnes continued to carry on business independently as a merchant of some kind at various addresses in the town.[2] Two or three instances will suffice. In 1787 we find 'Barnes and Cotter, China Manufacturers, Haymarket' and 'Zachariah Barnes, flour merchant, Button Street'. In 1790, the Directory entry leaves out Cotter's name, which does not again appear and we read 'Z. Barnes, china manufactory, 23 Haymarket'; 'Z. Barnes, Merchant, 58 Whitechapel'; and a third entry which reads 'Z. Barnes, Corn and Flour warehouse, 2 Button Street'.

Whether with Cotter's disappearance from the scene, his place was taken by another potter of experience we do not know. There may be no significance in the change from 'China Manufacturers' in 1787 to 'China Manufactory' in 1790. It is certain, however, that Barnes continued to carry on his business as a merchant from other addresses in the town as late as 1811, many years after the closure of the china works which seems to have taken place about the year 1800. Many Directory entries bear witness to this. That Barnes was engaged in active business during all this time is shown by the fact that he owned a corn and flour warehouse which adjoined the potworks at the time they closed.

On this evidence, Barnes' business activities are probably best described

---

[1]Holt & Gregson MSS.   [2]Liverpool Directory.

as those of a broker and on one occasion at least he so referred to himself.[1] His reputation as a potter must therefore be largely posthumous and is surely one of the most remarkable anomalies among many in the history of Liverpool pottery. For the plain fact is that there is no evidence that he ever potted anything in his life or knew how to do so.

In this matter, Mayer, usually fairly reliable, is partly to blame in accepting without reserve some of the statements made by the descendants he interviewed,[2] although it will be seen that if we substitute the partnership for the name of Barnes, there is little in his narrative to find fault with. Reference has been made to the blue-printed porcelain plate with a characteristic border, which was given to Mayer by Barnes' youngest daughter, Mrs Aaron Wedgwood and vouched for by her as her father's manufacture. Long known to be an incorrect attribution, it would be strange if this plate alone could be held responsible for the great 'build up' which has taken place around this man's name. Yet it may indeed be so, for its border[3] is associated with a number of designs in common use during the decade 1770–80 and a little later and, by the links so provided, with a great many more. In this way, the recognition of a whole group of pieces which were thought to be Barnes' porcelain became an easy matter.

Nor can Gatty's contribution to the Barnes legend be overlooked, for he describes a personal interview with Mrs Lyon, of Claughton, a grand-daughter who 'remembered seeing the young men painting the blue designs on the tiles etc., at the Old Haymarket Pottery'.[4] The impossibility of this becomes apparent when we learn that the first of Barnes' daughters to marry was Ellen, who married John Smallshaw in 1797, just three years before the pottery closed. It is true this has no bearing on the credibility or otherwise of Barnes as a maker of porcelain, but it serves to throw into perspective the doubtful value of oral tradition. In the midst of so much romance it is refreshing to turn to a letter in my possession written in 1907 by one of the next generation, a great grand-daughter, Mrs Smallshaw-Jackson. It ends thus: 'I have never seen any of Zachariah Barnes pottery. There is none of it in our family. Please excuse mistakes'.

It has long been part of the Barnes legend that he made porcelain at first but gave it up to become a maker of delftware. The reason for such a statement is difficult to understand. In effect, it stamps him at once as no ordinary man and must have contributed materially to the position he came to occupy in the temple of fame. The only question which need concern us is whether porcelain was ever made by the firm of Barnes and Cotter, as their advertisement of

[1] *W.L.A.*, 27th September 1789. [2] Mayer op. cit., page 38.
[3] See Plate II, No. 17 and Plate 46 (b). Its best known association is probably with the 'prawn-tailed' exotic bird. [4] Gatty, op. cit., page 25.

1783 claims. We have no authenticated piece of porcelain in support of such a claim, but neither have we in the case of many other Liverpool potters whose *bona fides* as china makers is not in doubt. There is the negative evidence of Sadler's *Note Book*, which mentions the presence of a delft kiln at these potworks in 1784, but not of any other. Yet it seems unlikely that such a claim would be made and even more so that it *could* be made, were it untrue; and with that we must leave the matter.

Delftware was without doubt the chief production of this potworks. Mayer tell us — and there is no reason to doubt the accuracy of the statement — that quantities of delftware of Barnes' manufacture were sent to fairs at Chester, thence finding its way into North Wales.[1] In addition to numerous articles for ordinary domestic use, drug jars[2] and 'pots for char' were made.[3] The statement, often repeated, that Sadler obtained tiles from Barnes may clearly be dismissed as an impossibility, for Sadler had retired from business ten years before Barnes had anything to do with a potworks. There is no mention of Barnes in Sadler's *Note Book*, as is only to be expected; and while it is possible that Green may have bought tiles 'in the white' from this firm, I believe there is no record that he actually did so.[4]

Concerning the management of this pottery during the last ten years of its life, we can only guess. In the absence of any evidence that a new partnership was formed, one must assume that it was placed under the management of an experienced potter in Barnes' employ. 'Industrious money making man', he was described by his grand-daughter, and though he may have been, assuming that he had managed to pick up a smattering of the potter's art, it seems hardly likely that he would be able to include this among his many other pre-occupations.

He carried on business as a merchant at No. 21 Shaw's Brow within two years of his death, which took place at his country house in 1820 when he was 77 years of age. He is spoken of as pious, as well as money making, taking an active part in the socio-religious life of the day. We find him on the committee of the Day and Sunday Free School in Circus Street, to which he gave an annual subscription of two guineas; and when he died he was its benefactor to the extent of another ten.

His name does not appear on any voting list and he was not a Freeman;

[1]Op. cit., page 38.

[2]Two well authenticated specimens were included in the Mayer bequest to Liverpool Museum and suffered its fate.

[3]Small fish of the trout family found in a few deep water lakes in this country and in North Wales.

[4]Mayer's remarks on this are ambiguous (op. cit., page 38) and inaccurate in that he refers to 'Sadler and Green'.   [2]Gatty, op. cit., page 28.

146

nor have I been able to trace the names of any apprentices. The pottery stood at the corner of the old Haymarket and Dale Street, on a frontage of about thirty yards. Mayer, addressing the Historical Society in 1854,[1] referred to it as 'the last pottery of the old-established locality carried on in Liverpool, of which that part of the premises occupied as the showroom and warehouses are still standing'.

JOHN SADLER

John Sadler, 1720–89, was born at Aintree, the son of Adam Sadler (1682–1765) who fought in Marlborough's wars and subsequently settled on a farm at Aintree. According to Mayer, 'being of an active turn of mind, he shortly afterwards commenced business as a printer in the New Market, in Liverpool, where he printed a great number of books, amongst which was one called *The Muse's Delight,* containing a large collection of songs set to music . . . . His son, John Sadler, having learned the art of engraving and being out of his apprenticeship, bought from his father, Adam Sadler, a house in Harrington Street, nominally for the sum of 5/- and there he commenced business on his own account in 1748.' From this, Mayer's narrative continues, with more or less accuracy, until the date of the great tile-printing demonstration on 27th July 1756.

Some of these intervening years may well have been spent in formulating ideas and experimenting in the application of printing to the decoration of pottery. Mainly, Sadler seems to have been engaged in the ordinary work of a printer which, as he was a Roman Catholic, included devotional literature of the Roman Church. It was he who printed *The Muse's Delight*, published in 1754 and not Adam, his father, as Mayer tells us; and he also published the first Hospital Reports of the 'New Infirmary' opened in 1749. Mayer would also seem to be at fault in saying that Sadler learned the art of engraving, although, be it noted, he does not state that he worked as an engraver. If Sadler had this knowledge, his letters to Wedgwood give no indication of it and there can be no possible doubt that he never made use of it at any time.

One of his publishing activities during these early years got him into trouble. He published anonymously a pamphlet in September 1753 which was signed 'Freeman' and which purported to be an address to the Freemen of Liverpool, who considered that many of their ancient privileges were being usurped by the burgesses who constituted the Common Council. Sadler himself was not a Freeman, certain qualifications of birth and apprenticeship

---

[1]While Mayer is the authority for stating that, at the date in question, portions of the old potworks belonging to both Barnes and to Seth Pennington were still in existence, the evidence of the Liverpool Directory goes to show that to Seth Pennington belongs the honour of being the last of the old potters to close down. (See under Seth P.).

being necessary which he did not possess.[1] But it is more than possible that he had refused to pay certain fees which apparently were equally necessary, according to the civic status of the applicant (perhaps more so), before the privilege was granted. The issue was doubtless complicated. As the result of an enquiry which took place, it was ordered that 'the author, printer and publisher of a most infamous and scandalous paper, lately printed at Liverpool and highly reflecting on and most maliciously defaming the character, reputation and integrity of the Common Council of this borough and corporation . . . be prosecuted at law with effect and that this Order be made publick'. This was evidently too much for Sadler who owned up and 'on account of his open and candid confession and on his signing his submission to the Council which is now ordered to be published in the newspapers'[2], he was forgiven and escaped further punishment.

In the year following the tile experiment of 1756 and in the midst of the intense activities in which he must have found himself engaged as a result, it is surprising to find that he had time to start a weekly newspaper of his own. The first number of the *Liverpool Chronicle and Marine Gazetteer* appeared on Friday 6th May 1757[3]. It ran for exactly a year, the last issue being on 28th April 1758. It would seem that Sadler quickly found he had taken on too much, for, on 18th November he announced in the paper that Mr Owen would in future be responsible for printing it.[4]

One of our sources of information about Sadler is an ancient and battered note book which was once his property. This relic is available for inspection in the Records Office of the Liverpool Public Library. In its present state it measures some six by four-and-a-half inches and contains about sixty pages, many of which have suffered mutilation by re-binding and which are obviously no longer in their original order. The earliest date extant seems to be 1st January 1766 and the last a date in January 1788.

It is a remarkable document. In it Sadler has jotted down a miscellany of facts and ideas embracing a multitude of topics. Formulae for porcelain bodies, colours and glazes jostle with quack remedies and home brews for ailments of all kinds. On the same page with a formula for aquatint engraving we find Mr Willhead's infallible cure for a cough, followed a little further on by notes on Lawrence Harrison's yellow varnish for japanning on earthenware,

[1]Appendix VII.

[2]Evidently a reference to news-sheets which appeared at irregular intervals. There was no regular newspaper until *Williamson's Liverpool Advertiser*, 28th May 1756.

[3]Six numbers are missing. It contained the usual information about the arrival of ships from Ireland and Devon with potters' clay, notices about Societies and their doings, potters' announcements by Reid & Co., Chaffers, etc.

[4]Sadler announced that 'he will continue the Printing Business in all its branches except the News print'.

Ball's best white glaze and a memo on Hannah's wages. Practical potters who have made trial of these porcelain formulae say that they are useless and will make nothing recognizable as porcelain.[1] In days when the greatest secrecy in these matters was preserved, such disclosures are as remarkable as they appear to be unnecessary. A moment's reflection will show that there was no good reason why Sadler, a pottery printer, should possess this knowledge, nor possessing it, should find it necessary to run the risk of writing down something far less complicated than the cooking recipes which the average housewife carries from day to day in her head. Whether the remedies would be more likely to achieve their object it would be hard to say, although it is perhaps easier to understand why they should be recorded.

The 'note-book' is also a diary, recording social engagements with Sadler's comments thereon and in addition, it throws interesting side lights on trivial contemporary events. But its greatest value probably lies in the information it provides about Sadler's business affairs and, more importantly perhaps by inference, about Sadler, the man himself. From its pages we learn that he sold his printing presses at the end of 1765 to Messrs Everard and Gore for £257.[2] John Gore was the publisher of a newspaper (*The Liverpool Advertiser, or the Commercial Register*)[3] which had just appeared and he clearly wanted Sadler's plant in connection with it and with the publication of Liverpool's first Directory, shortly to appear in 1766. Sadler's father had died in October 1765 and this may have brought about some of the changes which now seem to be taking place, although apart from any change in his financial position which this may have resulted in, the pottery-printing side of Sadler's business must have become so profitable he could afford to give up Press-printing entirely.

The note book also tells us that about this time the partners were looking for a third partner, the sole reason being that John Sadler was 'not chusing to confine himself to business so much as heretofore'. In this they were not successful, almost certainly because the terms were not sufficiently attractive. The offer was a third share for £200, but included no participation in any profit until a year spent in instruction had elapsed.

A very full advertisement of the business and its scope appeared in the local Press on 1st May 1767 and again one month later.[4] These are the only two occasions on which the firm appears to have advertised. Possibly as a result of this publicity, Richard Abbey was taken on as an apprentice on 4th November 1767 on payment of £100.[5]

---

[1]See Appendix for extracts from correspondence on this matter.
[2]Holt & Gregson MSS., volume 16, give the name as Nevett and say that he was an 'overseer' in Sadler's office. It is clear enough as Everard in the note book.
[3]Became *Gore's Liverpool General Advertiser* after 1788.
[4]Appendix V.   [5]Toppin, Trans. E.P.C., 1929, page 44.

In May 1769, an event of profound importance occurred in Sadler's life. His mother, to whom he was deeply attached, died at the age of 87.[1] Eighteen months later, at the early age of fifty, he retired from business, leaving Green to carry on alone, but not before he had taken on another apprentice, Henry Tatlock, for a further indenture fee of £100. From a page of the note book on which are jotted down a collection of figures showing Sadler's assets, we learn that his half share of the warehouse goods was valued at £300, the copper plates (all Sadler's) at £250 and cash £200. Of great interest also is the statement of business transacted with Wedgwood which was called for in the winding up proceedings. Figures have already been given showing the size of the trade which developed so rapidly between these two men. The final account in September 1770 showed a yearly turnover on both sides of the account of over £4,600 at wholesale prices, a sum of money which, by standards of the day, shows the working of a very profitable business undertaking.

Sadler was a sociable man who remained a bachelor for the greater part of his life, looked after by his housekeeper, Hannah, who came to him in 1763 and remained with him many years at £4 per annum, later on raised to £5, paid quarterly. We catch glimpses of the names of many personages connected with Liverpool potting interests recorded in the note book — Christian, Edward Chaffers, Pennington, William Ball, Lawrence Harrison and many others — sometimes clearly in a business connection, but quite frequently forming part of the social round of Sadler's daily life. It is here that we so often have occasion to regret the mutilation, in some cases quite deliberate, which the entries have suffered. Who, for instance, were 'Pinto and Perkins', who occupied his bed on a certain night in April 1766 and why were they there. Perhaps the answer is to be found in the fact that his bill for beer from Mr Unsworth, presumably for one year, was £5 3s. 6d. — no very great sum until you read further on that two gallons of rum cost but seventeen shillings. This in turn may also provide the answer to the puzzle provided by the fact that so many entries, obviously of a social nature, end abruptly with the single letter 'd', followed by '—'. His health cannot have been good, if the number of jottings about cures for various complaints are any guide. He married late in life in 1777 at the age of 57, Elizabeth Parker, daughter of G. Parker, who kept a 'toy shop' in Castle Street, a young woman some thirty-five years younger than he was, by whom he had three children. The eldest, John Adam Sadler, born in 1778, entered the Royal Navy and died in 1816. A daughter, Elizabeth Mary, was born in 1782. This was the descendant visited by Mayer

[1]'Mr Sadler has been abroad a fortnight and came home post on Sunday to the burial of his Mother. She was a most deserving old Woman, and has left us in the greatest affliction for her loss' (Green to Wedgwood, 16th May, 1769).

in 1854 at the family farm at Aintree, from whom he obtained the documents concerning the tile printing experiment carried out by her father almost a hundred years earlier. The third child was a son, James, who was born in 1786 and died in 1794.

Some time after his retirement, Sadler moved to St. Pauls Square, at that time a newly-built fashionable residential area. He died in 1789 and was buried in Sefton churchyard in the same grave with other members of his family, his widow dying in 1842 at the age of 88 years. His daughter, Elizabeth Mary, the last surviving member of the family, died in 1857.

GUY GREEN

Little more is known of Guy Green than has appeared as the result of his association with Sadler, from which it would be correct to infer that Sadler's personality dominated their relationship throughout. He was born in 1729 and to Mayer we are indebted for the information that he was a poor boy who used to spend his spare pennies in buying ballads from Adam Sadler, who, seeing that he was a sharp lad, took him into his employment. In what capacity it is not stated and it seems likely that, employed as an errand boy at first, he proved himself so valuable that before long he enjoyed a confidential position in Sadler senior's publishing business. That he could ever be correctly described as a printer appears unlikely; and whether, as seems to be inferred in Mayer's account, he succeeded to Adam Sadler's business is equally open to doubt. If he did so, there are many gaps in the narrative and in our knowledge which are not easy to fill, for Adam did not die until 1765 by which time the partnership with John Sadler had been established many years.

If there is any mention of Green in Sadler's note book, it has escaped the writer's notice. Our knowledge of him is such as can be gleaned from reading his letters to Wedgwood, to whom he was always deferential and strictly correct. The tone of these is in marked contrast to Sadler's outspoken expressions of opinion couched in the language used in speaking to an equal. We get the impression that Green was rather a colourless personality, always feeling inferior and behaving generally in the manner of the poor relation. The only mention of his name in connection with any public service occurred when he became a member of the Committee of the Society for Promoting Art and Design in Liverpool (1783).

He was married and in 1765 a son John was born, subsequently apprenticed to his father, for we know that he worked in the business. Many of the later letters to Wedgwood (after 1785) are written by John, acting for his father and so signed. He died in 1795. On reaching the age of 70, Guy Green retired from active participation in the business (1799), which, however, was carried on for another four years until his death in 1803 at 74 years of age.

Changes in methods and management may have been taking place in these later years, for new premises were taken on Brownlow Hill, which receive the description of 'China manufactory' in the Directories of 1796 and 1800, evidently additional to the Harrington Street premises which were retained. It is doubtful to what extent one can rely on Directory entries as an accurate record and it is easy to see how they can mislead when historical veracity is at stake. 'Caution marks the guarded way' nowhere acquires greater significance than in such cases, for obviously no responsibility can be accepted by the publisher for the description of an entrant given by himself; and clearly any entry must always refer to a state of affairs existing in the year previous to publication. In these circumstances, we think there can be no question that the entry 'China manufactory' should not be regarded literally as the use to which these premises were put; and the same applies to the description of Green as a 'China manufacturer' at the old addresses in Harrington Street in the Directories for 1781 and 1790. The entries in the 1790 Directory seem to provide the reason for all this which was to show that the ware was printed at 15 Harrington Street, received its painted decoration (if any) at No. 39 and sold in the finished state at No. 13 Harrington Street, later at Brownlow Hill.

JEREMIAH EVANS

There is no record of the date of birth or death. Apparently he came from London and the first reference to him in Liverpool is in 1755 in connection with alterations to the plates of the *Chart of the Sea-coast from Chester to Formby*. This chart was first published in 1738 by Fearon and Eyes. The next re-engraving took place in 1767, when it was undertaken by Billinge and it is therefore possible that Evans was not living in Liverpool at that date.

He was attracted early by the prospect which pottery-print engraving offered at the time and must have been one of the first to try his hand at it in Liverpool, where he was already well established when he inserted an announcement in Sadler's newly-issued newspaper, the *Liverpool Chronicle*.[1] This read, 'J. Evans, engraver from London, at his house in Williamson's Fields, Liverpool, executes Copper plates, seals and other Engraving in the most elegant manner, and teaches Young Gentlemen, etc., to draw on moderate terms'. While it is perhaps significant that he should make this announcement in Sadler's paper at such a time, it seems hardly safe to assume that his energies were immediately diverted to pottery-print engraving. The Seven Years War had barely started and Frederick the Great, national hero though

[1] 3rd June 1757.

he was destined to become, did nothing of importance until his Rossbach victory in November of 1757.[1] I have said elsewhere that, in Liverpool as at Worcester, Frederick started the portrait gallery on pottery and porcelain which was to enjoy such popularity for so many years; but whereas Hancock's engraving, which is dated 1757 and was probably issued in December of that year, is a finished product of many years' experience, that of Evans, taken from the same portrait by Pesne, is not nearly as good. It probably represents his first attempt. The portrait of Frederick in Court dress has received mention already and it is a regrettable fact that these portraits constitute the only signed examples of Evans' work which remain. For reference, these may be tabled as follows: Frederick in armour, 1, a small bell-shaped mug (Plate 29 (a)); 2, a cylindrical mug with expanding base, an unsigned example of which is shown on Plate 27 (a), but of which, as in the case of the preceding, there is a signed example in the collection of Mr E. Allman; 3, cylindrical mug, formerly in the Dykes Collection.[2] The only signed portrait of Frederick in Court dress was the 'Gilbody' mug (Plate 35 (a)) destroyed in 1941 by enemy action.

If we had to judge Evans' work from these examples, we should form a wrong impression. Entwistle, however, observed that the figures of Fame and Justice which flank the Gilbody mug portrait were identical with the same two figures flanking a red printed 'Bucks' mug in the Merton Thoms collection, an observation which can be confirmed by the writer from a 'Bucks' mug in his possession (Plate 37 (c)); and close examination makes it probable that all these prints, of which there are a considerable number, are Evans' work. Entwistle tells us that there is a signed and dated (1758) 'Bucks' plate. But he goes much further than most of us would be prepared to follow when he claims that 'we are able to locate the whole of the large number of porcelain mugs with a Worcester-like body and printing to be the work of Sadler, with the plates engraved by Evans'. Perhaps 'the whole of a large number' is sufficiently indefinite to allay alarm and allow room for the work of Thomas Billinge who assuredly had left sufficient proof of his ability to warrant a good share of credit in this matter. It is no easier to agree with him when, a little further on, he states that 'the porcelain mugs on which these prints occur are of local manufacture.'

It seems likely that for a short time, Evans may have been in the whole-time employment of Sadler and worked in his office; and he may be 'the Engraver under our own eye' referred to by Sadler in a letter to Wedgwood

[1] England gave no support to Frederick II until 1757 although, on the Continent, the war had begun in the summer of 1756.
[2] This mug is referred to in letter Ent. MSS. 7/30, dated 7th October 1922. The mug is described as 5 inches high, $3\frac{1}{2}$ inches wide with loop handle having thumb rest.

dated August 1763. That he was a free lance for a considerable time is shown by the outside work, including work for Liverpool Corporation, which he was able to undertake. He was commissioned by the Council to engrave 'the Freeman's Oath', the document headed by the City Arms[1] which used to be called 'the Free Burghers Form'. This particular issue was signed by Evans and dated 1758. He also engraved a membership form for the Society of Bucks and certain maps, e.g., the chart of the Mersey (already mentioned) in 1755 and later, in 1785, when the plates again required alteration. From this it may be inferred that he was living in Liverpool at that date. Among book plates engraved by him may be mentioned those of James Clegg, the attorney, Sir Robert Cunliffe of Saighton Tower and the Liverpool Library.

THOMAS BILLINGE

Thomas Billinge was a well-known printer of newspapers in Liverpool from an early date. He was also an engraver of some repute. There is no record either of his birth or death.

He first comes into notice in the first issue of Gore's Directory in 1766, wherein he is described as an engraver living in Rainsford's Buildings. Allowing for a normal apprenticeship, it is not therefore unlikely that he was born in the early 1740's. In 1767, he again receives mention as an engraver and 'glass flowerer', with an address in Pool Lane. By 1772, he had become an engraver and 'druggist' and had now moved to Castle Street. Continuing to follow his career through the pages of the Directory, the next entry, in 1774, reveals him as a 'druggist, engraver and copper-plate printer' at the same address, from which it is not a big step to 'printer, stationer and engraver' which describes him in the Directory issue for 1790. The last entry which need concern us is in 1803 when, still in Castle Street, he appears as 'stationer, printer and publisher'. We are therefore safe in assuming that whatever else he may have done, he was an engraver for the greater part of his life.

Never far from a newspaper office, he acquired an interest in Williamson's *Liverpool Advertiser* between 1780 and 1790, but no change in title occurred until 1794, when the paper became known as '*Billinge's Liverpool Advertiser and Marine Intelligencer* and continued thus until 1829.

From the available evidence, as will appear later, it seems certain that Billinge worked for Sadler and Green during some part of the early years of the partnership, leaving in order to set up in business for himself about 1765, the year in which Sadler gave up press printing. There is a bell-shaped

[1]There is a well-known Liverpool creamware plate (photograph Ent. MSS. 5/20) now in the possession of Mr E. Allman, the sole decoration of which is formed by the City Arms in the centre, with Liver crest on the rim. It is probably Evans' work.

porcelain mug of Chaffers' make, with flat strap handle, which bears a black printed portrait of Pitt, signed at the bottom left corner, 'T. Billinge Sc'. (Victoria and Albert Museum, *C.940/1924*); and there used to be a large Chaffers jug in the Liverpool Museum carrying a black printed portrait of George III with a crown overhead, which was also signed in the same way, but the signature was centrally placed. Unfortunately this was lost by enemy action, but good photographs remain[1] from which its close resemblance to the portrait on the mug shown on Plate B.27 (*b*) can be seen. This is, therefore, also taken from a Billinge engraving. A third signed example occurs on a cream-ware jug, carrying a print of Europa and the motto 'Let wisdom unite us' on one side, the other side showing a print of 'The Masons' Arms' which is signed in the bottom right-hand corner 'Billinge Sc. Liverpool'.[2]

From one of Sadler's letters (16th September 1763) we learn that 'The Masons' Arms' engraving was executed in the autumn of 1763 and that the engraver was working in Sadler's office. Whether that fact justifies the conclusion that Billinge, at that date, was in Sadler's whole-time employment is doubtful. If so, it is surprising that his signature had been allowed to remain and that Sadler's does not appear on this particular example. That he did execute many engravings for pottery use is clear, for although these are the only signed examples I have been able to trace, several others can be iden-tified from these as his work, notably a Pitt portrait on a creamware mug (Schr. II.366), a portrait of John Wilkes on a creamware teapot (Schr. II.372), a portrait of Rodney on a cylindrical mug in the Willett Collection (Brighton) and a late portrait of George III on a creamware jug, bearing date 1798.[3]

A brief record of his other engraving activities may be useful. He re-engraved the plates (previously done by Evans) of a new survey of the coast from Chester Bay to Formby Point (Fearon and Eyes, 1767). A chart of the Harbour of Liverpool, 1771 and 1781, also bears his name. He was an engraver of bookplates and executed designs for P. Salusbury, R. Varick, P. V. Rensse-laer and John Ashton, the latter a Liverpool merchant and subscriber to the Infirmary Building Fund. The Arkle Collection contained a print of the North Front of the Infirmary engraved by Billinge.

[1] Recorded height 7 inches. Illustrated *Apollo*, July 1942, Lancaster. This may be the one previously in Hurst Collection.

[2] Formerly regarded as Leeds.

[3] Illustrated in *John Sadler, Liverpool Pottery Printer*, (E. Price). The distinctive feature on all these is the scrollwork, characteristic in line and frequently containing an inscription which flanks the portrait. Entwistle MSS. contains photographs of several such, e.g., two pottery bowls bearing portraits of Washington and Benjamin Franklin, (Entwistle MSS 5/4) and a red-printed portrait of Frederick of Prussia on a creamware mug, height $6\frac{3}{4}$ inches (same reference, a note saying that it was purchased from Mr Lloyd of 14 Blackfriars, Chester).

155

He married a daughter of Guy Green. There is a record of a son who was buried at St. Peter's Church in 1772, but none of any surviving children. John Waring and Thomas Wheatcroft were apprenticed to him.

RICHARD ABBEY

Richard Abbey was born at Aintree and died there in 1801. In 1767 he was apprenticed to Sadler & Green on payment of £100; and in 1773 he set up in business on his own account in Clieveland Square. We give the wording of the announcement in full, as it is of some importance.

'December 17th 1773. Richard Abbey, late apprentice to Messrs Sadler & Green, begs leave to inform his friends and the Public that he has opened his shop at No. 11 Clieveland Square where he manufactures and sells all sorts of Queen's Ware, printed in the neatest manner and in variety of colour. Orders for Exportation. Also Coats of Arms, Tiles, or any other particular device will be completed at the shortest notice.'

It will be noted that (a) he claims to be a manufacturer of creamware, (b) he mentions printing in polychrome and, (c), he does not call himself an engraver.

With regard to the first, this must be regarded loosely. There is no evidence that he did any such thing, but bought creamware from a nearby maker in Park Lane as his raw material, processed it and sold it as a fully-manufactured article. The second point is very interesting. There is no doubt he learned the art of polychrome printing at Sadler's, but where are the examples which might be expected to have survived? Pieces decorated in this way are uncommon by any standards and those we come across all seem to belong to earlier years. They match up with the porcelain of the printed portraits and some, as already mentioned, show affinity with the 'scratch-cross' group of wares. These must, therefore, be Sadler printed (Plate 33 (d)). Occasionally, however, one comes across pieces of later date in which a foundation of printing in colour may be suspected, but so concealed is it by over-painting that detection, even with the aid of a lens, is difficult. (Plate 31 (d) may be an example). It is to be remembered that re-inforcement of polychrome printing with enamel colours was always resorted to in the early days and the practice, no doubt, would persist. Abbey only seems to have remained in business here for some four years and his output of ware decorated in this way was probably quite small, accounting for the paucity of surviving examples.

The omission to refer to himself as an engraver may have no significance. It does not justify the assumption that the 'Coats of Arms' were the work of an employee, for there are several signed examples of his work of later date. It can be assumed that he learned the engraver's art in the school of engraving run in connection with Sadler's business and although no signed prints by him on porcelain have come to light, there can be little doubt that such did exist. Signed pottery prints include 'Hudibras and the bear'; 'the Death of Wolfe'; 'Hibernia', which may have commemorated the raising of the Irish Volunteers in 1779, all of which occur on jugs; 'Toby the Filpot' on a cream-ware mug and two signed tiles of actors which were in the Greg Collection. Entwistle states that 'many pieces are signed "R. Abbey, Sculpt., J. Robinson Burslem pinxt".', but according to Lancaster, the Hudibras jug is the only Robinson-signed piece known. Other printed jugs credibly attributed to Abbey are 'The careless lover', depicting a young man asleep and his girl companion fishing in his place, with the Masonic Arms on the reverse; 'the Man with a load of Mischief', depicting a man carrying an apparently intoxicated woman on his shoulders; landscapes with house and waterwheel, with, on the reverse, 'Gretna Green or the red-hot marriage' with couplet; 'Youth' with landscapes on reverse; and a very large six-gallon harvest jug, sixteen-and-a-half inches in height, showing various scenes.[1]

Richard Abbey was therefore principally an engraver to the pottery printing trade. He seems to have left Liverpool in 1777 from when, until 1794, the record is sketchy. During part of this time he was in Glasgow, where it is said he was teaching his art and later on in Paris with Mons. Potter, the first man to practice transfer printing on pottery in France. Abbey apparently assisted him at the 'Prince of Wales' pottery in the Rue de Crussol. Returning to this country in 1794, he founded, in conjunction with John Graham, the Herculaneum Pottery on the present site of the dock of the same name. But he sold out two years later to Messrs Worthington, Humble and Holland, and retired, dying as stated, in 1801.

HENRY BAKER

Came from Malahow near Dublin, the son of Henry Baker and was among Sadler's earliest competitors. The date of his birth in unknown, but as it is recorded that he died in 1823, he must have been a very young man when, on 28th May 1756, he put an announcement in the very first number of Williamson's *Liverpool Advertiser*, sixty-seven years previously. It said, 'Henry Baker, enameller, having finished several flower pieces in Basso-relievo in imitation of the Dublin patterns, yet not inferior to them, proposes to sell them at reasonable rates and to continue to carry on this branch of the business. Specimens of his performance may be seen at Mr Robert Williamson's, bookseller and printer near the Exchange'.

Baker, it will be observed, calls himself an 'enameller', as did Sadler but pottery print engraving was in its infancy in 1756 and one would think from

[1]Entwistle records that the Greg Collection (Manchester Art Gallery) contains two rare tiles with prints of Actors, signed by Abbey and that others were in the Hodgkin Collection.

the context that this meaning of the word cannot properly attach to it here. This 'Basso-relievo' work consisted in taking cardboard-pulp impressions from moulds of flowers, birds, etc, and hand-colouring them. We do not hear of Baker again until 1763 when he was still in Liverpool, at that date a pottery printer whose activities had reached Wedgwood's ears. Evidently in reply to an enquiry from Wedgwood, Sadler wrote on 11th October 1763, 'I know Baker does a deal of Pencilled teapots, etc., for the work here and I have seen some pieces of his printing, but I'm sure the Londoners would buy none of 'em at any price. As I told you before, He cannot hurt us.'

It would be unsafe to assume from this that Baker was engraving, but it is likely; and Sadler's wording does not rule it out. Clearly, if he was not engraving himself, somebody was doing it for him. But he was a versatile and gifted man as his subsequent career proves. Before long he left Liverpool and went to Hanley Green (Staffordshire) as we learn first of all from a notice issued by him about a runaway apprentice, Edward Gerrard, which appeared in the *Liverpool Advertiser* in 1770. He was still there seven years later, as can be seen from a letter from Wedgwood to Bentley (January 1777), 'I am told this morning that H. Palmer, of Hanley Green set out for London again yesterday and has taken his head enameller Baker, late of Liverpool, along with him'. It will be noted that in none of these references is the word 'engraver' used.

His name appears in the Liverpool Directory for 1781 with an address at 32 Mersey Street as 'Enameller, painter on glass'. This was the year in which he applied for a patent (Patent No. 1296 of 1781) in respect of 'A new method of ornamenting glass by a composition of Colours or materials imprinted or made upon the glass by means of copper or other plates and wooden cuts'. The patent was for fourteen years to Henry Baker, his Exors, etc. The description of Baker in the patent — presumably by himself — is still 'Enameller', which now begins to appear strange. One would have thought that an entirely new process such as printing in colours on glass must involve an engraving technique intrinsically part of the secret process which depends upon it and which would be known only to the patentee. It is interesting to note that at the Septcentenary celebrations and exhibition at Liverpool in 1907, two squares of glass were exhibited, measuring six by five inches and decorated with purple prints of classical subjects in which the grounds were coloured a deep ochre. The prints were not line engravings like Sadler's, but had a 'Bartolozzi' appearance. Both were signed 'H. Baker Liverpool'.

Baker's new process seems to have been allied to aquatint engraving of which it may have been a development suitable for colour printing on glass. This method of engraving, a French discovery, had been brought to this country about 1770 by Paul Sandby and was used here as early as 1772 (see under Burdett). The use of transfer printing on glass would appear to have been more general at this time than we are apt to suppose, witness the advertisement by John Mackay & Co. in the *Advertiser* on 5th December 1782: 'Printed and Stained Glass Manufactory, Liverpool, 28 November 1782. The Public are desired to take notice that this Manufactory of Printed and Stained Glass carried on in the name of John Mackay and Company is discontinued....'

THOMAS LAWRENSON

Little is known of this Liverpool engraver. He was living in Lombard Street in 1756 when the parish registers show the death of a son and the baptism of a daughter Annie. It was the following year that he announced the forthcoming publication of *The Secrets of Art and Nature*, which, as I have already stated, has never been traced and was probably never published. This remains one of the many unsolved mysteries of the early days of pottery printing. The full advertisement reads:[1]

'Proposal for printing by subscription in a pamphlet 8vo, containing about six sheets letter-press besides copper-plates, some of the most valuable Secrets of Art and Nature. (Chapter iv). The new and curious art of printing or rather re-printing from copper-plate, Prints upon porcelaine, enamel and earthenwares, as lately practiced at Chelsea, Birmingham, etc., With a true preparation of suitable Colours and necessary rules of baking. The contents of these chapters are not collected from any other authors or taken upon Hearsay as too frequently things of like nature are; being the result of innumerable experiments in every branch they tend to. By Thomas Lawrenson, Engraver. Private subscribers half a crown. Subscriptions from the Author in Lombard Street (Liverpool) and Williamson's, Liverpool'.

This reads, as no doubt was intended, like a communication from someone with first-hand knowledge — if the apparent inaccuracies can be explained. The most obvious conclusion to be drawn from it is Lawrenson's interest in ceramic printing and therefore his responsibility for some share of the print-decorated ware which was shortly to appear in such quantity. It is likely that he engraved for Sadler, quite possibly on a whole-time basis and that he was amongst those whose identity was swallowed up and digested by the great maw of this eighteenth-century centre of mass production.

The parish registers show the baptism of another daughter, Fanny, in 1761. His death was announced (*W.L.A.*) on 7th July 1769, when he was referred to as an engraver living in Dale Street. No examples of his work are known.

[1] *W.L.A.*, 11th February 1757, quoted by Gatty, op. cit., page 10.

LAWRENCE HARRISON

From an announcement in the *Liverpool Advertiser* in 1794, recording the date of Harrison's death at the age of 71, we infer that he was born in 1723. In 1749 he is described as a potter living in Princes Street, in which year a son, Thomas, was baptized in St. Nicholas' Church. Twenty years later, he appears in the Directory as a 'Potter and Victualler with an address in Williamson Street. This was a not uncommon combination of businesses during the latter part of the eighteenth century. His name occurs on the bottom of a large delftware bowl with the date 1748, decorated inside with 'Hogarth's Midnight Modern Conversation' and on the outside with a stag hunt, views of the Mersey and Bidston Hill in the distance (Greg Collection, Manchester). The obituary notice refers to him as 'an eminent delftware manufacturer'.

There are records of a HENRY HARRISON, potter, who was made a Freeman in 1760 and whose name occurs in the Poll Books for 1761, 1784 and 1790. He is described as a 'china enameller' in a lease of property on 'the north side of the road leading from the Haymarket'.

THE LIVERPOOL JOHNSONS

The sorting out of the Liverpool Johnsons of the second half of the eighteenth century presents considerable difficulty, for some twenty-five persons of this name could be classed as potters, pot-painters, printers, engravers or artists between the years 1755 and 1800. Of these, we may mention JOSEPH JOHNSON, whose name occurs in the Town Records as an engraver in 1773, in which year he was made a Freeman. He was the son of Joseph Johnson. In the Liverpool Directory for 1777, he appears as a 'tallow chandler and earthenware printer' with an address at 25 Edmond Street. This clearly shows that he is to be thought of otherwise than as an engraver whose work was confined to the Herculaneum period of late Liverpool wares, a view widely held because of the evidence of the known signed examples. He was still in Edmund Street in 1794.

It can hardly be a coincidence that this address was also that of Richard Walker, 'copper-plate engraver'; and there is a creamware jug decorated with a print depicting the 'Death of Wolfe' on which both their names occur.[1] There is also an 'Abbey' jug bearing this print (*q.v.*) and there is no doubt that all three men collaborated in pottery decoration to a considerable extent.

Johnson's name is found on many pottery prints and we may mention a mug of the 'Bidston Hill Signals' of date 1790, on which forty-three flags (uncoloured) are displayed.[2] There is another showing 'The Tars Farewell',

[1] Adapted from the painting by Benjamin West.
[2] Bidston Hill lighthouse and its signals, with numbered flags and a list of the various arms represented thereby. It was a frequent subject of pottery decoration at the time.

and another of Colonel Tarleton, a very popular local hero, member of an old established Liverpool family and the Member of Parliament for Liverpool from 1790 to 1812.[1] Tarleton on horseback is depicted on another Johnson-signed jug and yet another, also signed, bears a print of the 'Shipwrights Arms'.

No examples of Joseph Johnson's work on porcelain are known to us, possibly because they have not survived, but possibly also because of the anonymity forced by custom in many cases on an engraver who was not a free lance. I record the little that is known of him, because, at this date, printed porcelain had not completely lost the battle to a creamware which could be produced for about one-fourth the cost and examples may yet come to light.

Brief mention of a few of the other Johnsons must suffice. There is Nathaniel, variously met with under the description potter, printer, engraver and enameller on as many different occasions over a period covering rather more then twenty years. It seems certain that reference is not always to the same person and the temptation to draw conclusions on insufficient evidence must be resisted. The Nathaniel who was made a Freeman in 1767, served an apprenticeship with James Cotter & Co. and may be identified with a Directory entry of a potter of this name who was living at 11 Charles Street in 1781, interests us because of Cotter's later partnership with Zachariah Barnes.[2] Another Nathaniel was made a Freeman in 1761 and it may have been he who exhibited (as an engraver?) 'Two groups of Landscapes,' at the Liverpool Society of Arts (No. 39) in 1774. All this is very confusing and although this assortment may conceal an identity which would be of interest to us, in the absence of anything signed, the claim of Nathaniel Johnson to a place in the 'gallery' must be rejected.

One, Robert Johnson, makes a brief appearance as also serving apprenticeship with James Cotter & Co. in 1759 and was probably therefore a potter. Another Robert appears in the Directory for 1796 as a 'painter'.

The Thomas Johnsons' provide another puzzle and here at least three different identities seem to be involved in the records. One such person, described as an engraver, was living in Basnett Street from 1774 to 1780 as can be seen by his regular appearances at St. Peter's Church from this address, for the purpose of baptising children. Another of the same name and also an engraver, advertised (February 1776) that he had lately been with Mr Gore[3]

[1] From a portrait by Sir Joshua Reynolds, then P.R.A., contributed to an exhibition held in Liverpool in 1784. Colonel Tarleton of the Liverpool Blues, is standing with his left foot on a cannon.
[2] Gore's Directory for 1777 shows a Nathaniel Johnson as an 'enameller' living at 8 Charles St.
[3] Gore, the printer and publisher, who bought Sadler's press printing machinery in December 1765, published the first issue of the Directory the following year and *The Liverpool Advertiser or Commercial Register*.

and had a general printing office, including copper-plate printing, at Fenwick Alley, Castle Street. The mention of copper-plate printing introduces the possibility of pottery printing; yet there was a Thomas Johnson, printer, with an address at Crowder Court, Water Street, in 1777, and at 6 Castle Street in 1790, while a fourth person of the name is described as an engraver who was living in Bachelor Street. The last was probably a watch engraver whose identity should be merged with that of number one of the list and who was elected a Freeman in 1770; but which it was who was buried at St. Peter's Church in 1792 is still a matter for speculation.

In addition to all these there is mention of Isaac, another copper-plate engraver living in Bakehouse Court; Uriah, a potter, whose name is recorded under date 1761 and Josiah, described as a 'pot-painter', whose will was proved at Chester in 1786. Lastly, William, 'an earthenware printer of this town', whose marriage to a lady of Cowbridge, near Newcastle, in 1791, may perhaps indicate the trend of affairs in Liverpool's potting industry. Somewhere in this tangle may lie the clue to an obscure problem in Liverpool's potting history which still awaits solution.

PETER PEREZ BURDETT

Peter Perez Burdett seems to have been a native of Leicestershire and is described as an engraver and drawing master. Most of our knowledge of him is derived from Bemrose's biography of Joseph Wright of Derby. He lived in Derby for some time and became on friendly terms with Wright. In his earlier years a cartographer, with maps of Cheshire, Lancashire and Cheshire (1767) to his credit, he later came to Liverpool and was there elected President of the newly formed Society of Arts in 1769. He exhibited various drawings of architectural subjects about this time, including 'an etching in imitation of a wash drawing'. This may have been his earliest essay in the aquatint process of which later, with the assistance of Samuel Chubbard, he claimed to be the inventor. While there seems little doubt that this was a French invention introduced into this country by Paul Sandby from whom Burdett gained his knowledge of the subject, Burdett lost little time in approaching Guy Green — and through him, Josiah Wedgwood — with the object of inducing them to use his 'discovery' for the decoration of pottery.

In November 1771 he submitted, for use on borders, some engraved plates of shells and seaweed, for printing from which a patent inking device of his own invention was necessary.[1] Green's praise seems to have been rather lukewarm, limiting his remarks to Wedgwood to his opinion that it was pretty and might succeed better than flowers.[2] But Burdett's charges were high and

[1] Holt & Gregson MSS., volume 23, page 40.
[2] Appendix IV A (25).

his attitude haughty; and although Wedgwood, in his letter to Bentley,[1] would clearly like to have disputed the amount of the bill, discretion won the day.

He must have been a remarkable character, very self-assertive and well able to look after his own interests. Wedgwood was clearly afraid of him and handled him cautiously, although it is likely that his fears were aroused as much by the new printing process itself and the effect which he thought it might produce on the public as by the unfavourable opinion he had formed of its 'inventor'.[2] Wedgwood's business instinct comes out strongly here. The monochrome aquatint print would closely resemble the flat monochrome washes of a water colour drawing *before* colours were added. How close this resemblance might be can be inferred from Wedgwood's letter in which he clearly thinks that, used as a form of decoration applied to vases, the public would have difficulty in distinguishing between printed and painted examples[3] That he overcame his scruples concerning its use at some later date emerges from the fact that, in 1784, he was undertaking to instruct young John Pennington in this particular art.[4]

Jewitt tells us that Burdett worked for Wedgwood and introduced the process of transferring aquatints to pottery and porcelain.[5] Whether, having read Wedgwood's letters on the subject, it will be considered that the relationship between these two men is thus accurately described is a matter of opinion. We can perhaps agree that there may be some truth in the latter part of Jewitt's statement.[6]

Burdett's name probably lives in the memories of most as the author of that sublime act of effrontery, when in 1773 he wrote to H.M. King of Prussia seeking the Royal patronage in respect of his discovery, whereby he claimed he could 'make impressions transferable to porcelain which, when vitrified, resemble and equal the most delicate paintings'.[7] He seems to have left Liverpool shortly after this letter was written and nothing more is heard of him. It is reasonable to infer from the latter that, by 1773, porcelain had been so decorated. In that case, the close association of Liverpool with the developments of the process in this country renders it likely that the earliest examples of its use on porcelain would be found on Liverpool wares. None, however, are known to exist.

[1]Appendix VI c (9).
[2]Appendix VI c (8).   [3]Appendix VI c (7).
[4]*John Pennington jnr* (Biography).   [5]*Ceramic Art in Great Britain*, volume ii, page 50.
[6]In his petition to H.M. King of Prussia (see later), Burdett implies that porcelain had already been so decorated.
[7]The sole evidence of this is a letter which came into Joseph Mayer's possession, dated 21st February 1773, at Liverpool. A transcription of it is given in full in the 'History' among a collection of miscellaneous memoranda, without any comment or note saying whence it had been obtained. It may never have been dispatched. It is signed Peter *Pever* Burdett.

CHAPTER SEVEN

FACTORY WASTERS AND MARKS

ROM TIME TO TIME, excavation has taken place on and around the old Liverpool pottery sites for one reason or another, but always, as might be expected, because new constructional work made it necessary and never for archaeological reasons. As a result, the collection of shards was a matter of chance and the records show that it is mainly if not entirely due to the enthusiasm of the late Peter Entwistle that we owe the scanty knowledge we possess on this subject.

By far the greater number of fragments unearthed were of pottery, mainly delftware, with a sprinkling of lead-glazed and saltglazed wares; and except indirectly they do not concern us here. But porcelain fragments were unearthed at the Smithfield pottery site (marked C on plan) in December 1924 and early 1925. Entwistle tells us that this work was under observation by him throughout and his description of what he saw forms a valuable record.[1] This pottery, at first worked by John Dunbavan & Co. (Dunbibin) and later by Thomas Deare, was at the bottom of Patrick's Hill, at the east corner of Smithfield Street and Tithebarn Street. At the date in question, Messrs Burrows, the occupiers of the site, began excavating for an extension of their works southwards. At a depth of about eleven feet was a layer of greyish-green clay, 'presumably Irish'. Fragments of saggers, triangular struts, and parts of bowls, plates and tiles, both finished and unfinished, were laid bare. In a layer higher up, fragments of blue-painted porcelain cups (Plate 12 (h)) and of 'palm tree' type teapots were uncovered (Plate 20 (e, f).

Now there is no record that chinaware was ever made at this pottery and the evidence that the fragments unearthed at this time could be regarded as factory wasters is not stated. But writing not long afterwards, Mr Bernard Rackham had evidently satisfied himself on this point regarding the cups, but not, apparently, in the case of the teapot fragments, from which it may be inferred that the criteria in the two cases differed. Both types, however, are now firmly established as Liverpool wares on many other grounds. Strong support for this is provided by the fact that, although these pieces exhibit

[1]Entwistle MSS., 8/1.

no obvious relationship, resemblances can be shown to exist by a chain of argument which not only links them together but can be made to embrace a large cross-section of the wares of the middle period.

The only other finds of porcelain shards which have been recorded relate to some tin-glazed fragments found by Entwistle on the Trueman Street site in February 1916. The locality corresponded with the western boundary of Alderman Shaw's pottery (marked A on plan) and yielded quantities of shards of every kind of earthenware.[1] Here again there is no record that Shaw ever made porcelain, although he certainly made delftware; nor does Entwistle state the circumstances which would entitle these particular fragments to be classed as factory wasters. A contemporary photograph which is reproduced in this book seems to show that they are fully decorated. But there is nothing improbable in supposing that a maker of delftware at this time tried his hand at making porcelain, which he would naturally glaze with tin. This is, however, of less importance than the undoubted fact that the finding of shards of this type on a Liverpool pottery site confirms, if confirmation were needed, that examples of this uncommon type of porcelain may claim a Liverpool origin.

MARKS

There is no Liverpool factory mark and, if we except pieces of the 'scratch-cross' class and certain others of presumed Podmore origin which may bear 'painters' marks', very little Liverpool porcelain is marked in any way (Plate 50). The Worcester open crescent was occasionally copied (Plate 48 (c)), and various forms of cross occur – in red (Plate 42 (c)), in slate-blue with a numeral (Plates 15 (b), 50 (m)) and sometimes incised (Plate 13 (c)). A mark in blue, like a large capital C, is found on the bowl seen on Plate 23 (m), while the often discussed letters H P in blue underglaze occur on a bowl which is itself painted in colours only (Plate 50 (g)). The mock oriental marks which are not infrequently seen on pieces blue-painted with the 'jumping boy' subject (Plate 50 (c)) and very occasionally on small vases, have received notice.

ANALYSIS

We have, at present, no means of testing porcelain for the presence of soap-rock except complete analysis. This is a mutilating process because it requires the removal of an appreciable portion of the specimen if any degree of accuracy is to be attained. Analysis of the mug shown on Plate 9 (c) was undertaken for me by Dr Reginald Milton, who reported as follows: Silica

[1]Thomas Shaw, bailiff of Liverpool 1738, Mayor 1747, potter, retired in 1774 on selling his works to John Chorley and died in 1779.

165

50·2; Alumina 7·8; Phosphate 13·2; Magnesia 0·5; Potash 1·2; Soda 1·2; Lime 25·9. This shows about thirty-five per cent bone-ash, but no soaprock.

'Spot-testing' for the presence of bone-ash or lead may yield valuable information, particularly in the case of the former substance. The results of my use of this method for detecting bone-ash, when known, are given with the description of each piece here illustrated (P, phosphatic; NP, non-phosphatic). The appearance of an appreciable yellow precipitate after three or four minutes was regarded as a positive result.

'Spot-testing' for lead proved less satisfactory in my hands, the test being seemingly too delicate for practical use, however carefully one attempted to remove all traces of glaze. But analysis has shown that some soft-paste Bristol and early Worcester wares may contain this metal in appreciable quantity[1] and its presence has been reported in wares of the 'scratch-cross' group to the extent of about four per cent. Many of the latter are heavy in the hand (pages 47, 48) and the possibility that these more heavily potted pieces, both 'scratch-cross' and others of seemingly early type, might have a different composition (? more lead) which could be correlated with a higher specific gravity was considered and investigated.

With this in view, the specific gravity of about eighty pieces, covering a wide assortment, was estimated. The variation noted, however, was small in the great majority of cases, ranging between 2·41 and 2·49. No correlation was found to exist, indeed, in some few instances, the more heavily potted piece had a lower density.

[1]*Analysed specimens of English Porcelain*, 1922, No. 24 (Herbert Eccles and Bernard Rackham).

NOTES ON THE PLATES

The result of examination by transmitted light is given in each case, when known, in order to make the information as complete as possible. Its possible value in helping to make attribution will be read in the light of the remarks on translucency on pages 28, 29.

p—*phosphatic.*   NP—*non-phosphatic.*

Plate 1

(*a*) Page 118. The 'Thomas Spencer' jug, n.d. According to Mayer, Thomas Spencer worked a pottery at the bottom of Richmond Row, whence he removed to Prescot. Translucency, green. Chaffers. 1756–65.

By permission of the City Museum, Stoke-on-Trent

(*b*) Similar jug, painted in colours, 'Cocks at main'. Height 8½ inches. Translucency, green. Chaffers. 1756–65.

By courtesy of E. Allman, Esq.

(*c*) Similar jug, blue painted. Page 118. Chaffers & Co. are the only Liverpool china makers known with certainty to have been in production in 1762. Translucency, green, 1756–65.

Bootle Museum, by courtesy of the museum authorities and the executors of A. Collington Bishop, decd.

Plate 2

(*a*) Page 119. The porcelain 'Plumper mug' of the 1761 Parliamentary Election Very green glaze with flat unglazed base and plain loop handle. Translucency, green. Height 3½ inches. Diameter at top 2⅞ inches. 1761.

By courtesy of E. Allman, Esq.

(*b*) Cylindrical mug, with plain loop handle, flat unglazed base chamfered at the edge. Painted with coat of arms and motto 'In this is my hope'. Translucency, green, showing small flaws in paste, but no glazing defects. Height 4½ inches. A similar mug is in the Victoria and Albert Museum. Chaffers. *circa* 1760. NP.

(*c*) Jug of baluster shape, painted in colours with flower sprays and a coat of arms. Flat unglazed base, loop handle, back-turned at lower end with impress of potter's thumb. Translucency, green. Height 8 inches. Chaffers. 1756–65.

By courtesy of E. Allman, Esq.

(*d*) Jug, similar to preceding, painted in colours with the subject known as the 'beckoning Chinaman'. Translucency, green. Height 8½ inches. 1756–65. NP.

Plate 3

(*a*) Cup with ribbed moulding and scroll handle. Blue painted border of the type seen on Plate 12 (*h*). Translucency, yellow-green. No glaze shrinkage. Height 2⅛ inches. 1756–65. NP.

(*b*) Coffee cup, lobed and chevron-moulded, with blue painted border. Translucency, yellow-green. Many small flaws in paste and glazing defects on base. Height 2⅝ inches. Painter's mark in blue. 1756–65.

(*c*) Cup with bulbous body, everted rim and peaked scroll handle, painted in blue with

167

flowering shrubs and fence. Of pronounced greyish-blue appearance, it has a pure blue translucency. The base shows peppering and no glaze shrinkage. Height $2\frac{5}{8}$ inches. *circa* 1760. N P.
(*d*) Coffee cup, lobed and chevron-moulded with blue painted border. Translucency, yellowish-green. Height $2\frac{1}{4}$ inches. Painter's mark in blue under handle. 1756–65. N P.
(*e*) Tea bowl and saucer, rib-moulded with blue painted border. Translucency, yellowish-
green, with many flaws in paste. The saucer shows marked peppering. No shrinkage. Saucer
diameter $4\frac{3}{4}$ inches. Painter's mark in blue. Cup height $1\frac{3}{4}$ inches, painter's mark in blue
resembling letter C. N P.

All the foregoing may represent Podmore's early work at Liverpool. Chevron-moulded cups
of this type (type (*b*)) are sometimes found with printed decoration (birds), a fact which may
indicate a date considerably later than that usually allotted to them.

(*f*) Tea bowl and saucer, showing eversion with a footring which is not undercut. Blue
painted with two figures on a river bank within a Liverpool border (No. 7) copied from the
oriental. Translucency, green. No glaze shrinkage. Saucer diameter $4\frac{5}{8}$ inches. Cup height
$1\frac{3}{4}$ inches. *circa* 1760.
(*g*) Plate of Chien Lung shape, blue painted in delft style. Translucency green, poor. Diameter, 9 inches. Possibly Chaffers (page 34). *circa* 1760. N P.
(*h*) Cup with bulbous body and everted rim. Peaked scroll handle. Blue painted in conven-
tionally Chinese manner. Translucency, green, good, with a few flaws. No glaze shrinkage.
Fire crack in handle. Base peppered. General appearance bluish-green. Height $2\frac{3}{8}$ inches.
Painter's mark in blue. *circa* 1760.
(*i*) Cylindrical mug, slightly waisted, with recessed base, blue painted in 'Chinese' manner
with well-known early design. Loop handle almost U-shaped (page 30) with very weak groove.
Translucency, green, good. Glaze shrinkage present. Height $2\frac{3}{8}$ inches. Painter's mark in blue.
Podmore. *circa* 1760.
(*j*) Hexagonal cup, the panels blue painted with conventional florets beneath an interrupted
trellis border. Translucency, yellowish-green. A few flaws are present in the paste. Base shows
pin-pitting and peppering. Appearance very bluish-green. Height $2\frac{1}{2}$ inches. 1756–65.
(*k*) Cylindrical mug with plain loop handle and flat unglazed base, blue painted with trees
and foliage. Translucency, yellowish-green and general appearance very bluish-green. Peppering slight. Height $2\frac{1}{2}$ inches. These 'coffee cans' are generally attributed to Reid & Co. Those
made by Chaffers are heavier, greyer looking, less translucent and have a typical handle
attachment. Height $2\frac{1}{2}$ inches. 1756–60. N P.

Plate 4

(*a*) Coffee pot with plain curving spout and strap handle, the base recessed from a short
bevel. Blue painted with English-looking trees. Translucency, green, poor. Height $8\frac{1}{4}$ inches.
Chaffers. 1756–65. N P.
(*b*) Coffee pot similar to preceding, painted in colours with English flowers. Translucency,
green, poor. Very green glaze. Height $8\frac{3}{4}$ inches. Chaffers. 1756–65. N P.
(*c*, *d*) Cup and saucer similarly decorated in colours and with similar green glaze. Translucency, green with flaws in paste (cup) and considerable pin-pitting present. Saucer diameter
$4\frac{1}{2}$ inches. Cup height $1\frac{3}{4}$ inches. 1756–65. Slightly phosphatic.
(*e*) Coffee can with plain strap handle and flat unglazed base, similarly painted. The paste
shows wreathing, but no flaws. Translucency, yellowish-green. Height $2\frac{3}{8}$ inches. 1756–65.

(*f*) Bowl painted in colours with a spray of flowers by a different hand. The glaze has but a slightly green cast. Translucency, yellowish-green, with no flaws. Very undercut footring with no glaze shrinkage. Diameter 6¾ inches. 1760–5.

The attribution of ware of this type to Chaffers is traditional.

Plate 5

(*a*) Saucer, blue painted in pseudo-Chinese manner. Everted rim. Small footring, not undercut. No glaze shrinkage. Translucency very good, green. Diameter 5⅛ inches. Painters mark in blue. (see Plate 3 (*e*)). Podmore. *circa* 1760.

(*b*) Coffee cup and saucer, blue painted in 'Chinese' manner and having a very green glaze. Translucency, yellowish-green, poor, with no flaws. Glaze shrinkage. Saucer diameter 5⅛ inches. Cup height 2½ inches. ?Chaffers. *circa* 1760. N P.

(*c*) Coffee can with plain loop handle and flat unglazed base, painted with trees and foliage in red and blue, with sparse gilding. Translucency, green, poor. No glazing defects. Height 2⅜ inches. *circa* 1760.

(*d*) Coffee can, blue painted with unglazed base and chamfered edge, the plain round loop handle attached in the manner shown on Plate 8 (*c*). Glaze very grey. Translucency, almost pure blue, good. Height 2¼ inches. Chaffers. *circa* 1760.

(*e*) Sauce boat, moulded and blue painted with double C-scrolled handle, in silver-shape. Translucency, green. Slightly recessed base, with peppering but no shrinkage of glaze. Length 7¼ inches. *circa* 1760. P.

(*f*) Mug, bell-shaped with scroll handle, blue painted in 'Chinese' manner. Translucency, yellow-green, good. Some peppering of base but no glaze shrinkage. Height 5 inches. An unusual shape, probably Chaffers. 1760–5. N P.

Plate 6

(*a*) Coffee cup, with plain flat loop handle and Liverpool type of footring (page 36), blue painted in 'Chinese' taste. Translucency, yellow-green, fair. Slight wreathing. Height 2⅜ inches. *circa* 1760. P.

(*b*) Coffee cup, similar to preceding, painted with the 'stag hunt'. Height 2⅜ inches. See Plate 16 (*b*) for teapot and Plate 50 (*a*) for base. *circa* 1760. N P.

(*c*) Teapot and cover, with fluted bulbous body, ribbed handle and a curved spout seated on a moulded decagonal escutcheon (better seen on Plate 10 (*b*)). The ground colour is pink, with gruyère cheese-like holes in it and the enamel colours generally are of great clearness and brilliance. Translucency, yellow-green, good, with no flaws. No glaze shrinkage, but much peppering present everywhere. Height 6⅛ inches.   *circa* 1760.

(*d*) Coffee cup, in shape similar to (*a*) and (*b*) above, painted in brilliant enamel colours. Translucency, yellow-green. Height 2⅜ inches. *circa* 1760.

(*e*) Coffee cup, vertically fluted, with scroll handle and cusped base-ring, painted with floral sprays in Japanese manner beneath a red-brown border of scrolls. Translucency, green without flaws. Slight pin-pitting. Height 2 inches. The type is customarily attributed to early Worcester. It is borderline and perhaps 'Podmore' might be a better nomenclature. Compare with (*h*) below, with Plate 31 (*j*), and with others on Plate 3. 1756–65.

(*f*) Cup with bulbous body, everted rim and peaked scroll handle, painted in colours with large root ornament, peony-type flower, a quacking duck and a white (enamelled) flower.

Within, a linear red and gold border, interrupted by fleur-de-lys. Translucency, green, good, with one or two flaws. Some peppering inside, with much pin-pitting on base. No glaze shrinkage. Height 2⅜ inches. A Liverpool attribution rests mainly on 1, the palette, and 2, the 'hand', which is well known on Liverpool wares. *circa* 1760.

(*g*) Bowl, of flat-sided delftware shape, painted with a battle between dragons amid flowering shrubs, in the oriental manner. Translucency, green, very good. Glaze bluish, no shrinkage, no defect. Grey-blue appearance. Undercut footring of 'un-Worcester' look. Diameter 7 inches. Podmore. 1756–65.

(*h*) Coffee cup, octagonal, with everted rim, weak footring and scrolled handle, the panels painted in colours in oriental manner. Similar figure painting is found on 'scratch-cross' wares. Translucency, greenish and very poor. A grey looking porcelain. Height 2¼ inches. Mark: an arrow and annulet in black. Podmore. 1756–65.

(*i*) Coffee can with flat unglazed base and shallow-grooved loop handle, showing marked wreathing and painted with 'Chinese' figures in bright enamel colours. Translucency, yellow-green, with many flaws. No glazing defects. Height 2⅝ inches. *circa* 1760. N P.

(*j*) Teapot and cover, globular shape with Liverpool footring (page 36). Greyish colour. Painted with Chinese interior scenes almost entirely in sepia and gold, the gilding being of good matt quality resembling that of Sèvres or Worcester. Translucency, yellow-green, with no flaws. Glaze shrinkage is present and some peppering is noticeable, chiefly on the handle. Height 5½ inches. *circa* 1760. N P.

(*k*) Cream jug with grooved loop handle, pinched lip and grooved foot, painted in colours. Translucency, green. 1760–5.

By courtesy of H. R. M. King, Esq.

Plate 7

(*a*) Coffee cup and saucer, the cup with grooved loop handle, both showing eversion and painted in red and blue with traces of gilding. Translucency, pale green and good without flaws. No glaze shrinkage, slight peppering. Saucer diameter 4½ inches. Cup height 2½ inches. Podmore. 1756–65.

(*b, c*) Tea bowl and saucer of octagonal shape and grey appearance. Small footrings. Painted in oriental manner in enamel colours. Translucency, green, very poor. No shrinkage and no glazing defects. Saucer diameter 4¼ inches. Cup height 1¾ inches. Podmore. 1756–65.

(*d*) Coffee can, with weakly grooved loop handle and narrow glazed footring enclosing a depressed and glazed base. No glaze shrinkage, but much pin-pitting and blackening all over base. Painted in oriental manner in bright colours. Oriental border in use at Liverpool (No. 7 and see Plate 3 (*f*)). Translucency, green. Height 2¼ inches. 1756–65.

(*e*) Bowl with undercut footring, painted in colours with Japanese goldfish and seaweed. Translucency, pale green, very good. No shrinkage. Diameter 4¾ inches. *circa* 1760.

(*f*) Teapot (no cover) of globular shape, painted in blue in oriental manner. The footring slopes inwardly in Liverpool manner, there is no glaze shrinkage and glazing defects (cloudiness and discolouration) on the base are present. Translucency, green, good. The design is well known (Plate 3 (*c*) is a version) and is seen on a cider mug in the Victoria and Albert Museum, C/807/1924 (Liverpool case). Podmore. 1756–65.

By courtesy of National Museum of Wales

(*g*) Saucer with crenated rim, blue painted with two fishermen, rocks and willow tree. Small undercut footring. Bluish glaze showing no shrinkage. Translucency, yellowish-green, good, with no flaws. Diameter 4¾ inches. *circa* 1760. P.

Plate 8

(*a*) Bowl of grey appearance, painted in 'Chinese' manner in enamel colours (see Plate 26 (*d*)). Translucency, yellowish-green, very poor. No undercutting and no glaze shrinkage. Diameter 4⅜ inches. Chaffers. 1756–65.

(*b*) Bell-shaped mug, with scroll handle and Scotia-moulded foot, of grey appearance, painted with a burlesque Chinoiserie in enamel colours. Glaze on base is thin in places. No shrinkage. Translucency, yellowish, poor. Height 3½ inches. Chaffers. 1756–65.

(*c*) Coffee can with flat unglazed base and round loop handle, painted in smudgy-blue under-glaze. Grey appearance. Translucency, yellowish, poor. Height 2⅝ inches. Chaffers. 1756–65.

(*d*) Mug of bell shape, with scroll handle and Scotia-moulded foot, blue-painted with the same design as (*c*) to which further foliage in red with sparse gilding has been added. Translucency very poor, almost opaque. Pin-pitting and peppering on base. Height 5 inches. Chaffers. This and the preceding pieces are among the greyest of Liverpool porcelains. 1756–65. P.

(*e*) Bell-shaped mug, with scroll handle and Scotia-moulded foot, painted with a 'Chinese' figure in a garden setting in colours. Translucency, yellowish-straw and better than preceding mugs of this type, to which it clearly belongs. No glazing defects. Height 4⅞ inches. Chaffers. 1756–65. See page 62.

(*f*) Bell-shaped mug, with plain loop handle having back-turned lower end showing impress of potter's thumb and Scotia-moulded foot, painted in underglaze-blue and red with willow trees, flowering shrubs and insects. Translucency, green, with no flaws. No glaze shrinkage. Height 6⅛ inches. Probably Chaffers. *circa* 1760–5.

(*g*) Teapot and cover with glazed flange. Globular shape, painted in 'Chinese' manner in famille verte colours. Translucency, green, fair. The base shows glaze shrinkage, with some pin-pitting. Seven holes. Height 5¼ inches. *circa* 1760. N P.

(*h*) Cup, with plain loop handle having back-turned lower end, painted in colours with a figure in Chinese dress, standing over a fire upon which is a vessel. The cup of the Mayer bequest. A documentary piece, for reasons given in the text. Chaffers. 1756–65. (Page 62).

By permission of the Libraries, Museums and Arts Committee, Corporation of Liverpool

Plate 9

(*a*) Mug, bell or cider-shaped, with ribbed loop handle, painted in colours with 'mei jen' figures in panels separated by a broad band of trellis. Translucency, green, good with a few flaws. No glaze shrinkage. Peppering present (seen in photograph). Footring has ground edge. Height 6 inches. *circa* 1760.

(*b*) Cylindrical mug with ribbed loop handle and recessed base, painted in colours with foliage, etc, in a style not recognizable as Worcester and in a non-Worcester pallette. Trans-lucency, green, good, showing many flaws. Footring narrow, glazed all over, with no shrinkage. Heavily peppered on base and (less so) within. Base shown on Plate 50 (*c*). Height 4½ inches. 1760–5.

(*c*) Bell-shaped mug with scroll handle and Scotia-moulded foot, painted in enamel colours with the 'lady and parrot'. Very grey appearance. Rim edged with chocolate line (unusual on Liverpool). Translucency, greenish-yellow, fair, showing a few flaws. No shrinkage. Height 4¾ inches. Chaffers. The type piece of this class. 1756–65.

(*d*) Bell-shaped mug, of grey appearance, with scroll handle and Scotia mould foot, painted with a burlesque Chinoiserie in enamel colours. Translucency, yellow-green, poor. No flaws. Height 4⅞ inches. Chaffers. 1756–65.

Plate 10

(*a*) Jug of baluster shape, with scroll handle and lip moulded with foliate scrolls, painted with flower sprays in natural colours. The base is flat and unglazed, except for patches due to kiln volatilization. Translucency, green, good. No glazing defects. Height $8\frac{3}{8}$ inches. This might be called the 'Liverpool' handle. 1765–75.

(*b*) Teapot and cover. Bulbous shape with fluted sides, ribbed handle and curving octagonally moulded spout seated on a raised decagonal escutcheon, painted in enamel colours in a salt-glaze manner. On one side, the subject known as the 'beckoning Chinaman' with a spray of flowers; on the other, a 'Chinese' lady in a garden setting, talking to a boy with outstretched arms. Translucency, green, good, with some flaws. Small footring with no glaze shrinkage. Peppering on base. Six holes. Flattened cover, also fluted, with button knop and the under side of the flange glazed. For shape, see Plate 60 (*c*). *circa* 1760. Base shown on Plate 50 (*d*).

(*c*) Bowl, painted in enamel colours with a Chinoiserie of two Chinamen sawing branches off a tree; inside, near the rim, a brick red line. The ground treatment, in washes of purple-brown and bluish-green, resembles closely that seen on some examples of the 'red cow' print. Translucency, bluish-green, fair. Footring undercut, with some glaze shrinkage. No glazing defect. Diameter $4\frac{3}{4}$ inches. Exhibited English Ceramic Circle, 1948, Catalogue No. 495. 1760–5.

(*d*) Bowl, painted with the Chinese river scene, which might conveniently be called the 'ramp' pattern, in underglaze-blue and red. Translucency, yellowish-green, poor. No shrinkage. Diameter $6\frac{1}{2}$ inches. 1760–5.

(*e*) Coffee cup and saucer, painted with a spray of English flowers and several florets in natural colours. 'Beans' border in red. Translucency, green and good. The cup has a grooved loop handle and is square shaped, with glaze shrinkage and slight peppering. Height $2\frac{1}{2}$ inches. The saucer shows no shrinkage. Diameter 5 inches. Probably Chaffers, but of later date than the cup and saucer on Plate 4 (*c, d*), with similar decoration. *circa* 1765. N P.

Plate 11

(*a*) Jug, of baluster shape, with mask lip, scroll handle and flat unglazed base, blue-painted, with the well-known 'peony and dots' design. The border is probably better known on Bow pieces than on Liverpool. Translucency, green. Height $7\frac{1}{8}$ inches, 1765–70.

(*b*) Tea bowl and saucer painted in underglaze blue in conventional oriental style, within a trellis border. Both pieces show undercutting and good glazing without defects. Translucency, green, good, with one or two flaws. Saucer diameter $4\frac{3}{4}$ inches. Cup height $1\frac{3}{4}$ inches. *circa* 1760–5.

(*c*) Bowl with ribbed moulding, blue painted hexagonal cell border outside, blue-printed inside with a boy holding a sunshade over a lady in Chinese dress, in a garden setting. Translucent, yellow-green. Very undercut footring. Glaze on base clouded. Diameter $7\frac{1}{4}$ inches. The subject of the print (*e*) occurs as a 'smoky primitive' on those sauce boats in silver shape furnished with high foot and splay lip. *circa* 1765. P.

(*d*) Bowl, blue-painted with the more usual version of 'peony and dots' design. Footring irregular, slightly undercut. Bluish glaze. Translucency, blue, good. Diameter $6\frac{3}{8}$ inches. *circa* 1765.

Plate 12

(*a, b*) Tea bowl and saucer carrying a lightly impressed geometrical design (moulded), the decoration being completed with a floral pattern in blue, printed on the bowl, but painted on the saucer, each having a blue-painted running floral border. The glaze is everywhere even and free from defect. Translucency, green, good. Saucer diameter $4\frac{3}{4}$ inches. Cup height $1\frac{5}{8}$ inches. This cup and saucer is one of a pair, both of which show the same peculiarity. *circa* 1765. P.

(*c*) Coffee cup with wavy chevron moulding and scroll handle, painted with a rose spray in natural colours beneath a blue-painted border. The rose is faintly outlined in carmine in an unusual manner. The footring is formed by small cusps which project downwards from the side of the cup and kinship with Plate 3 (*b*) is obvious. General appearance bluish-grey, with translucency of bluish tint. Much clouding and blackening of the basal glaze. Mark: Three dots in the form of a triangle in blue under glaze. *circa* 1760.

(*d*) Sauce boat, probably deriving from silver-shape, moulded externally with rococo scrolls enclosing panels which are painted with rocks, bamboo trees and flowering shrubs in blue-underglaze and red, with a touch of gilding. Wavy rim, scroll handle and a flat base from which rises a moulding of acanthus. The base is unglazed except for patchy volatilization. Inside, the rim is painted with an interrupted trellis in red-brown, while at the base is a mosaic in green and red. Translucency, yellowish-green, poor. General appearance bluish-grey. Length $6\frac{1}{2}$ inches. The counterpart of this in saltglaze no doubt exists but I have not come across it. 1760–70. P.

(*e*) Tea bowl externally moulded with an elaborate pattern. This consists of vertical pleats surmounted by a wavy line and which are overlaid with foliage so as to enclose three reserved panels. There is no further decoration, though it seems likely that the panels were intended to receive vignettes after the manner of the coffee pot of Plate 15 (*b*). Translucency, bluish-green and very good, with an occasional flaw. Footring undercut. No glazing defects. Height $1\frac{3}{4}$ inches. One of a pair, with matching saucers. 1765–70. N P.

(*f*) Sauce boat on low foot, with crenated edge and ear-shaped handle, showing a moulded pattern of vertical reeding overpainted in colours on both sides with a formal spray of flowers in red and blue, surmounted by two turret-like buds. Translucency, yellowish-green, with flaws. Recessed base. Length $5\frac{5}{8}$ inches. 1765–70.

(*g*) Mug of inverted bell shape, with grooved foot and scroll handle, having a moulded ground pattern of leaves and flowers on which are reserved three panels picked out in rococo scrolls and painted in 'Chinese' manner with vignettes in underglaze blue. Translucency, green, very good with no flaws. Footring unglazed and base deeply recessed without glaze shrinkage. No glazing defects. Height $5\frac{1}{4}$ inches. 1765–70. N P.

(*h*) Tea bowl and saucer, moulded externally, with a characteristic blue painted border. The moulding takes the form of a narrow reeding, crested with small scrolls and overlaid with sprays of flowers. It closely resembles that of the sauce boat (Plate 12 (*f*)). Translucency, yellowish-green. Heavy wedge-shaped foot, blue glaze with no shrinkage. Saucer diameter 5 inches. Cup height $1\frac{3}{4}$ inches. Fragments of a cup of this pattern were found by Entwisle near the site of the Patrick Hill pottery (C on map) in circumstances which permitted the conclusion that it was a factory waster, although there is no reason to think that porcelain was ever made here. The evidence is not stated. Date about 1775 and therefore later than the other moulded wares on this Plate.

Plate 13

(*a*) Bowl, the underglaze blue ground diapered with a gold trellis and interrupted by four reserved panels, semi-circular in shape and painted with flowers in natural colours. Inside the rim is a narrow band of blue, diapered in gold with small rosettes and terminating with a wavy edge. A single line of gilding encircles the footring. Translucency, cream-yellow, good. Diameter 7½ inches. *circa* 1770.

By courtesy of National Museum of Wales

(*b*) Vase, pear shaped and cover, on which flowering shrubs and insects have been applied in raised slip of bianco paste. The glaze is almost of celadon greenness. Translucency, yellowish, poor. Recessed base, glazed, with no shrinkage and no defect. Height 6½ inches. 1760–70. N P.
(*c*) Teapot and cover, depressed globular shape, painted with rose spray and projecting bud. The rose is faintly outlined in carmine (Plate 12 (*c*)). Plain handle and spout. Footring shallow with no glaze shrinkage and no glazing defect on base, which is marked with an incised cross. Conical knop. Cover flange glazed. 1760–5.
  The painting is reminiscent of the rose-engraved Jacobite glass and may have that significance. See page 69.

By courtesy of National Museum of Wales

(*d*) Cylindrical mug with ribbed loop handle and recessed base, painted in a manner similar to the preceding. Translucency, green, good. No glaze shrinkage. Height 3⅜ inches. 1760–5.
(*e*) Bowl of yellowish-green appearance, painted with fence and flowering trees in colour and white enamel. Translucency, yellow-green, poor, with flaws. Wreathing also present. Diameter 6¼ inches. 1765–70. N P.
(*f*) Bowl of greyish-blue look, painted with peony, bird, fence and rocks in a famille rose palette, the heron-like bird picked out in white enamel. Heavily potted, poor translucency of yellowish-green colour. Slight glaze shrinkage, with much pin-pitting and peppering all over base. Diameter 5⅛ inches. 1760–5.

Plate 14

(*a*) Bowl, similar to Plate 13 (*a*), but painted with fruit instead of flowers and having a trellis diaper throughout. Translucency, yellowish. Diameter 9 inches. *circa* 1770.

By courtesy of National Museum of Wales

(*b*) Teacup, with plain loop handle, painted in colours. Very green glaze. Translucency, greenish-yellow, with flaws. Ground footring. Small glaze-filled depressions here and there in paste. From the Hurst Collection (regarded as Chaffers). Height 1⅝ inches. Diameter 3¼ inches. 1760–5. N P.
(*c*) Coffee can, with rounded loop handle and flat unglazed base showing a chamfered edge, painted in colours with a peony and flowering branch. Very grey appearance. Translucency, green. Height 2⅝ inches. Chaffers. 1760–5.
(*d*) Coffee cup and saucer, both painted and gilded by the same hand but the underglaze blue of the cup shows the streakiness characteristic of Liverpool, whereas that of the saucer is evenly applied. Cup, brown translucency, no glaze shrinkage. Height 2⅞ inches. Saucer, green translucency with shrinkage. Diameter 5¾ inches. Probably 'married' in the decorating shop. *circa* 1765.
(*e*) Jug of inverted bell shape, with splay lip, grooved foot and plain strap handle showing the potter's thumb mark, painted with peacocks in a marshy landscape. Grey appearance. Recessed base with glaze shrinkage. Translucency, green, poor. Glazing defects are confined to the interior (blackening). Height 6½ inches. Well painted by an unknown hand. Chaffers. 1760–5.

Plate 15

(a) Coffee pot on a foot, with reeded and grooved loop handle showing the potter's thumb mark, externally moulded (including the spout) with an interlocking 'onion' pattern and painted in underglaze blue with a floral pattern and dragonflies. Recessed base with sloping bevel. Translucency, yellow. Height $10\frac{5}{8}$ inches. 1770–5. P.

(b) Coffee pot, with domed cover, scroll handle and moulded spout, externally moulded with a pleated pattern overlaid with flower sprays in which are reserves painted in blue in 'Chinese' manner. Wedge-shaped footring with recessed base and no shrinkage. Translucency, green, good. Height $9\frac{5}{8}$ inches. Marked in *underglaze* slate, X7. The resemblance to the mark found on H.P. Bristol coloured wares is too close to be accidental. It therefore has a dating value (?1772–5). For the moulded pattern, see Plate 12 (e).

(c) Teapot of globular shape with ribbed handle and plain spout, painted in natural colours with flower sprays containing roses, a very variegated tulip and bent-over leaves. Translucency, green, good. No glaze shrinkage, but glaze good with scattered pin-pitting. Cover with conical knop and glazed flange. Border No. 27. Height $6\frac{1}{2}$ inches. 1760–5. NP.

(d) Coffee pot with domed cover, scroll handle, moulded spout and grooved foot, painted in colours (with Chinese figures). Translucency, greenish-yellow. Recessed base with no shrinkage. Height 10 inches. 1770–5.

Plate 16

(a) Tea bowl and saucer depicting the 'stag hunt', with a formal border in red and gold. The Chinese original is seen on the left from which it can be seen how closely, and with what pains, the potter attempted to copy the diapered ground of white enamel, which is overglaze on the saucer but underglaze on the cup. Very grey look, with good green translucency. Markedly undercut footring. No shrinkage. Saucer diameter 5 inches. Cup height $1\frac{7}{8}$ inches. *circa* 1765.

(b) Teapot of depressed globular shape, with plain handle and spout painted in colour with the 'stag hunt' empanelled on a plain ground. Very grey look. Translucency, green, very poor. Type of base is described on page 36. See Plate 50 (a), which also shows the thundercloud glazing. Pin-pitting marked. Height $4\frac{7}{8}$ inches. *circa* 1760.

(c) Bowl, painted with a jointed meandering branch and flowers in natural colours, with the use of white enamel. Border No. 25 in dark red. Translucency, pure blue, with many flaws. Footring irregular (see Plate 50 (d)). No shrinkage and no glazing defects. Diameter $6\frac{1}{8}$ inches. 1765–70.

(d) Coffee cup from the same service as (c). Note the square look. Translucency, blue. Footring irregular. Height $2\frac{1}{8}$ inches. Reverse side of (c) is seen.

(e) Tea bowl similarly decorated. Height $1\frac{5}{8}$ inches. 1765–70.

(f) Tea bowl, coffee cup and saucer, showing bird painting. Greyish appearance. Translucency, pale green, showing flaws. Glaze shrinkage. The saucer shows overfiring, all greens appearing as yellow. Saucer diameter $4\frac{3}{4}$ inches. Coffee cup height $1\frac{5}{8}$ inches. 1765–70.

Plate 17

(a) Bowl, painted in colours in 'Chinese' manner, in which grass is indicated by a wash of green over rows of dots and leaves by a wash of very dark green over an umbrella-like framework. Possibly a saltglaze painter. Translucency, green. Glaze shrinkage on base, with blistering and wreathing present. Diameter 4½ inches. 1760–5. N P.

(b) Teapot made by a saltglaze potter, with crabstock handle and spout and painted in red and gold with flowering branch and fence in oriental style. Translucency, yellow, fair. Greyish look. Small footring with slightly depressed base, showing much sanding. Height 4¾ inches. *circa* 1760. P

(c) Dish, of oval shape with wavy rim, painted in red and blue with gilding, with peonies and trees, by a delft hand imitating a Chinese Imari style. Blue glaze with much pin-pitting and practically opaque. 14 inches × 11½ inches. 1765–70.

(d) Pear-shaped vase (no cover) painted in a delft manner in blue underglaze. Flat unglazed base. Translucency, greenish. Height 5¼ inches. *circa* 1765. P.

(e) Sauce boat in silver shape, on four lion-mask and claw feet, painted in colours in 'famille rose' manner. Inside are depicted three Japanese goldfish in red and gold. Grey appearance with good glazing. Practically opaque. Length 7½ inches. Probably Christian. 1765–70.

(f) Bowl, with an appearance suggesting saltglaze, painted in bright enamel colours in 'famille rose' manner. Translucency, yellow, good. No glaze shrinkage. Glaze bluish with bare patch inside footring. Diameter 4¼/4⅛ inches (not quite circular). 1756–60. P.

Plate 18

(a) Bowl, painted in colours by a saltglaze painter, with a large peony in 'famille rose' manner. Translucency, green, with many flaws. Pin-pitting present. No shrinkage, but markedly undercut footring. Diameter 7¾ inches. Chaffers. 1760–5. N P.

(b) Vase, of flask shape with wide neck, painted in saltglaze manner in bright enamel colours. It has an ivory appearance, with yellow translucency (good). Footring small, shallow and peppered base. Height 5 inches. 1756–60. P.

(c) The interior of (a). Trellis border in red-brown, interrupted by passages of floral ornament in colours. A flower spray on the base. A saltglaze hand.

(d) Bowl and saucer, both painted in colours with the same subject and probably by the same hand. The bowl is of saltglaze and here replaces the porcelain bowl which matches the saucer, in order to show the influence of a saltglaze background on Liverpool china. The saucer has green translucency with patchy brown staining due to iron impurity. Both the saucer and its porcelain cup have grey surface appearance, pin-pitting and no glaze shrinkage with moderate undercutting. Saucer diameter 4⅞ inches. Perhaps an early essay in china making by the maker of the bowl. 1756–60. N P.

Plate 19

(a) Plate with scalloped and fluted rim, painted with flower spray in colours. Translucency, yellowish, showing flaws. Starch blue glaze collecting inside footring. Diameter 6¾ inches. Border No. 3 in red-brown. 1770–5.

(b) Bowl painted in colours with Chinese figures, including Pu Tai and a bull, in an outdoor setting. Border inside rim No. 6 (blue). Translucency, pure blue, good. No Shrinkage. Pin-pitting on base with discolouration. Diameter 6 inches. 1765–75.

(c) Teapot and cover painted with flower sprays in natural colours. Plain handle and spout. No glazing defects and no shrinkage. Greyish appearance. Eight holes. Cover with conical knop and glazed flange. Translucency, blue-green, good. Height 5¼ inches. Border No. 27. *circa* 1765. N P.

176

(*d*) Teapot and cover painted with flower sprays in colours. Plain handle and spout. Bluish glaze, tending to collect inside footring. Translucency, yellow-straw, good. Conical knop and glazed flange. Border No. 27. Height 6 inches. 1765–70.

(*e*) Bowl, with sloping and undercut footring, painted with a large spreading tree having red and blue leaves. Translucency, green with flaws. No shrinkage and no glazing defects. Diameter 6 inches. 1765–70.

(*f*) Cream jug, with pinched lip and grooved loop handle, painted with a flower spray in colours. Border No. 27. Translucency, bluish green, good. No shrinkage. Height 4 inches. *circa* 1765. N P.

(*g*) Cream jug, with pinched lip and grooved loop handle, painted with the Liverpool exotic bird perched among foliage with red twiggy branches and leaves of metallic green, in which the veining is present, but no outline. Translucency, dirty yellow but good, with flaws. Blue glaze collecting inside footring with clouding. Border No. 28. Height $3\frac{7}{8}$ inches. *circa* 1770. N P.

Plate 20

(*a*) Coffee pot of pear shape, with moulded spout, scroll handle, grooved foot and cover with conical knop, painted with a floral design in colours and the use of white enamel. The base is flat but glazed, an unusual feature. Translucency, bluish-green. Height 9 inches. There is an overlapping scale moulding between the thumb rest and the point of handle attachment of a type sometimes seen on 'scratch-cross' jugs (Plate 29 (*d*)) and this, together with a weakly domed cover and the unusual base, suggest that this is an early example of the type — possibly 1760–5. Border No. 33.

(*b*) Sauce boat on grooved foot, with wavy rim, biting snake handle and moulded panels on either side painted with flower sprays in natural colours. Translucency, dirty yellow, good. Slightly recessed base with no glaze shrinkage, but showing a large bare area. Length 6 inches. Border No. 28. 1770–5.

(*c*) Bowl, of decidedly grey appearance, painted with ducks in fancy colours (one in gold) in a marshy landscape, part of which is pencilled in black. The 'jointed branch' painter. Translucency, bluish-green, showing flaws: poor. Mild undercutting, with no shrinkage. Diameter $5\frac{5}{8}$ inches. 1765–70.

(*d*) Sauce boat on a low moulded foot, with scroll handle and moulded sides on which are reserved panels outlined in scrolls and painted in colours. Border No. 21. Translucency, bluish-green, showing flaws. Length 8 inches. There is kinship with Plate 20 (*a*) in both potting and decoration. 1760–5.

(*e*) Teapot with domed cover, the body moulded externally on either side with three palm trees forming panels on which are painted figures in Chinese dress, in colour. Below these is a row of leaves springing from the base, each outlined in green with a red midrib. The spout is ribbed and has a moulding of overlapping lanceolate leaves at the base, similarly coloured, while the handle is also ribbed. On the shoulder and round the edge of the cover is a tracery of scrollwork in red-brown. Translucency, yellowish-brown. Height $7\frac{1}{2}$ inches. The palm-tree or 'Liverpool' teapot. 1770–5. P.

(*f*) Teapot, moulded in manner similar to (*d*), the panels blue printed with convolvulus, anemones and moss roses and the leaves at base outlined in blue. Border No. 9. Translucency, yellow. Height $7\frac{3}{4}$ inches. 1770–5.

(*g*) Bowl, painted with the Liverpool exotic bird, in colours. The appearance is creamy, but the glaze is blue and collects inside the footring. Translucency, yellowish-brown. Diameter 6 inches. 1770–5.

Plate 21

(a) Teapot of globular shape, with plain spout and ribbed handle, the body moulded with reeds of alternating width and painted in colours by the painter of flowers with hard black outlines. On the shoulder and round the edge of the cover are bands of 'marbled blue'. The cover flange is glazed. Knop in the form of Worcester flower bud. Nine holes to spout. Translucency, yellowish-green, good, with no flaws. Glaze shrinkage present. Height 5½ inches. 1765–75.

(b) Teapot of similar type, but with conical knop on cover, painted in colours with the formal design used by the 'turretted bud' painter. Translucency, yellowish-green, good, with no flaws. No glaze shrinkage. Height 5¾ inches. 1765–75.

(c) Cream jug on foot and with 'biting snake' handle, showing moulding and painting similar to (a). The base is recessed, with collection of blue glaze in pools. Translucency, dirty yellow, good. Height 4¼ inches. 1765–75.

(d) Cylindrical mug, of glassy paste, with plain loop handle and very shallow recessed base, painted on both sides with a burlesque Chinoiserie in colours among which a strong pink is prominent. The scenes are empanelled in purple coloured feathery scrollwork. Border No. 27. Translucency, green and extremely good. Height 4¼ inches. Regarded formerly as Longton Hall (*Bemrose, L.H.P., Plate XXVI, Plate XLVII*). 1765–70. P.

(e) Tea bowl and saucer, the bowl ribbed, the saucer fluted and both painted in colours matching (a) and (c) with 'marbled blue' borders. Cups of this type have heavily wedged but narrow footrings in the angle of which the glaze collects. Translucency, yellowish, good. Blue glaze. Potting from the same moulds is seen with pilgrim shell decoration in blue on Plate 45 (b). Saucer diameter 5¼ inches. Cup height 2 inches. 1770–5. P.

(f) Teapot and cover, the body of depressed globular shape with plain handle and spout and shallow recessed base, painted in colours and with the use of white enamel in an oriental manner. General appearance greenish. Loopline border in dark red on shoulder and edge of cover. The type of base is shown on Plate 50 (a). Seven holes. Cover flange glazed. Translucency, green, poor, without flaws. The glazed base shows shrinkage, pin-pitting and bare areas. Height 4⅞ inches. 1760–5. N P.

(g) Bowl painted in colours with a peony, rocks and meandering branch on which a bird is perched. Translucency, blue, very good and showing flaws. No shrinkage and no glazing defect. Diameter 6 inches. Border No. 3 in red. *circa* 1765.

Plate 22

(a) Teapot and cover with conical knop, the body of globular shape with ribbed handle and painted in colours with four musicians playing instruments. Greyish look. Translucency, green. Footring of irregular outline, undercut but with no glaze shrinkage. Border No. 24. Height 5¾ inches. *circa* 1765.

(b) Coffee can with round loop handle and flat underglazed base, painted with Chinese figures in colours and with the use of white enamel. Translucency, yellowish-green and very good, without flaws. Border inside No. 3 in red. Height 2½ inches. 1760–75. P.

(c) Sauce boat on low foot, with wavy rim and scroll handle in the form of a debased biting snake, the sides moulded with three arched panels and painted in red and gold in a Chinese Imari manner. Translucency, green, with numerous flaws. Length 4¾ inches. 1770–5. N P.

(d) Cup and saucer, painted with small flowers in natural colours in panels outlined in rococo scrollwork reserved on an overglaze scale blue ground. Translucency, pale greenish-white.

Undercut footring. Unglazed area on back of saucer. Saucer diameter $4\frac{7}{8}$ inches. Cup height $1\frac{3}{4}$ inches. 1765–75.

(e) Bowl, with glaze of bluish cast, painted in red, blue and gold in pseudo-Imari style. Translucency, greenish-yellow, good and showing flaws. Base slightly undercut, no shrinkage but with marked pin-pitting. The blue is 'washy' and the gilding, particularly the diagonal work on the vertical bands, is poor. Diameter $5\frac{5}{8}$ inches. *circa* 1765. N P.

(f) Teapot and cover with conical knop, the body of globular shape, with ear-shaped ribbed handle, painted in colours with figures in Chinese dress. Translucency, yellowish-green, showing flaws. The footring is irregular and slightly undercut. No shrinkage of glaze, but much pin-pitting and peppering, most marked on base. Seven holes. Cover flange glazed. Height $5\frac{7}{8}$ inches. 1765–70. N P.

Plate 23

(a) Bowl painted with a conventional floral pattern in colours. Translucency, dirty yellow. Wedge-shaped footring, with blue glaze collecting in angle. Diameter 6 inches. *circa* 1775.

(b) Coffee cup, painted in colours with a flower spray featuring small tightly packed rosebuds. Plain round loop handle. Blue glaze collecting inside footring. Translucency, yellowish, brown. Height $2\frac{1}{2}$ inches. Border No. 28 in red. 1770–5.

(c) Cream jug, with pinched lip and round loop handle, painted with flowers in colours by the same hand as (b). Translucency, yellowish-green. Glaze blue, collecting inside footring. Border No. 27 in red. Height $2\frac{7}{8}$ inches. 1770–5.

(d) Cream jug with pinched lip and grooved loop handle, painted with willow tree in Chinese garden scene, in red and blue with spare gilding. Border No. 3 beneath a cell border, all in blue. Ttanslucency, brown. Blue glaze which collects inside footring. Height $3\frac{7}{8}$ inches. 1770–80.

(e) Cream jug of similar shape to (d), painted with 'ramp' pattern in red and blue. Translucency, bluish-green. Glaze, blue, thin and even. Trellis border in red and blue. Height $3\frac{1}{2}$ inches. Of earlier date than (d). 1760–5.

(f) Coffee can, with flat unglazed base and grooved loop handle, painted with flowers in natural colours. Translucency, dirty yellow. Border No. 31. Height $2\frac{1}{2}$ inches. *circa* 1775.

(g) Coffee cup, with ribbed loop handle, painted with a flower spray in colours. Translucency, yellowish-brown. Heavy wedge footring, with blue glaze collecting. Border No. 32 in red and blue. Height $2\frac{5}{8}$ inches. *circa* 1775.

(h) Coffee cup, with cusped rim and round loop handle, painted in colours with a version of the design known as 'La peche'. 1760–5.

By courtesy of E. Allman, Esq.

(i) Coffee cup with round loop handle, painted in colours with figures in Chinese dress. Translucency, yellow. Glaze collects. Height $2\frac{1}{2}$ inches. 1770–5. P.

(j) Cream jug, moulded with spiral volutes springing from acanthus leaves. Scroll handle and shallow recessed base. Painted with the Liverpool exotic bird in bright colours, perched on red twiggy foliage. Border No. 28. Translucency, yellow. Height $3\frac{1}{2}$ inches. 1770–5. N P.

(k) Cream jug, similarly moulded, but painted with small flower sprays and having the mid ribs of the acanthus picked out in brown. No border. Translucency, yellow. Height $3\frac{1}{2}$ inches. 1770–5.

(l) Bowl painted with flower spray and small sprigs in colours. The pattern resembles that formerly used by Chaffers (Plate 4 (f)). from which it clearly derives. Wedge footring, blue glaze tending to collect. Translucency, pale dirty yellow, but very good. Diameter $6\frac{1}{4}$ inches. Border No. 28. Probably Christian of about 1775.

179

(*m*) Bowl, of creamy colour, painted in red and blue with sparse gilding. Trellis border in red and blue inside. Translucency, dirty yellow. This blue glaze. In spite of its comparatively late date, the footring shows mild undercutting. Mark on the base resembling a large C and, some distance away, a large dot, both in underglaze blue. Diameter 6¼ inches. ?1775–80. NP.

Plate 24

(*a*) Cup, coffee can and plate, painted in underglaze blue with the 'jumping boy'. The cup is octagonal, with plain loop handle and small footring. Mock oriental mark. Height 1¾ inches. Base pin-pitted. Coffee can, plain loop handle and flat unglazed base. Height 2½ inches. Plate of Chien Lung shape, with a border of interrupted trellis, also in blue. Mock oriental mark. Diameter 4⅜ inches. All three show a strong blue glaze with good green translucency. 1760–5. The coffee can is phosphatic.

(*b*) Mug of inverted bell shape, with fluted loop handle and shallow recessed base, painted in underglaze blue, iron red and green with the 'peony and fence' pattern. Border No. 7 in red and green. Translucency, yellowish-green, fair, with no flaws. Marks: an incised stroke and painter's mark in blue. Height 3⅝ inches. 'Scratch-cross'. 1756–65.

(*c*) Mug similar to (*b*), pattern in blue only and blue border of interrupted trellis, its usual accompaniment. Translucency, yellowish-green, fair. Marks as (*b*) with the addition of an incised cross. 'Scratch-cross'. 1756–65.

(*d*) Tea bowl and saucer, both showing everted rims, painted with the 'jumping boy' in blue, with the addition of iron red and a little gilding. Translucency, yellowish-green, no flaws. Greenish-blue glaze with shrinkage. Saucer diameter 4⅝ inches. Cup height 1⅝ inches. 1760–5.

(*e*) Sauce boat of well-known Meissen type, with grey surface appearance. These sauce boats are sometimes found with painter's mark in blue. One such appearing in the third edition of the *Jermyn Street Catalogue* had a footnote suggesting that the mark stood for Pennington. Overfiring has led to gross discolouration of the painting. Translucency, green, very poor. Length 8⅛ inches. The kinship of many pieces of this type with the 'scratch-cross' group has been noted. (*Honey, O.E.P., 1946, page 160*). Podmore. 1756–65.

(*f*) Dish in the form of a leaf, moulded with a spray of flowers and another leaf, the veining and edges of the latter picked out in slate blue. 'Dash' border in the same colour. The glaze has a yellowish-green cast. Translucency, green, very good. Length 4⅝ inches. 1760–5.

(*g*) Inverted bell-shaped mug, with scroll handle, deeply grooved foot and recessed base reached by a sloping bevel (Plate 50 (*k*)), blue painted with willow trees in Chinese style. Blue glaze. Translucency, yellowish green with no flaws. Marks: an upright cross in blue and a knife cut in the bevel. Height 3⅝ inches. 1756–65.

(*h*) Mug of shape similar to (*g*), but with D-shaped cross section of handle, blue painted in Chinese manner. Translucency, yellowish-green. Recessed base reached by sloping bevel. Marks: small incised cross and painter's mark in blue. Height 3¾ inches. 1756–65. NP.

The Liverpool attribution of mugs of this type is conjectural.

By courtesy of E. Allman, Esq.

Plate 25

(*a, b*) Jug of inverted bell shape, with pinched lip, scroll handle and grooved foot, painted in colours with the 'beckoning Chinaman' on one side and a bunch of flowers on the other. Translucency, green, fair, with no flaws. Depressed base, slightly peppered. Height 7 inches. No mark. 'Scratch-cross'. 1756–65.

(c) Coffee cup, with loop handle of U-shape, painted in colours in 'Chinese' manner. Translucency, yellowish-green. Weak footring with glaze shrinkage. Height $2\frac{1}{2}$ inches. *circa* 1760.
By courtesy of National Museum of Wales

(d) Cylindrical mug with ribbed handle and recessed base, painted in bright enamel colours with 'Chinese' figures in a garden setting. Translucency, light green. Base glazed all over, including the footring which shows much sanding. No shrinkage. Height $4\frac{3}{4}$ inches. *circa* 1760.

Plate 26

(a) Coffee pot, pear shaped, with scroll handle, grooved foot and flat cover with conical knop, painted in colours with figures crossing a bridge over a stream. Mark: an incised cross, 'Scratch-cross'. 1756–65.
By courtesy of the Victoria and Albert Museum. Crown copyright

(b) Coffee pot, pear-shaped (no cover), with scroll handle and grooved foot, painted in colours with 'Chinese' figures and a bird cage suspended from an elaborately scrolled stand in gold. The same hand and palette is seen on the coffee cup, Plate 6 (h). Translucency, green, fair, without flaws. Greyish appearance. Mark: an incised cross and a cut in footring. Height $5\frac{1}{2}$ inches. 'Scratch-cross'. 1756–65.

(c) Bell-shaped mug, with plain flat handle, back-turned at lower end, which shows impress of potter's thumb, grooved foot, painted with a coat of arms and flower sprays by the painter of Plate 4 (d). Translucency, pale greenish-white and not good, showing flaws. Footring $\frac{1}{4}$ inch wide, showing glaze shrinkage. No bevel. Height $3\frac{3}{4}$ inches. Chaffers. 1756–65.

(d) Teapot and cover, the body of globular shape with ribbed handle the cover flange glazed, painted in colours with figures in a garden setting, in Chinese style. Translucency, yellowish, poor. Spout with seven holes. Height $6\frac{1}{2}$ inches. Chaffers, 'lady and parrot' group. 1756–65.

(e) Cream jug, with pinched lip, grooved loop handle and grooved foot, printed in brownish-black and coloured (red cow pattern). Translucency, bluish-green and one or two flaws present. Shallow recessed base within narrow footring. Height $3\frac{1}{8}$ inches. 1760–5.

(f) Cream jug, with cornucopia lip, grooved loop handle and grooved foot, painted with flowering plants in colours in oriental style. Translucency, green, good. Height 3 inches. Its drooping lip and 'waisted' shape resemble (e); its footring closely copies (c). No mark. 'Scratch-cross'. 1756–65.

Plate 27

Jug, with cornucopia lip (restored), scroll handle with overlapping scale moulding between thumb rest and point of attachment and grooved foot, painted with figures and domestic animals in a landscape of European trees with a large house in the distance. Translucency practically nil. A shallow recessed base reached by a very steep bevel from an unglazed footring. Mark, an incised cross with an incised stroke at some distance. Height $9\frac{1}{2}$ inches. A heavily-potted jug (weight $4\frac{3}{4}$ lb.) of ungainly proportions, superbly painted by an unknown artist, in a manner characterized by good perspective and of which dark brown rocks in the foreground and purplish-blue mountains in the distance are features. Scratch cross. 1756–65.

Plate 28

(a) Punch pot and cover, the body globular, with plain round loop handle, curving spout and footring of greater depth on the outside; the cover with glazed flange and mushroom-shaped knop with projecting apex. Painted in blue underglaze with a version of the well known 'peony and fence' pattern, with an interrupted trellis border on the shoulder and around cover. Practically opaque. No glaze shrinkage. Mark: an incised stroke. Height $7\frac{1}{2}$ inches and weight 3 lb. 4 oz. Heavy and massive construction. 'Scratch-cross'. 1756–65.

(b) Cylindrical mug with spreading base and grooved loop handle, painted in blue underglaze with the 'peony and fence' pattern beneath a diapered border. Translucency, green, poor. Shallow recessed base with unglazed footring. Mark: incised cross and cut in footring Height $6\frac{1}{8}$ inches. 'Scratch-cross'. 1756–65.

(c) Cylindrical mug with slightly spreading base and fluted loop handle, painted in blue underglaze and iron red with the 'peony and fence' pattern beneath a border in blue and red similar to that of (b). Translucency, green, poor. Mark in blue under handle and a cut in footring. 'Scratch-cross'. 1756–65.

By courtesy of National Museum of Wales

Plate 29

(a) Saucer, radially ribbed to within $\frac{1}{2}$ inch of the rim, printed in dark brown and overpainted in colours with a design of peonies, flowering shrubs and two geese. Translucency, pale bluish-green, very good and showing no flaws. No glaze shrinkage or other imperfection. Small footring. Rim slightly everted (and that of the companion cup also). Diameter $4\frac{1}{8}$ inches. Both the engraving line and the palette are identical with that of the 'red cow' print. The decoration is that of the mug referred to on page 41, footnote 2. *circa* 1760–5.

(b) Plate, blue painted by a delft hand in Chinese manner. Chien Lung shape. Blue glaze, showing slight crazing in one place. Translucency, green, poor. Diameter $8\frac{7}{8}$ inches. 1765–70.

(c) Jug, pear shaped, with scroll handle, pinched lip and grooved foot, painted in colours with ladies in Chinese dress, furniture and gilded bird cage supported on a tall scrolled stand. The palette is seen on the coffee pot (Plate 26 (b)) and the cup (4 (h). Translucency, green, almost opaque. Mark: two incised strokes. Height $7\frac{1}{8}$ inches. 'Scratch-cross'. 1756–65.

(d) Jug, pear shaped, with scroll handle showing overlapping scale moulding between thumb rest and point of attachment, cornucopia spout and grooved foot, painted in colours with the 'Fox and grapes'. A more heavily potted jug than (c). Translucency, green and very poor. Height $8\frac{1}{4}$ inches. Mark, incised cross and incised stroke. 'Scratch-cross'. 1756–65.

Plate 30

(a) Jug, pear shaped, with scroll handle, mask spout and grooved foot, blue-painted with a bamboo tree, large chrysanthemum and root ornament (page 66) of an unusual type. The shade of blue is light, as generally seen on 'scratch-cross' pieces (much lighter than on the 'John Fell' jug). Translucency, green, fair. Bluish glaze. 'Orange peel' appearance in many places. Mark, incised cross and a mark in blue on the base. Height $6\frac{7}{8}$ inches. 'Scratch cross.' 1756–65.

(b) Jug, baluster shaped, with plain strap handle, the back-turned lower end showing the potter's thumb impress, wide mouth, splayed lip and flat unglazed base, blue-painted with a willow tree, bridge over stream and figures in the Chinese manner. Translucency, green, showing numerous circular flaws. Height 6⅞ inches. Chaffers. 1756–65. N P.

(c) Teapot and cover, the body high shouldered and slightly bulbous, with ribbed loop handle and curving hexagonal spout. The cover, with flower knop is completely glazed. Painted in smudgy underglaze blue (see Plate 5 (f)). General appearance very grey. Translucency, pale grey and good with no flaws. Slightly bluish glaze with no defects. Height 4¼ inches. *circa* 1760.

Plate 31

(a) Plate, painted in blue in Chinese manner, within an interrupted trellis border. Translucency, dirty straw colour, with one or two flaws. Chien Lung shape. Diameter 9⅛ inches. 1760–5.

(b) Teapot and cover with button knop, the body with the flattened sides and curving spout associated with pottery shapes, the handle plain and rounded and carrying very small thumb rest, painted in blue with countryside scenes and figures of European type by the painter of the 'horsemen' mug in the Schreiber Collection (I.781). The glaze is slightly blue, even and free from defect. Height 4½ inches. *circa* 1760.

(c) Cream jug, with curving rim and lip and flattened loop handle, the lower part of the body moulded with fine vertical reeding surmounted with a cresting of scrolls and overlaid with flower sprays in relief, the neck hexagonally moulded and blue bordered within and without. The design is a late adaptation of that of the cup and saucer on Plate 12 (h). Translucency, straw colour. Base recessed, with no shrinkage. Height 4 inches. 1775–85. N P.

(d) Cream jug with pinched lip and grooved loop handle, painted in colours, the ground treatment suggesting that seen on Plate 16 (f). There is definite evidence of a printed outline. Border No. 23. Translucency, straw. Glaze bluish, with thundercloud patch on base, but no shrinkage. Height 3⅞ inches. 1770–80.

(e) Coffee cup with grooved loop handle and weak footring, painted in a pseudo-Imari manner. No glaze shrinkage. Height 2½ inches. Compare with bowl of Plate 22 (f). *circa* 1765.

(f) Coffee cup, with grooved loop handle and weak footring, painted in colours, with the sparing use of enamel. General appearance bluish-grey. Translucency, green, with iron staining in one place. Some shrinkage, but no glazing defects. Height 2½ inches. The design was in use at Worcester. *circa* 1765. N P.

(g) Bucket, on four cusped feet, with shaped rim and rococo scrolled handle, the sides moulded in relief with leaf scrolls and shell ornament enclosing on either side panels painted with formal sprays in colour. Glaze pale bluish-white, with no defect. Translucency, yellowish green. Height to rim 2¼ inches, to top of handle 3¼ inches. Spoon, with reeded bowl and small moulded pattern on handle, with painting to match. Length 5 inches. *circa* 1770.

(h) Cream jug, with tip-tilted lip and rounded scroll handle of unusual type, painted in colours by the hand seen on the preceding piece. Bluish glaze, with no shrinkage. Bare area on base. Translucency, yellowish-green. Height 3 inches. From the same factory as (g). *circa* 1770. P.

(i) Saucer, blue printed with a 'lambrequin' surround. Translucency, straw. Dirty looking glaze, with sanding near rim. Diameter 5¾ inches. 1780–5.

(j) Tea bowl with powder blue ground, the reserves painted in Chinese manner and having smudgy outlines. Translucency, bluish-green, good. Footring small, no shrinkage. Height 1¾ inches. *circa* 1765.

(k) Coffee cup, with grooved loop handle and smallish footring, painted with formalized flowers in colours within a cartouche outlined in gold. Greyish appearance. Translucency, blue-green, good. No shrinkage. Height $2\frac{1}{2}$ inches. *circa* 1765.

Plate 32

(*a*) Bowl, octagonal, the ogee curved panels forming an everted rim, printed and over-painted with the 'red cow' in enamel colours. Inside, an interrupted trellis border in red and green; at the bottom, a small green leaf at junction of base with one of the panels. Translucency, bluish-green, poor. Greyish appearance. Glaze shows blistering and some sanding. Recessed base. Height $2\frac{1}{2}$ inches. Diameter $4\frac{7}{8}$ inches. 1760–5.

(*b*) Hexagonal bottle flask, with slightly flared neck, printed and painted with Chinese figures, accoutrements and insects in enamel colours. Formal iron-red border. Translucency, green, fairly good. Base slightly expanded, flat, unglazed. Height $4\frac{5}{8}$ inches. 1760–5.

(*c*) Flask similar in every respect to (*b*). Opposite side. 1760–5.

(*d*) Cup and cover, the body bulbous, with recessed base and square peaked handle, printed and painted with the same design and employing the technique used in the preceding examples; the cover with rounded knop and glazed flange. Translucency, green. No glaze shrinkage and no glazing defects. Height 3 inches. 1760–5.

(*e*) Hexagonal bottle flask, of similar shape and potting features to (*b*) and (*c*), but slightly more bulbous, painted with the design known as 'the acrobats' in colours; on the other side is a small landscape and buildings. Below the rim, a loop and line border in iron red. Translucency, green. General appearance very slightly less grey than (*b*) and (*c*). Height $4\frac{5}{8}$ inches. 1760–5.

(*f*) Cream jug of silver shape, with high peaked handle decorated with the 'red cow' print. Translucency, blue-green, a few flaws and one small area of iron staining. Glaze bluish with defects including bare area close to upper attachment of handle. No shrinkage. Height $3\frac{5}{8}$ inches. 1760–5.

(*g*) Coffee cup, with grooved loop handle, small irregular footring and everted rim. Translucency, blue without flaws. Glaze bluish with many black specks (visible in plate). No shrinkage. Height $2\frac{1}{4}$ inches. 1760–5.

(*h*) Cream jug of squat appearance, with pinched lip, grooved loop handle and grooved foot, decorated with the 'red cow' print. Translucency, pale green. No shrinkage. Height $2\frac{3}{4}$ inches. 1760–5.

(*i*) Mustard pot (no cover), with square peaked handle, decorated with the 'red cow' print. Translucency, pale green with many flaws. Greyish appearance. Recessed base with no shrinkage. Height $2\frac{1}{2}$ inches. 1760–5.

(*j*) Coffee cup, octagonal, with scroll handle and weak footring, decorated with the 'red cow' print. Translucency, bluish-green with no flaws. Slightly recessed base, completely glazed. Height $2\frac{1}{4}$ inches. 1760–5.

(*k*) Coffee cup, with grooved loop handle, decorated with the 'red cow' print. Creamy appearance. Translucency, very pale green, good, with no flaws. Height 2 inches. Type 2, with both cows red, no sun and no ground colouring. Photograph to show shallow grooving of handle. 1760–5.

(*l*) Saucer with slightly everted rim, decorated with the 'red cow' print. Translucency, bluish-green, good, no flaws. Bluish-grey appearance. No shrinkage. Slight undercutting. Diameter $4\frac{5}{8}$ inches. 1760–5.

All the above are type 1 ware, with the exception of (*k*). See pages 37, 97, 98, 99.

Plate 33

(*a*) Plate with crenated rim. In the centre, an oval panel outlined in scrollwork, printed in brown and overpainted in colours. Surrounding it are many small florets, sprays and insects, all of which are polychrome printed. Grey surface appearance. Translucency, straw coloured, not good. Diameter 7¾ inches. Mark: an incised stroke. 1760–70.

By courtesy Victoria and Albert Museum, Schr. I.469. Crown Copyright

(*b*) Plate, polychrome printed with insects, sprays and small detached flowers. Warped in firing. Translucency, straw, poor, the centre only being translucent. Bluish glaze. Chien Lung shape. Diameter 8¾ inches. 1760–70.

(*c*) Vase and cover, the body baluster shaped, with narrow footring and recessed base, printed in polychrome in the manner of the preceding. Translucency, straw, good, with many flaws. Blue glaze. Height 6 inches. 1760–70.

(*d*) Inkwell, printed in polychrome with insects and small flowers. Translucency, straw. Blue glaze. Narrow foot ring and recessed base showing deep knife cut, probably representing an incised stroke mark. Height 2¼ inches. 1760–70.

(*e*) Bowl, printed with sprays and small detached flowers in polychrome. Greenish appearance. Translucency, greenish-yellow. Ground footring, wedge shaped. Small circular depressions, and surface irregularities, glaze-filled. Diameter 4⅞ inches. (*cf.* Plate 14 (*b*)). 1760–70.

(*f*) Sauceboat on three lion mask and paw feet, with wavy rim, printed on both sides and within with large sprays in polychrome. Grey surface appearance. Translucency, straw, not good. Length 7¾ inches. 1760–70.

(*g*) Cream jug of squat shape, with pinched lip, small footring and plain round loop handle printed with sprays in polychrome. Bluish grey appearance. Translucency, yellowish green, poor. No shrinkage. Potting and glazing are of a high order. Height 3 inches. 1760–70.

(*h*) Sauce boat, with wavy rim peaked handle attached at the upper end by a lug and with recessed base, moulded on either side with a shield flanked by trophies, one enclosing a coloured portrait of the Duke of Marlborough in relief, the other, a portrait of Commodore Howe (afterwards Admiral Lord Howe), similarly treated. Below the spout and on the base inside, is printed a bouquet in polychrome. Translucency, yellowish, showing one or two small circular flaws. Length 6¼ inches. 1759–70.

The sauce boat commemorates combined operations carried out against the French Channel ports (Cherbourg, St. Malo, etc.,) in 1758 during the Seven Years War. (The Duke was the third Duke.) It is unlikely that this piece can correctly be dated before 1759.

By courtesy of Trustees of British Museum, No. 1938, 3–14, 68

Plate 34

(*a, b*) Coffee pot and cover, the body pear shaped, with curved spout, grooved handle, and grooved foot, printed in brownish line and washed with colours; on one side with the print of the long tailed macaw, perched on a parapet as originally drawn, on the other with the print of the quarrelling tom-tits. Recessed base, with no shrinkage. Translucency, greenish-yellow showing flaws. Green surface appearance, with small depressions in the paste. Cover with button knop and glazed flange. Height 7¼ inches. The rare tom-tit print occurs on a saucer dish (Trapnell Collection, No. 261) and on a jug and coffee pot, with enamel colours, of Plymouth porcelain in Plymouth City Art Gallery. 1760–5.

(*c*) Bell shaped mug, with grooved handle and grooved foot, black printed with the usual version of the long tailed macaw and fruit. Translucency greenish, poor and showing flaws.

Narrow footring with slightly recessed base, both thinly glazed. Grey surface appearance. A raised and over-inked print. Mark: incised cross and incised stroke. 'Scratch-cross'. Height $4\frac{1}{2}$ inches. 1760–5. Page 103.

(*d*) Coffee cup and saucer, black printed with a garden scene showing two young persons in conversation, seated under a tree. The print is found also on Liverpool teaware with loopline border, on 'hump-handled' teapots and on tea bowls of type (*e*) and (*f*) below. A Liverpool attribution for this example is conjectural. 1760–70.

By courtesy of E. Allman, Esq.

(*e*) Tea bowl, with everted rim and small undercut footring showing no shrinkage. Translucency, pale green and very good, with no flaws. Black printed in 'smoky primitive' manner with 'La Cascade'. Height $1\frac{1}{2}$ inches. *circa* 1760.

(*f*) Tea bowl similar to (*e*) printed in greyish-black with the subject known as the 'flute lesson'. Height $1\frac{1}{2}$ inches. Diameter 3 inches. *circa* 1760.

(*g*) Small scallop shell dish, printed in greyish-black with the same subject as (*f*). Greyish look and very poor green translucency. Length $3\frac{1}{8}$ inches. *circa* 1760.

(*h*) Bowl of greyish appearance, carrying three prints in black. On the outside, leapfrog and a milking scene; on the inside, a goat milking scene. Translucency, green, uneven and poor. Footring undercut with no glaze shrinkage. Height $2\frac{3}{8}$ inches. Diameter $4\frac{7}{8}$ inches. 1760–5.

(*i*) Saucer, black printed. Bluish grey surface appearance. Translucency, blue, with many flaws. Footring markedly undercut. Glaze good, with slight pin pitting and no shrinkage. Diameter $4\frac{3}{4}$ inches. *circa* 1765.

Plate 35

(*a*) Cylindrical mug, black printed with Frederick the Great in Court dress, signed below on left 'Gilbody maker' and on right 'Evans Sct'. No particulars available except Entwistle's statement that it had a plain handle (*Entwistle MSS. 5/79*). Height $4\frac{5}{8}$ inches. *circa* 1758.

By permission of the Libraries, Museums and Arts Committee, Corporation of Liverpool

(*b*) Jug, of baluster shape, with wide lip and plain strap handle, printed in black and over-painted with portrait of Frederick the Great within a wreath of scrollwork. Height $7\frac{1}{4}$ inches. Mayer bequest and destroyed, with the preceding example, by enemy action in 1941. Chaffers. *circa* 1760.

By Permission of the Libraries, Museums and Arts Committee, Corporation of Liverpool

(*c*) Mug of inverted bell shape with scroll handle and grooved foot with Scotia moulding, black printed with portrait of Frederick in Court dress flanked by trophies. Translucency, green and good, except at upper part of mug. Height 5 inches. Chaffers. 1760.

(*d*) Coffee cup and saucer, black printed with 'milkmaids'. Greyish porcelain. Translucency, blue, good. Saucer, cloudy glaze, no shrinkage, undercut; diameter $4\frac{5}{8}$ in. Cup with weak and slightly irregular footring, also no shrinkage. Height $2\frac{1}{4}$ inches. 1760–5. Probably a Hancock engraving. The potting characteristics, shape and glaze of this cup exactly tally with those of Plate 32 (*g*).

Plate 36

(*a*) Coffee cup and saucer, purple printed and colour washed with the sparing use of enamels. Translucency, blue, very good. No glaze shrinking, but no undercutting. Saucer diameter $4\frac{5}{8}$ inches. Cup height $2\frac{1}{4}$ inches. The most striking feature is the very pronounced blue-grey surface appearance. See note on Plate 35 (*d*). *circa* 1765.

(*b*) Teapot and cover, the body of globular shape, with ribbed handle, the cover with rounded knop and glazed flange, black printed with lovers seated under a tree. The print occurs on a Liverpool tile (signed) and on a teapot of barrel shape, now attributed to Longton Hall. 1765.

By permission of the Libraries, Museums and Arts Committee, Corporation of Liverpool

(*c*) Cylindrical mug, with expanding base and plain strap loop handle black printed with the 'Bucks Society' arms (a convivial and charitable organization centred in Liverpool during the eighteenth century, with branches in the Isle of Man). Running loop-line and dot border in black. Translucency, dirty yellow, good, with one or two flaws. Bare area near base, which is flat and unglazed. Height $4\frac{7}{8}$ inches. *circa* 1765.

(*d*) Jug, of baluster shape, with scroll handle, flat unglazed base and lip moulded with foliate scrolls, black printed with the Liverpool print 'dancing dwarfs'. Translucency, green, with one or two flaws. Height $8\frac{5}{8}$ inches. 1765–75. See Plate 39 (*e*). The subject occurs on a Liverpool tile.

Plate 37

(*a*) Bell shaped mug, with plain strap handle having the lower end back-turned, but without potter's thumb mark, black-printed with the arms of the Society of Bucks. This is a good example of over-inking, see front view (Plate 38 (*b*)). No particulars are available. 1760–70. No clue to maker.

By permission of the Libraries, Museums and Arts Committee, Corporation of Liverpool

(*b*) Cylindrical mug, with plain strap handle, the lower end backturned with potter's thumb mark and flat unglazed base, black-printed with a version of the 'haymakers' and dated 'Feb. 9 1768'. Translucency, green, moderately good with flaws present. Height $3\frac{3}{4}$ inches. Chaffers–Christian.

(*c*) Cylindrical mug, with an unusual type of scroll handle and flat unglazed base, black-printed with the arms of the Society of Bucks and signed 'Sadler Liverpool'. Translucency, very pale green and very poor. This is probably an Evans print (page 153). Height $3\frac{1}{2}$ inches. *circa* 1765.

(*d*) Tea bowl and saucer, of quatrefoil form and very grey appearance, black-printed with the Liverpool version of 'La Terre'. Almost opaque. Saucer diameter $4\frac{5}{8}$ inches. Cup diameter 3 inches, height $2\frac{1}{8}$ inches. The shape is a copy of the Chinese (Chien Lung), found also in Derby wares later. *circa* 1765.

(*e*) Bowl, with inward sloping footring, some glaze shrinkage but no undercutting, showing the version of 'La Terre' seen in (*d*), colour washed and touched with enamel colours. Translucency, green, good. On the reverse side, the 'red cow' print. Diameter 6 inches. 1760–5.

Plate 38

(*a*) Bell shaped mug, with scroll handle and Scotia moulded foot, black printed with a portrait of William Pitt, signed 'I Sadler Liverpool Enaml' below, centrally. After Rd. Houston's engraving of a portrait by Wm. Hoare (see footnote on page 57). To the right is a figure of Britannia surmounting numerous emblems; to the left, a shield bearing the Prussian Arms and surrounded by flags and trophies. Translucency, green, very poor. Sanding on and near base. Grey surface appearance. Height $6\frac{1}{4}$ inches. Chaffers. *circa* 1760. Probably from the Merton Thoms Collection (Exhibit No. 50, Liverpool Septcentenary Exhibition, 1907).

(*b*) Front view of mug shown on Plate 37 (*a*).

By permission of the Libraries, Museums and Arts Committee, Corporation of Liverpool

(*c*) Tea bowl, printed in sepia with a shepherd boy seated, minding sheep. Translucency, pale green. No shrinkage. Ht. $1\frac{5}{8}$ inches. 1760–70.

(d) Saucer, of deep shape, printed in purple with the 'tea party' (no servant, dog in foreground). Painted border in purple of feathered scrolls (No. 20). Translucency, blue, good. Diameter 4⅞ inches. 1765–70.

(e) Tea bowl and saucer, red printed with Harlequin and Columbine. Translucency, green and good, without flaws. Shrinkage present and no undercutting. Greyish appearance. Saucer diameter, 4⅝ inches. Cup diameter 2⅞ inches. 1760–70.

Plate 39

(a) Plate with scalloped edge and fluted rim, black printed with lovers seated under tree. Translucency, yellowish-green, good, with one or two flaws. Chien Lung shape, bluish-green glaze with bare areas on base. Diameter 6 inches. 1765–75.

(b) Cream jug with wavy rim, high lip and plain round loop handle having back-turned lower end, printed in brownish-black. On the reverse side — buildings in a small landscape. Footring small, no shrinkage. Grey surface appearance. Translucency, blue, good, with no flaws. Height 3½ inches. *circa* 1765. N P.

(c) Tea bowl, black printed. Translucency, blue, with one or two flaws. No shrinkage. Footring undercut: base very peppered. Diameter 3 inches. *circa* 1765.

(d) Plate similar to (a), black printed with a Liverpool version of the 'Tea party' (right-handed, page with kettle in right hand).

(e) Jug, of baluster shape showing 'L'Amour' black printed and in reverse. The other side of jug shown in Plate 36 (d). 1765–75.

(f) Mug of grey appearance, cylindrical, with flat strap handle and expanded base, black printed with Frederick II in armour and signed 'Sadler Liverp enaml' on the left. Engraved by Evans. Translucency, dirty grey, good. Narrow footring with shallow recessed base, some shrinkage and a few patches devoid of glaze. Height 4 inches. 1758–64.

(g) Mug or coffee can, with very small rounded loop handle and flat unglazed base, black printed with 'La Cascade', right handed and not reversed, as are most ceramic states of this print. Inside, a loopline border. Overfired to a light sepia in places. Translucency, pale straw, good. Height 2½ inches. *circa* 1760. P.

Plate 40

(a) Bowl, interior view. On the outside, a marine view and two men, one seated on an anchor holding a bowl, the other seated on a barrel, pistol in hand. Between them a chest labelled 'Spanish Gold'. No particulars except diameter 8½ inches. Traditionally Pennington. Dated 1779. See page 78.

By permission of the Libraries, Museums and Arts Committee, Corporation of Liverpool

(b) Vase, with ovoid body, slender neck rising to a cup-shaped expansion, pedestal foot and recessed base reached by a sloping bevel, printed in underglaze blue with convolvulus, pomegranates. Glaze even, greenish. Translucency, yellowish-green, good. Height 5 inches. 1770–?? P.

(c) Mug of cylindrical shape, with deeply grooved loop handle and flat unglazed base, painted in blue. Translucency, yellowish-green, with flaws. Glaze greenish-yellow and showing scum line at top. Height 4¾ inches. *circa* 1770. P.

(d) Vase, pear shaped with expanded base, recessed and bounded by a narrow footring, painted in blue. Translucency, yellowish-greency, good. Bluish glaze without defects. Height 3¾ inches. *circa* 1770. P.

(e) Vase of pear shape, with cover showing bird knop, blue painted in oriental manner.

The decoration is carried out with the greatest artistry and skill. Translucency, yellowish. Height 21 in. *circa* 1780. Pennington.

By courtesy of E. Allman, Esq.

Plate 41

(a) Jug, pear shaped, with mask spout, strap handle provided with thumb rest, a grooved foot and recessed base, blue painted and inscribed 'Robert Lewis 1783'. No particulars.

By courtesy of E. Allman, Esq.

(b) Vase and cover, the body pear shaped, the cover domed, with rounded knop, blue painted in semi-oriental style showing considerable artistry and skill. It is interesting to note that the blue band on the neck is marbled with brown instead of gold. Height 16½ inches. 1780–5.

(c) Punch pot with bird knop cover similar in form to that of the vase on Plate 40 (e) and intertwined handle, blue painted with a party scene in which figures a pot which is obviously meant to represent the article decorated. No particulars. See page 78.

By courtesy of E. Allman, Esq.

(d) Sauce boat on foot, with wavy rim and 'biting snake' handle, moulded externally on either side with a smiling 'mask' flanked by 'Livers' and below, a fruiting vine. Blue painted inside with formal scroll ornament. Translucency, greenish-yellow, showing flaws. Starch blue glaze. Length 7¼ inches. *circa* 1765.

Plate 42

(a) Coffee pot and cover, the body pear shaped, with pedestal foot, scroll handle with bifid lower end and showing feather moulding, painted with formal ornament in puce and green. Trellis border No. 34, the cover surmounted by a conical knop. Translucency, greenish-yellow, showing flaws. Height 7¾ inches. *circa* 1775.

(b) Plate, of tin glazed porcelain, painted in famille rose manner within a green trellis border. Slightly translucent in places. Diameter 8½ inches. Date uncertain. Page 34.

(c) Bowl, painted with stylized flowers: within, a border in red (28). Translucency, yellowish-green, good, showing many flaws. Starch blue glaze. No shrinkage. Undercut footring. Badly made, with many imperfections and badly decorated. Mark: cross in red. Diameter 6⅛ inches. *circa* 1775.

(d) Coffee cup, with grooved loop handle, printed in underglaze blue with addition of red and gold ('cut finger red'). Within, a trellis border in red and blue. Height 2¾ inches. *circa* 1785.

(e) Tea bowl painted in colours with a looped chain of small flowers suspended between borders Nos. 9 and 13 in blue. Translucency, dirty white, but good. Blue glaze, with no shrinkage. Strong footring. Height 1⅞ inches. 1780–90.

(f) Coffee cup, painted in oriental manner in iron red and blue. Within, a trellis border. Translucency, quite brown. Strong footring, no shrinkage. Height 2⅝ inches. 1780–95.

(g) Coffee cup, with grooved loop handle, painted in colours with the sparse use of gilding. Border inside of red and blue trellis interrupted by scrollwork. Translucency, brown. Height 2⅝ inches. 1785–95.

(h) Tea bowl painted with the 'pilgrim shell' in blue with the addition of iron red and yellow overglaze. Translucency, brownish, good. Height 1⅞ inches. 1785–95.

(i) Coffee cup, with grooved loop handle, painted in colours. Inside, a border in iron red (No. 29). Translucency, pale greenish-yellow, good, without flaws. Clear glaze and well potted. No shrinkage. Height 2¼ inches. 1765–75.

Plate 43

(*a*) Saucer painted in colours with 'the scolding woman'. Deep shape and dirty glaze. Translucency, whitish-brown, good. No shrinkage. Diameter $5\frac{1}{8}$ inches. 1790–1800.

(*b*) Saucer painted in colours, in mock Chinese style. Deep shape. Translucency, whitish-brown, good. Dirty glaze, with no shrinkage. Border No. 30. *circa* 1795.

(*c*) Plate painted in colours and inscribed w. m. mercer. No potting details available. *circa* 1792.

By courtesy of E. Allman, Esq.

(*d*) Tea bowl and saucer, painted in colours with 'Chinese' figures in a landscape. Translucency, yellowish-green. No glaze shrinkage. Thundercloud effect on base with peppering. Saucer diameter $4\frac{3}{4}$ inches. Cup height $1\frac{3}{4}$ inches. 1780–90.

(*e*) Bowl painted in red and blue with traces of gilding. Bluish-green glaze showing crazing. Translucency, brown. Good footring with no shrinkage. Diameter $4\frac{7}{8}$ inches. *circa* 1785.

(*f*) Mug, ogee shaped with grooved foot, painted in colours with a man seated at a table under a tree and inscribed 'James Boulton' with date 1792. Height $3\frac{3}{4}$ inches.

By courtesy of E. Allman, Esq.

(*g*) Cream jug on a high foot, helmet shaped and with 'biting snake' handle, painted in colours in the Chinese style. Within, a deep trellis border in pinkish-red. Translucency, pale greenish-white, good. Hollow based with narrow footring. Height $3\frac{7}{8}$ inches. *circa* 1785.

Plate 44

(*a*) Tea bowl and saucer, painted in underglaze blue and red, with trellis border in same colours. Translucency, greenish-white, good. Blue glaze with no shrinkage. No flaws. Saucer diameter $4\frac{3}{4}$ inches. Cup diameter $2\frac{7}{8}$ inches. Height $1\frac{1}{2}$ inches. 1765–75.

(*b*) Tea bowl and saucer, painted in underglaze blue and red, with trellis border in same colours. Translucency, green, good. No shrinkage. Footring undercut. Saucer diameter 5 inches. Cup height $1\frac{3}{4}$ inches. 1760–70. *cf.* Plate 11 (*b*).

(*c*) Teapot and cover, the body globular, with plain loop handle and plain curved spout, painted in underglaze blue and red. Good footring with no shrinkage. Cover knop conical, flange glazed. Seven holes in spout. Translucency? tea stained. Height $5\frac{3}{4}$ inches. 1770–80. *cf.* Plate 48 (*b*).

(*d*) Saucer painted in underglaze blue and red, with trellis border in same colours. A variation of (*a*). Translucency, blue, good, without flaws. No shrinkage. Diameter 5 inches. 1765–75.

Plate 45

(*a*) Tea bowl and saucer, the latter of deep shape, underglaze blue printed. Translucency, brownish-white, good, without flaws. Dirty bluish glaze, showing no shrinkage. Saucer diameter $5\frac{1}{8}$ inches. Cup diameter $3\frac{1}{4}$ inches. Height $1\frac{1}{2}$ inches. *circa* 1795.

(*b*) Tea bowl, coffee cup and saucer, reeded with crenate edges and blue painted with the 'pilgrim shell' pattern. Translucency, whitish-blue, good. Starch blue glaze tending to collect in pools. Saucer diameter $5\frac{1}{8}$ inches. Coffee cup height $2\frac{3}{8}$ inches. Bowl — no details. 1770–80. Same mould as Plate 21 (*f*).

(*c*) Cream jug on pedestal foot, with reeded body and 'biting snake' handle, blue painted with formal sprays. Border No. 12. Recessed base, greenish blue glaze. Translucency, yellowish-green, good, no flaws. Height 4 inches. *circa* 1775.

(d) Cream jug, with pinched lip and grooved loop handle, underglaze blue printed. Translucency, dirty greenish-yellow. Bluish-green glaze, with no shrinkage. Cell border surmounting chain of fleur de lys. Height $3\frac{1}{4}$ inches. 1780–90.

(e) Mug, bell shaped, with plain loop handle and deeply grooved foot blue printed (sticky blue). Translucency, pale green to brownish in thicker parts, good. Footring narrow, base recessed, bluish-green glaze. Height $3\frac{3}{4}$ inches. *circa* 1780.

Plate 46

(a) Tea bowl and deep saucer, blue painted. Translucency, dirty white becoming brownish in thicker parts. Dirty grey-green glaze, with no shrinkage. Borders Nos. 5, 13. Saucer diameter $5\frac{1}{4}$ inches. Cup height $1\frac{7}{8}$ inches. 1775–95.

(b) Tea bowl and deep saucer, blue printed (overglaze). Translucency and glaze as (a). Border No. 17. The 'sticky blue'. Saucer diameter $5\frac{3}{8}$ inches. Cup height $2\frac{1}{8}$ inches. 1775–95.

(c) Plate with fluted rim and crenate edge, blue printed (?underglaze) and overpainted in blue. The subject is from a painting by Gainsborough and versions of this print occur on Worcester porcelain. Translucency, yellowish-green, poor in thicker parts. Greenish glaze with bare areas on base. Chien Lung shape. Border No. 18. Diameter $6\frac{1}{4}$ inches. *circa* 1775.

(d) Saucer, underglaze blue printed. Translucency, green, fairly good, with flaws. Glaze greenish with thundercloud patches. Undercut. Diameter 5 inches. This probably represents an early underglaze print, 1765–70.

Plate 47

(a) Coffee pot and cover, the body pear shaped, with scroll handle, curving spout and deeply grooved foot, printed in underglaze blue, with printed border No. 17. In these later examples, the tag at the lower end of the handle has assumed a backward direction. Base recessed, one large hole for spout. Cover domed with conical knop. Dirty greenish glaze, with thundercloud patches. Translucency, straw to brownish. Height 9 inches. *circa* 1775–85.

(b) Tea bowl and saucer, blue painted. Translucency, straw, brownish in thicker parts. Starch blue glaze; tea bowl with wedge footring. Saucer diameter $5\frac{1}{4}$ inches. Cup diameter $3\frac{1}{4}$ inches, height $2\frac{1}{4}$ inches. 1775–85.

(c) Plate of Chien Lung shape, blue painted on a printed foundation. Interrupted trellis border in blue and brown edge. Greenish glaze, showing some bare areas on base. Translucency, brownish, very poor. Diameter $8\frac{1}{2}$ inches. 1775–90.

(d) Saucer, of deep shape, painted with 'Chinese' figures in colours. Translucency, pale greenish-white. Dirty greenish glaze, thin and showing bare areas within footring. Not undercut. Diameter $4\frac{7}{8}$ inches. 1780–90.

Plate 48

(a) Tea bowl and saucer, blue painted with 'peg top and ramp' pattern. Trellis border. Translucency, bluish-green, good. Dirty greenish glaze. Undercut footring. No shrinkage. Saucer diameter $4\frac{3}{4}$ inches. Cup height $1\frac{5}{8}$ inches. 1765–75. A well known pattern, used at many factories, including Worcester and Caughley, over probably a long period of time.

(b) Coffee cup and saucer, blue painted. Translucency, green. Glaze, dirty greyish-green (saucer), with no shrinkage. Saucer diameter 5 inches. Cup height $2\frac{3}{8}$ inches. 1770–85.

(c) Sauce boat, with narrow body on a pedestal foot and with high angular handle, the body moulded with acanthus foliage rising from the base and with a pearled beading on the rim.

A blue print partly overlaps the acanthus moulding (to its detriment); and within, a lace-like border (No. 8). The handle may be a development of 'biting snake'. Translucency, brownish (some examples show good green translucency). Length 6¼ inches. 1780–1800.

(*d*) Sauce boat similar to (*c*) in moulding, but less well made and having an incised cross on the base. Translucency, brownish. Length 6¼ inches.

Plate 49

(*a*) Sauce boat, with leaf moulding under the lip, a high scroll handle, flat unglazed base and a grooved foot edged with twisted rope moulding, printed in blue underglaze. Translucency, greenish-white, becoming brownish in thicker parts. Dirty green glaze. Length 6½ inches. 1780–1800.

(*b*) Tea bowl, blue painted with much smudging. A glassy paste, with good pale green translucency. Creamy glaze showing a scum line and sanding, but no shrinkage. Inside, a cell border surmounting a chain of fleur de lys. Height 3⅜ inches. 1780–1800.

(*c*) Coffee pot and cover, with potting features resembling Plate 47 (*a*), blue painted. Loopline border. Crazing present. Height 8½ inches. 1775–90.

(*d*) Teapot and cover, the body globular, with plain handle and spout, the cover with conical knop and glazed flange, blue painted. Creamy glaze showing crazing. Translucency — tea stained. Border No. 14. Height 6½ inches. 1780–1800. The appearance — and of (*c*) also — is that of creamware.

(*e*) Tea bowl, moulded externally with an encircling band of foliate scrolls above spiral reeding and surmounted by a cell border carrying a chain of fleur de lys in blue. Starch blue glaze filling the angles of a narrow but strong wedge-shaped footring. Translucency, green, becoming brownish towards base. Diameter 3½ inches. Height 2¼ inches. 1775–85.

(*f*) Mug, cylindrical, with grooved loop handle and flat unglazed base, blue-printed with 'fisherman and sail' pattern. Inside, a cell and fleur de lys border. Translucency, pale yellowish-green, good. Height 2⅝ inches. 1775–85.

(*g*) Coffee cup, with grooved loop handle, blue painted in Chinese manner. Translucency, yellowish-green. Strong foot. Starch blue glaze. No shrinkage. Crazing present. Height 2½ inches. 1770–90.

Plate 50

Bases and footrings referred to in the text, and some of the more unusual marks. On (*g*) the much talked-of letters 'H P' in under-glaze blue are indistinctly seen.

THE PLATES

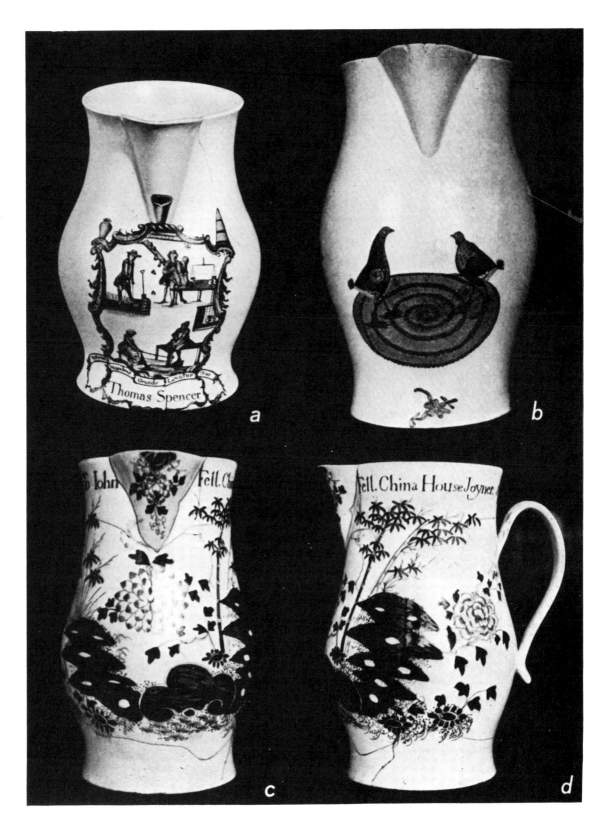

PLATE 1

PLATE 2

PLATE 3

PLATE 4

PLATE 5

PLATE 6

PLATE 7

PLATE 8

PLATE 9

PLATE 10

PLATE 11

PLATE 12

PLATE 13

PLATE 14

PLATE 15

PLATE 16

PLATE 17

PLATE 18

PLATE 19

PLATE 20

PLATE 21

PLATE 22

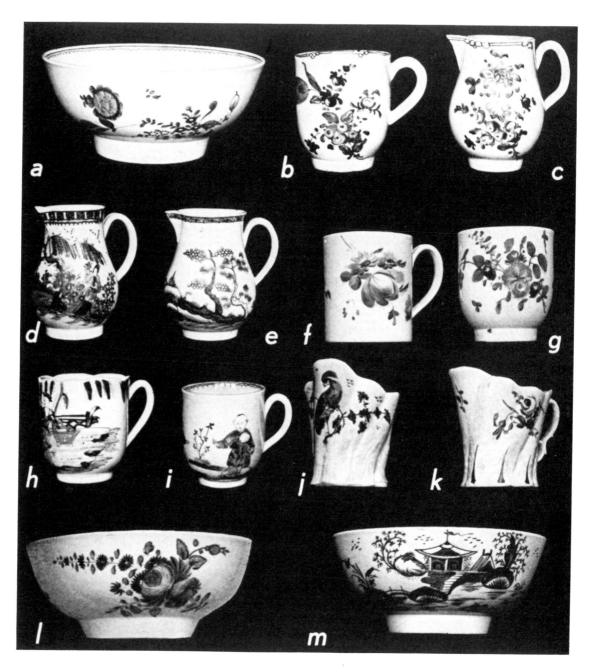

PLATE 23

PLATE 24

PLATE 25

PLATE 26

PLATE 27

PLATE 28

PLATE 29

PLATE 30

PLATE 31

PLATE 32

PLATE 33

PLATE 34

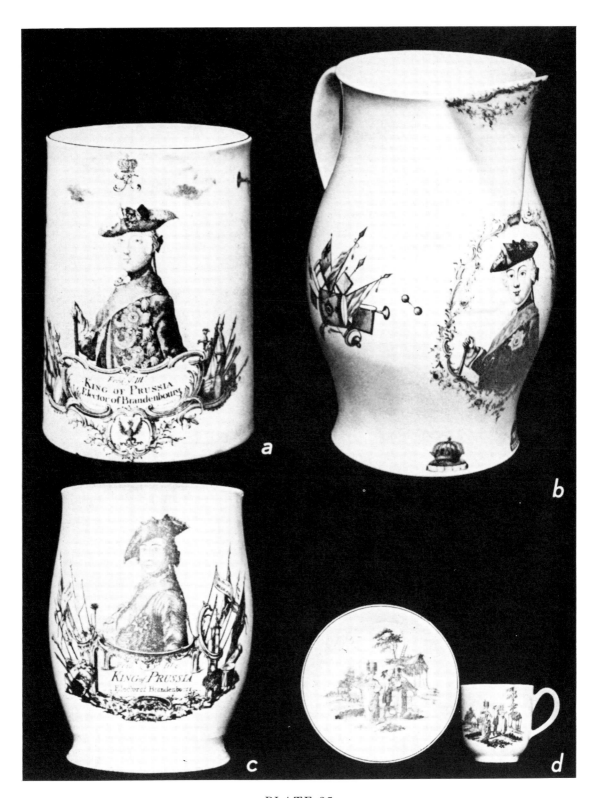

PLATE 35

PLATE 36

PLATE 37

PLATE 38

PLATE 39

PLATE 40

PLATE 41

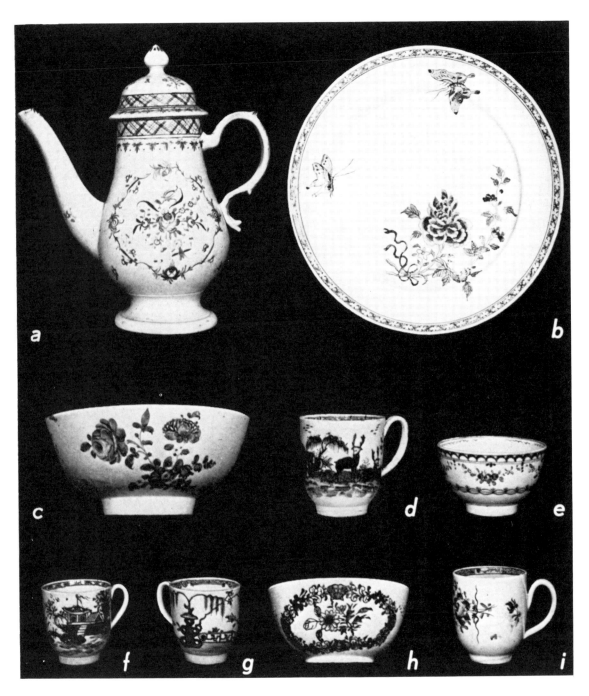

PLATE 42

PLATE 43

PLATE 44

PLATE 45

PLATE 46

PLATE 47

PLATE 48

PLATE 49

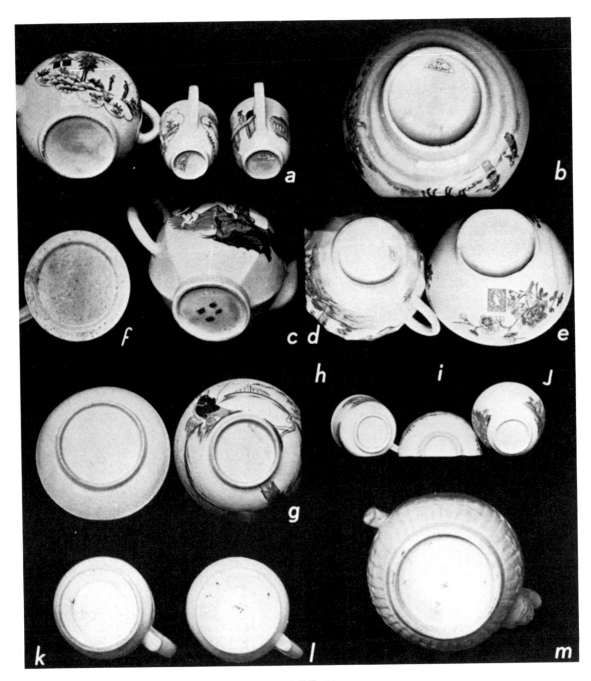

PLATE 50

THE AGREEMENT

ARTICLES OF AGREEMENT indented made concluded and fully agreed upon this fourteenth day of June One thousand seven hundred and fifty five BETWEEN ROBERT PADMORE of the city of Worcester Potter of the first part RICHARD CHAFFERS of Liverpool in the County of Lancaster Potter of the second part and PHILIP CHRISTIAN of Liverpoole aforesaid Potter of the third part

WHEREAS the said Robert Padmore is said to be very knowing and expert in the making painting and burning of earthenware in imitation of and to resemble Chinaware THEREFORE the said parties have agreed to be and Co-partners in carrying on the trade or business of making mending and selling of Earthenware in imitation of and to resemble Chinaware at such convenient place or places in Liverpoole aforesaid as shall be fixed and agreed upon by and between the said Parties for and during the Term and space of seven years next ensuing the date hereof upon the Terms Conditions and agreements hereinafter mentioned

AND FIRST the said Robert Padmore doth hereby for himself covenant promise grant and agree to and with the said Richard Chaffers and Philip Christian in manner following (that is to say that he the said Robert Padmore shall and will at all times during the said Term of seven years use his utmost care diligence skill knowledge and judgment in the making painting and complete finishing of the said Earthen ware in imitation of Chinaware and in the direction management and superintending of the said work and of the Labourers Servants and others to be employed in carrying on of said work

AND ALSO that he the said Robert Padmore shall and will with what expedition he can teach inform and instruct the said Richard Chaffers and Philip Christian in the Art and Mystery of making of the said Earthenware in imitation of or to resemble Chinaware in the best way or manner he can and fully communicate to them the secret thereof and shall not or will for or upon any Terms or considerations whatsoever in anywise discover publish communicate or make known the said Art to any other Person or Persons whatsoever or be concerned with any other person or persons in carrying on the said Trade or Business during the said Term of Seven years

AND the said Richard Chaffers and Philip Christian in consideration of the said Robert Padmore's working at the said business of making Earthen ware in imitation of Chinaware as aforesaid and in the management ordering and directing the carrying on of the said work they the said Richard Chaffers and Philip Christian shall and will provide a sufficient sum of money Stock and find for the said carrying on of the said Trade or Business extensively and to advantage and shall and will use their utmost endeavours therein for the good and benefit of the said Partnership

ALSO it is agreed between the said parties that the said Robert Padmore shall have and receive out of the said Partnership Stock and concern the sum of One pound one shilling weekly and every week for his Labour care diligence and superintending of the said work during the continuance of this Partnership

ALSO that the charge and expense of one or more building or buildings to be rented or taken and the Materials to be bought and used and workmen and Servants to be employed in the carrying on of the said work and all other charges and expenses attending the carrying on of the said Partnership Trade and Business shall be born and paid by and out of the said Partnership Stock and concern and the Accounts thereof and of all the buyings sellings charges and outgoings relating thereto shall be kept in a just fair and regular manner and settled and adjusted once in every year during the said Term and the said Robert Padmore shall have receive unto one twelfth part or share of the nett profits which shall arise or be gotten by or in the said Partnership Trade during the said Term of seven years and the said Richard Chaffers and Philip Christian shall have and be equally entitled unto the other eleven twelfth parts of the nett profits arising or to arise by or from the said Partnership Trade and a dividend of the said profits shall be made at the end of every year of the Term aforesaid

ALSO it is agreed between the said parties that if upon a Trial of the said Trade or Business it shall appear that the same will not answer the design of the said Copartners or bring in sufficient profit to the said parties with respect to the stock or Capital to be employed therein and to the said parties care trouble and expense in carrying on the said Business that then and in such case the said Richard Chaffers and Philip Christian shall have power to dissolve and put an end to the said Copartnership at any time during the said term upon giving three month notice thereof in writing to the said Robert Padmore.

ALSO the said Richard Chaffers and Philip Christian do hereby covenant promise and agree to and with the said Robert Padmore that they or either of them shall not or will communicate the secret of making the said Earthen ware which they shall be informed or learn from the said Robert Padmore to any person or persons whatsoever neither shall they or either of them be concerned to carry on the Trade of making such like Earthen ware with any other person or persons during the said Term of seven years AND LASTLY for the true performance of all and every the Covenants Clauses Articles and Agreements herein contained the Parties aforesaid do hereby bind and oblige themselves and each of them their and each of their Heirs Executors and Administrators unto the other of them in the penal sum of five hundred pounds of lawful money of Great Britain to be forfeited and paid by the party failing in the Performance of those presents unto the Party or parties performing the same IN WITNESS whereof the said parties to those presents their hands and seals have hereunto interchangeably set the day and year first above written SEALED and delivered (on paper duly stamped) in presence of us.

Eliz. Harrison
Jas. Rigby

Robert Padmore
Richard Chaffers
Philip Christian

*   *   *

AND it is hereby further agreed between the said parties before the execution of the within Articles that in case any of the said parties during the continuance of the said Copartnership shall happen to die that the principal Stock of the said Copartnership shall be valued and the share thereof of him or them so dying shall be forthwith paid to the Executors or Administrators of him or them so dying in full discharge of his or their share thereof.

Witnessed   Eliz. Harrison
             Jas. Rigby

Robert Padmore
Richard Chaffers
Philip Christian

We whose names are underwritten to be conformable to every article contained in the within articles of Partnership for the Term of three years to commence from the 22nd of January 1763 and to be complete and   22nd January 1766 as witness our hand this eighteenth day of April 1763.

    Witness

          William Heskin   Robert Padmore
                                                     Richard Chaffers
                                                       Philip Christian

* * *

NOTES

1 Reference has been made to the part played by Richard Holdship in the purchase of the Cornish soaprock lease from Benjamin Lund's Bristol company (page 13 and footnote). This company is said to have been engaged in using this soaprock in 'making Earthenware in imitation of China Ware' (A. J. Toppin, Trans. E.C.C., volume 3, 1954, page 134). The use of the same words in this Liverpool Agreement seems to represent a link with the older company for which only Podmore could be responsible.

2 The witnesses. Elizabeth Harrison was probably the wife of Lawrence Harrison, delftware potter (page 160). James Rigby, potter, was in partnership with John Roscoe, uncle of William Roscoe. Their pottery on Shaws Brow adjoined that of Samuel Gilbody on the east side. Rigby's name appears as a potter in the Voters List of 1761 and his Will was proved at Chester in 1768.

3 Although the original document of this Agreement has been lost, the copy in my possession here reproduced is clearly the document to which Gatty refers at the beginning of his letter of 28th December 1907 (Appendix IIIA (2). It is executed in copper plate and was made by an old-established firm of Dublin lawyers on paper watermarked with the firm's name on every sheet, thus establishing at once the accuracy of the copy and providing the strongest presumptive evidence of the authenticity of the document copied.

Letter from John Rosson, of Moor Hall, Ormskirk Lancashire, to the Editor of the *Liverpool Mercury*, dated 12th May 1854

The Arts and Manufactures of Liverpool from 1760–1780.

'Gentlemen:—In your impression of Tuesday, 18th ult. is a very interesting "Biographical sketch of Mr. John Wyke, with remarks on the Arts and Manufactures of Liverpool from 1760–1780", by Messrs Roberts and Pigeon. In the Society for the Promotion of the Fine Arts, established in 1769,[1] there were individuals whose talents and acquirements give a flat contradiction to the flippant observation of Derrick, the obsequious tuft hunter of my Lord Cork and other literary men of rank of the period.[2]

'Messrs Roberts and Pigeon in their excellent article, merely glance at the existence of a branch of industry at that time most extensively carried on in Liverpool, namely, the manufacture of earthenware, porcelain and blue-and-white earthenware. No doubt these gentlemen would have given a detailed description of the "eleven manufactories" had they been in possession of materials for such a purpose.

'A history of the porcelain and earthenware manufacture cultivated at that period in Liverpool has long been a desideratum in our local annals; and the great cause of the paucity of materials arose from the sudden death of Mr. Richard Chaffers, who, at that time, by his great talents, enterprise and industry had placed himself at the head of the art.

'It has often been a source of deep regret to me and other descendants of that distinguished individual that so few particulars of his life have come down to us. This partly arose from his sudden death at the early age of forty, in the midst of a career of unexampled success, promising the acquisition of wealth (to use an expression of Dr. Johnson) "beyond the dreams of avarice". That melancholy bereavement was viewed as a great calamity to the Town as well as to his family; and it might well be so designated, for the porcelain manufacture for which Liverpool was becoming so famed died with him.

'Mr. Chaffers resided at the bottom of Dale Street in a handsome house built for him by his father and removed a few years ago to make room for improvements. His manufactory consisted of a range of most extensive works situated on the North side of Shaws Brow and nearly occupying the whole of that locality. His mould houses were on the site of Islington Terrace. An idea may be formed of the extent of his business when it is stated that one hundred of his men polled for Sir William Meredith. His furnaces were watched by twenty-five firemen. Many of the small houses on the south side of Shaws Brow, recently removed, were occupied by his workmen. Mr. Chaffers, after having profitably carried on the manufacture of the more common blue and white earthenware which was largely exported to our American colonies, now the United States, began to feel the pressure of a most formidable rival in the person of the celebrated Mr. Wedgwood of Staffordshire, whose ingenious labours and the genius and skill of those who followed him have achieved a world-wide fame. At that period the knowledge and use of the clay called soaprock were confined to few. The districts in the county of *Cornwall* where that invaluable article *existed were leased out to others.* In truth, *Mr. Chaffers saw that the days of the Liverpool manufacture were numbered unless the same material could be procured.* In this *he was confirmed by a very clever person of the name*

---

[1] Liverpool's first Society of Art was founded in 1769, only one year after the Royal Academy, with P. P. Burdett as its first President.

[2] The reference is not clear, perhaps to something in the criticized article, but is not pertinent to the matter in hand.

of Podmore, who, although not a scientific person or a geologist (Mr. Chaffers was both) *was nevertheless a very superior practical man.*

'*Mr. Podmore had been in the service of Mr. Wedgwood, but left it from a wish to establish himself as a manufacturer in America. On coming to Liverpool to embark for that country, he called upon Mr. Chaffers as the leading man in the trade. They entered into a long conversation, in the course of which Podmore exhibited so much intelligence and practical knowledge, that Mr. Chaffers, by a most liberal offer, induced him to forego his American project and enter into his service.*

'*Mr. Chaffers object now was to come into the field with Staffordshire, pari materia, if I may be allowed that play upon words. He therefore determined to set out for Cornwall upon the forlorn hope of discovering a vein of soaprock. The operations would be most expensive and laborious, somewhat akin to the process of boring for coal in our county. But where was he to begin? On whose estate was it to be found? What description of men was he to employ. He was, however, in the prime of manhood, of untiring energy, of fine address and, what was then necessary, an excellent horseman. He obtained letters of intro-duction from the Earl of Derby, Lord Strange, his eldest son and other men of consequence in our county, to some of the leading landowners in Cornwall, then attending their duty in Parliament.*

'*In those days there were no mail coaches and railways to aid the weary traveller. A stout horse was the only means of conveyance for a man of the higher class. Imagine Mr. Chaffers, having taken leave of his wife and numerous family and friends, mounted with a pair of saddle-bags under him containing a supply of linen, etc., a thousand guineas, the first instalment, to pay the wages of the miners, a brace of pistols in his holsters, pur-suing his journey to London. He had made considerable progress in practical geology, though the science was then but little cultivated. Having during his stay in London obtained permission to bore for soaprock from more than one of the principal proprietors of mountain land he judged most likely to yield it, he proceeded to Cornwall and commenced operations. His first efforts were not successful. He moved to another quarter with no better result: in a word, he expended large sums of money without finding the wished-for vein. Somewhat disheartened, but not subdued, he determined to return home, where his presence was much wanted. He did not, however, intend to abandon but only to suspend his operations. He accordingly assembled all the miners in his employ and announced to them, to their great regret, his determination. Previously to his departure, he scrupulously paid every man his wages. One of them was missing; he was told the man in question had gone up the mountain to try another place. He then left that man's wages in the hands of the "captain of the gang", and, mounting his horse with a heavy heart, took leave of the men, to whom his animated and conciliatory manners had greatly endeared him.*

'*The road to the nearest town, the name of which I never could learn, was precipitous and rugged. A traveller on horseback made so little progress that a mountaineer on foot, by taking a short cut over the rocky crags, could easily come within earshot of him. After journeying for some little time, he thought he heard a faint cry in the distance. He dis-mounted and, ascending a hill, plainly saw the signal of discovery flying from a lofty peak. It appeared that the man, who had separated from his fellow miners and pursued his researches alone, had discovered a vein and on coming back to headquarters and finding that Mr. Chaffers had left them, he hoisted the pre-concerted signal and pursued him across the mountain with the pleasing intelligence, shouting at times to attract the somewhat dispirited traveller's attention.*

'*Mr. Chaffers immediately returned, took the whole gang into permanent employment and obtained an ample supply of the long sought for clay, which was conveyed to the nearest port and shipped thence to Liverpool. On its arrival, the vessel entered with its precious freight into the Old Dock, dressed in colours amidst the cheers of the assembled spectators.*

'*Mr. Chaffers had regularly corresponded with his wife during his absence but on his arrival in London on his return home, the continued fatigue he had endured, together with anxiety of mind, brought on a dangerous fever, under which he laboured for several weeks. He was unknown at the inn, but the landlord, seeing that his guest — a very hand-some man — had the dress and demeanour of a gentleman, called in an eminent physician who sedulously and skilfully attended his patient. The doctor examined his* portmanteau *and, having ascertained his name and address from the letters and papers therein, commu-nicated to his anxious wife all the particulars of his illness and concluded with the con-soling intelligence that* "*he could that day pronounce him out of danger*". *As soon as he could travel he delighted his family and friends with his presence in Liverpool* and com-menced that career which, if his life had been spared, would have made his native town famous for her porcelain and given her as high a rank in the manufacturing as she has since attained in the commercial world.

'*The sad tale of the sudden death of this eminent citizen remains to be told. Podmore, his favourite foreman, was seized some years after the events narrated with a malignant fever, without hope of recovery. The unfortunate sufferer sent a message declaring* "*his wish to see his dear master once more before their final separation*". *Mr. Chaffers, a man of full and sanguine habit, most imprudently complied and shortly after took the fever, to which he fell a victim. He was interred in the old churchyard of St. Nicholas, near the grave of his faithful servant,* leaving an agonised wife and numerous family to bewail his untimely death.

'*This unfortunate event, by taking away both master and principal assistant, put an end to the prosecution of the trade and was the commencement of the breaking up of that branch of the art which Mr. Chaffers had mainly brought to such a high state of perfection. A great number of the potters ultimately emigrated to America* and the business was ultimately transferred to Staffordshire.

'*It is said that when Mr. Wedgwood heard of the death of Mr. Chaffers, like a generous competitor he exhibited very sincere regret and acknowledged that he must ultimately have yielded the palm to his rival in certain branches, from his experience as a chemist, his pro-found knowledge of the art of compounding colours and their more economical preparation.*

'I have now, gentlemen, simply narrated what I have heard from an excellent mother, a daughter of Mr. Chaffers. It was always a most painful subject, for his death entailed many calamities on his surviving family. I have given this slight sketch with a view of eliciting from a better chronicler something more of the doings of Richard Chaffers than I, the last surviving grandson, am able to narrate.

'Mr. Chaffers had the pen of a ready writer and was an accomplished sportsman. He en-joyed the honour of the acquaintance and friendship of Lord Strange, the grandfather of the present Earl of Derby. At that time as you are aware, Mr. Editor, the eldest son of the Stanleys of Knowsley took that title. Lord Strange, a universal sportsman, patronised the cock pit; and the punch bowls then so much in use manufactured by Mr. Chaffers blazed with repre-sentations of the gallant battles of the spurred favourites of the noble lord, who imbued his son Edward, the accomplished sporting Earl as he was called, with all that love of the chase, the turf and the cockpit for which he was so long and so deservedly celebrated

Yours etc.,

Moorhall. 9th May 1854.   John Rosson.'

The italicized words indicate the extent of Mayer's copying in his *History*.

'P.S. I possess a portrait of Mr. Chaffers, "Kit-cat" size. The costume resembles the court dress of a private gentleman of the present day. I have only one specimen of his blue-and-white ware and one cup of his porcelain. I have been told that there are specimens of his manufacture in the old china collections of Knowsley; also at Wrightington Hall near Wigan, the ancient seat of the Dicconsons, now the property of Charles Scarisbrick Esq.'

Letters referring to the 1755 Agreement

1   Lord Cross to C. T. Gatty.   Entwistle MSS. 7/190.

Eccles Riggs,
Broughton in Furness.
November 27th 1907

'Replying to yours of 23rd, I have looked over such papers as I can find here about
Richard Chaffers. I perfectly remember the letters to which you allude and I believe
that I sent them many years ago to Mr. Mayer, silversmith, Lord Street, Liverpool,
who was writing something on the subject of Liverpool potteries. I know that he sent
them back but I cannot find them now, and am afraid they may have either been mislaid or destroyed as of no value. However I enclose two papers which are all I can find.
The letter to the *Liverpool Mercury* was, I believe, written by a Mr. Rosson, who lived
at Ormskirk.

Faithfully yours,
Cross.

*   *   *

2   C. T. Gatty to Peter Entwistle.   Entwistle MSS. 7/146.

Irish Art Companions,
28 Clare Street, DUBLIN.
December 28th 1907.

'He enclosed a good agreement between Chaffers, Christian and Podmore which I am
copying and a most interesting account of Chaffers sent to the *Liverpool Mercury*
years ago by Rosson. Do you know this?
The copy Lord Cross sends me is on paper with watermark 1852 so I suppose Rosson's
letter was then or thereabouts. It is not dated itself. Can you look up the old *Mercuries*.
Have written to encourage him to find the letters. It is a disaster if they are lost. Sending
copies of documents later. Return Cross' letter and keep copy. . . .

*   *   *

3   Richard Assheton Cross. 1823–1914. First Baron Cross, born at Preston. Third son of
    William Cross by his wife, Ellen, eldest daughter of Edward Chaffers of Liverpool
    and Everton, a collateral relative of Richard Chaffers. Educ. Rugby under Arnold
    and Trinity Coll. Cambs. Rowed in First Trinity boat. Pres. C.U. Called to Bar 1849.
    Father and grand father had held legal office in the County Palatine Court of Common
    Pleas at Preston. He became leader of the Preston and Salford Quarter Sessions Bar.
    Returned to Parliament as Conservative member 1857–1862. The death of his father in
    1860 led to his becoming a partner in Parr's Bank, Warrington and to the giving up
    of his Bar practice and his seat in Parliament later. He defeated Gladstone in 1868,
    became Chairman of Parr's Bank in 1870 and was Home Secretary in 1874. (N.D.B.)

4 Comments on this correspondence.

It will be noticed that in Gatty's letter to Entwistle, the words occur, 'The copy Lord Cross sends me is on paper with watermark 1852, so I suppose Rosson's letter was then or thereabouts. It is not dated itself'.

This does not refer to the Agreement, as might at first be thought, but to Rosson's letter, which had been copied and sent to Lord Cross. It is reasonable to suppose that Mayer did this at the time he returned whatever it was he had borrowed (presumably Teppit's letters). At the date Rosson wrote to the *Mercury*, Mayer was advertising regularly in its pages as a silversmith, giving good reason for believing that he would know if such a letter were written.

*   *   *

The equanimity with which the discovery of this original document is greeted seems strangely contrasted with the loss of Teppit's letters, which is viewed as a disaster. Were this loss confirmed, these letters had been thoroughly examined, reported upon and extracts made from their contents. One would think that, as Mayer presumably saw them after the notice they received in 'M. & M', if anything of importance had been overlooked, he would have published it.

Extracts from *Marks and Monograms,* Fourth Edition, 1874, by William Chaffers

1 P.733. 'Through the kindness of R. Assheton Cross Esq., M.P., we are enabled to give the date of his operations in Cornwall; he has favoured us with the perusal of a bundle of letters from one, Gauregan Teppit, a miner, addressed to Mr. Chaffers in Liverpool, by whom he was engaged to draw soap-rock at Mullion, Cornwall, on some land which he had leased for the purpose. These letters range over a period of eleven years, from July 1756 to December 1767; it was therefore about 1755 that the expedition to Cornwall just described was undertaken'.

*   *   *

2 Referring to Teppit's letters (page 733), the author of M. & M. goes on to say, 'These letters show that in 1756 he was procuring soap-rock from Mullion in large quantities, for making his porcelain at Liverpool . . . '. Extracts from some fifteen or sixteen are given, with a note that the last of the series, addressed to Edward Chaffers, was dated December 10th 1767.

No very accurate estimate of the total amount of soap-rock sent to Liverpool during this time can be made from these letters. The work took place mainly in the summer months. In one letter it is stated (1760) 'We began in April and left over in November'. In August of that year Teppit writes, 'Hope to hear the last parcel of clay arrived safe and well, will send ten tun in the next'. The following year (May), he talks about raising two or three hundred a day, while in 1762 he writes, 'We raise half a tun of a day'. The amount seems to have varied considerably and doubtless depended on the size of the pocket being worked at the time. A shipload was about ten tons, packed in thirty-five casks. Between 14th July 1763 and 5th October of that year, no less than thirty-two tons were sent. This may have been an unusual year, but perusal of this correspondence leads one to think that up to the date of Chaffers' death, something between two and three hundred tons of soaprock were dispatched, perhaps averaging twenty-five tons a year. (According to information obtained from Holdship's bankruptcy proceedings, published by A. J. Toppin in E. C. C. Transactions, 1954, volume 3, page 135, the annual amount taken by the Worcester factory was twenty tons.)

APPENDIX IVA

Extracts from Sadler's letters to Wedgwood

1 In a contra account of S. & G. to Wedgwood, the following entries occur.

1761.	Dec. 9.	To a china Pint Tythe Pig	.	.	.	.	.	.	.	3–6
		a K. Pruss. Enam, blank.	.	.	.	.	.	.		2–6
		a Mid. size print T. Pot.	.	.	.	.	.	.		1–0
1762.	Jan. 1.	A China Pint .	.	.	.	.	.	.	.	3–6
	Feb. 26.	Pd. for a Mill	.	.	.	.	.	.	.	2–18–9
	Nov. 26.	Apparatus for Tiles	.	.	.	.	.	.	.	1–14–6
1763.	April 15.	Crate of Tiles	.	.	.	.	.	.	.	5–13–4

* * *

2 26th January 1763. '. . . I wanted also to have talked a little about the prices we must sell at. Pray send me your Wholesale and Retail prices. We shall only supply Liverpool Shops & Exportation.'

* * *

3 6th February 1763. '. . . In one of the Red Crates you'll find a few red half pints, Heads — should be glad of your opinion of 'em — We think they'll be as saleable as the black'.

* * *

4 11th March 1763. '. . . We shall try further to improve our Red — we shall open our shop (Nr. Reid's) in a few weeks . . .'.

* * *

5 29th April 1763. '. . . Prints will be of more service to us than any subjects we can get designed on purpose, because a Designer will take more pains when, the sale, and consequently his advantage, depends on the Merit of his Performance, than he would when he expects to be paid for it, good or bad — Besides, the top draughts men will not copy anything that is publish'd, unless particularly insisted on. . . .'

* * *

6 27th March 1763. '. . . In the next parcel of ware you send us, don't fail to send a Doz. Pint Mugs — and two Doz. Half Pint Mugs (half straight and half bellied) of your best biscuit- We are trying for a white Glaze, wch. may be of Advantage — Don't fail. . . .'

* * *

7 31st March 1763. '. . . Mr. Sam. Wale (who lives in Little Court, Castle St. near Newport Street) is the principal Person that designs for us. He is a good natur'd Man, and of great Merit. Should you see him, I dare say he Wd. sketch you a Pattern or two exactly to your Taste; for he is very obliging.'

* * *

8 5th April 1763. '. . . The landskip is Mr. Wale's Design and I think a very good one in every kind . . .'

203

9 8th May 1763. ' . . . Have this day recd. some Drawings from Mr. Wale, among wch. is Harvest Home. We have finished our tiles and shall set hard to cream colour. . . . '

* * *

10 10th June 1763. ' . . . Mr. Ball tells me the Pint Mugs will take sixpence each in powder Gold to gild them on the edge. You'll find some pints edg'd with red. We think it is no addition, but if you like, it may easily be done . . . '

* * *

11 2nd July 1763. ' . . . I rec'd the Purple and shall make a mark or two with it, as far as it will go. . . . We are going on very rapidly, having an extraordinary draughtsman who has done us a many subjects . . . '

* * *

12 2nd August 1763. ' . . . We have often been asked for Bute's head and shall get it done with all possible dispatch. Could Mr. Wedgwood direct us in the choice of the print to take it from . . . '

* * *

13 13th August 1763. ' . . . but we have neither Quart nor Pint Prussia — nor any plate at all of Wolfe . . . '. ' . . . We have got all the sizes of Bute drawn from a Mezzotinto painted by Ramsey — they'll do — and the others will be done as fast as possible, we having the engraver under our own eye — I assure you we are hard at it early and late'.

* * *

14 16th September 1763. ' . . . We shall have the Masons Arms completed by the next firing, as the person who engraves them works in my own office. We have two engravers and a draughtsman under our own eyes! . . . You may think we fear no rivals by the Expenses we have already been at in Engraving only, which believe me is (since August was 12 months) £250 and upwards, besides what plates we had before that time . . . '

* * *

15 26th March 1764. ' . . . I have been disappointed of some cash due in Liverpool for work done in the old way. The Engravers give us no quarter — If we do not send them a Remittce in 3 or 4 days after we receive the Work, we are sure to have a Requesting Letter from 'em. . . . '

* * *

16 26th May 1764. ' . . . Have got a new colour (a kind of dark Purple) which I think beats the black. Shall send you some mugs done with it — It is as glossy and fine as possible . . . '

* * *

17 6th October 1764. ' . . . have unpacked the 13 Crates we recd. and the Ware is very good — It is of a pale Colour in general, which is liked vastly better by everybody than the deep Yellow . . . '

18 30th November 1764. ' . . . Mr. Luffingham brought a salt glaze plate from Worcester, Printed Blue, and glazed after — He boasted much of it, and told us Mr. Holdship said we could Print everything but Blue as well as himself, but that we could not manage. However we got the same Pattern engraved and Printed, glaz'd and burnt two Plates and 3 Mugs — Our Blue is much better than the Worcester (owing to its being firmer laid on) and our Glaze is whiter — Our Blue is as good as any I have seen on China. We shall send you some of the first pieces we do. You know the transparent Glaze for Blue and the Glaze for a fine White to print upon will be very different — As to the Glaze for Blue, I would not desire a better than I think ours is. But as to the fine White Glaze to print Black, Red, etc., upon, we have not made a thorough Trial yet, but we shall acquaint you with our Progress (if we can make any) as we go on; for we would you partake with us of every Thing that is likely to afford either Honour or Profit. I recd. the Zaffer, but have not tried it yet & We shall always be obliged to you for your thoughts on the above Matters'.

*   *   *

19 27th March 1769. (Invoice of the table service printed for Lady Warburton). 'For printing a Table Service Lady Warburton's Arms, viz. (then follows list of articles and separate prices of them, amounting to £3. 17. 7.). The expenses for Engraving this Service was £1. 17. 6. total £5. 15. 1. 'We have delivered the above Ware to Messrs Bentley & Boardman, the prices to Lady Warburton you must fix yourselves'.

*   *   *

20 24th October 1769. Another Invoice of goods 'For Lady Isabella Stanley delivered to Mr. Bentley's'. A crest is mentioned.

*   *   *

21 25th April 1770. 'We received yours and have made several essays towards a Purple colour some time ago, but find it very difficult. We shall however, not give it up . . . If you can give us any hint shall be obliged to you. Have seen several Prints of heads etc., in imitation of chalk drawings and when we receive the plates you mention shall make a trial of 'em with a new Colour; and if the weather is good shall probably bring 'em you myself'. (See Wedgwood letter, Appendix VII.A (7).

*   *   *

22 22nd September 1769. 'Your favour by your Modeller gave us great pleasure to hear you are so well and hearty . . . I have been with three different persons that make tiles (particularly Billy Nichols, who was Mr. Dunbibin's Tile Maker) but as they all have families, they'll none of 'em leave Liverpool without being engaged for 12 months certain. But Billy Nichols promised me he would go to Burslem for a fortnight and put your men in the way, for a Gratuity. You may guess at their suspicions. We think the cream Colour for Queens' tiles would have a great run, though there are some objections to them which we have hinted to your Modeller. If you send us a few we'll print open Landskips on them which will look very pretty. Flower pots for windows wd. undoubtedly sell; but really we are hard set to fire what articles we have at present. And yet we are every now and then trying at a Blue and a Green colour that wd. be good and print as well as old Black. I cannot at present accept your kind invitation, but next Spring, please God, I'll pay you a visit'.

23   —1771. Green to W. ' . . . I have not yet been able to procure a Purple to please me tho I have minded a good deal. I think the greatest difficulty lies in making a good solution of tin and a proper flux. I observe what I take to be white Enamel in the Purple you have sent for edging and the other parts seem to have been run into a glass. *Pray inform me in your next whether this is of Mr. Rhodes making, for I think it is made on a different principle to any I have tried.*

*   *   *

24   11th October 1763. ' . . . You may rest assured we never printed a piece for any person but yourself . . . '

*   *   *

25   29th November 1771. Green to W. ' . . . Mr Burdett has just brought a small shell to have a first print proof taken off on paper. It looks pretty and I think we will succeed in them better than flowers. As to the tool for edges, he says that he has altered his plan and proposes a pencil fastened to a tube which is to supply it with colour as it flows from the point'.

*   *   *

26   19th October 1774.   Green to W. ' . . . This is principally to acquaint you that the crates No. 98, 99, 100, are not yet come to hand, nor the small box for Mr. Radcliffe. Have been obliged to send his order away without it. If the new conveyance cannot be established on a footing so as to deliver goods in a more regular manner, I am inclined to think it will never answer, as the delay occasioned by it will be of greater loss than the difference of carriage as on the old footing. But perhaps it may be more owing to the neglect of carriers than unavoidable delays on the Canal, for the weather has been very favourable ever since . . . '. (Reference is to Trent-Mersey Canal, a section of which had recently been opened.)

*   *   *

Josiah Wedgwood

On 12th January 1795, Josiah Wedgwood, the greatest potting figure of the century, died. The last letter of Green's in this correspondence with Wedgwood is dated 1st June 1793, although there is an invoice of goods which bears a date two months later in my possession. It may be assumed, therefore, that this potter-printer association, which had an unbroken run of over thirty years, came to an end about this time. It had met with the most remarkable success. From the comparatively small and insignificant beginnings in the early 1760's, Sadler's business, with Wedgwood's backing, grew so rapidly that in a comparatively small space of time it completely dwarfed the efforts of all other pottery printing centres in the country for many years. It was the result of a relationship, one of those not infrequently met with in the pages of history, based on mutual trust and respect, in which each recognized that the other could contribute something to their common advantage. That the development which took place was beneficial to the Liverpool potting industry as a whole few would care to maintain, for it enabled Wedgwood to maintain close contact with Liverpool potters and their affairs and infiltrate their markets in a way which otherwise would have been impossible. The immediate effect was to hasten the decline of a declining industry; more remotely, it must be held to be largely responsible for the popular present day belief that Liverpool was mainly a pottery printing centre for other people's wares and made little of her own worthy of serious attention.

APPENDIX V

From Gore's *General Advertiser*, 1st May 1767

'Printed Ware Manufactory, Sadler & Green'

'At their PRINTED WARE MANUFACTORY in Harrington Street, continue to sell Wholesale and Retail, at very moderate prices, Printed, Enamelled and Japann'd CHINA; also CREAM COLOUR WARE, TILES, etc., viz: Complete Table Services of Cream Colour as Terrines, Dishes and Plates of all sizes; Bowls, Decanters, Mugs, Coffee-pots, Tea-pots and every other article.

Fine Copper-plate Printed and Enamelled TILES of different Colours, viz: Black, Red, Chocolate, Blue-and-white and coloured after Nature.

N.B. The Cream Colour Ware is the best and of the most elegant Shapes and Patterns, made in England and ornamented with a very great variety of Masterly Subjects, properly adapted to each piece of ware; and the Tiles are neater than any done in Holland or else where, consisting of upwards of a hundred different patterns of Landskips, Ruins, Ship pieces, Rural figures, etc., the Engravings for which have cost upwards of Eight Hundred Pounds; and the printing is as good as it is possible to be done.

Merchants may be supplied with quantities for Exportation on the shortest Notice and have a large Discount allowed.

Coats of Arms, Crests, etc., done on Table Services, Bowls, Decanters, etc., in the neatest manner, by

J. SADLER and G. GREEN.'

Extracts from Wedgwood letters

TRANSFER PRINTING

1 29th July 1765. To his brother John in London. 'I committed a very great blunder in
my directions about the plate designed by Mr. Wale, which obliges me to return it
to have it altered if that can be done, if not, to have a new one. Mr. Wale knows that
all plates engraved for the purpose of enamelling should not be reversed on the plate,
that is, the figures should not be left-handed but should be the same on the plate as
they are designed to be on the vessel. All that is wanted in the present plate is to have
the boys made to work with their right hands, which I believe may be done very easily
with the Smith and Mason.' (See note at end of this Section.)

*   *   *

2 18th July 1766. Burslem. ?To Bentley. 'What do you think of sending Mr. Pitt upon
crockery to America. A quantity might certainly be sold there now and some advantage
made of the American prejudice in favour of that great man. Ld. Gower brought his
family to see my works the other day and asked me if I had not sent Mr. Pitt over in
shoals to America. If you happen to do anything in that way we can divide a tolerable
profit and sell at the same price to Sadler'.

*   *   *

3 25th September 1766. To ?. 'Crests are very bad things for us potters to meddle with
and I never take any orders for services so ornamented. Plain ware, if it should not
happen to be firsts, you will take it off my hands as seconds, which, if crested, would be
as useless as most other crests and Crest wearers are. For this and other reasons the
additional expense is more the buyer can be persuaded to believe it ought to be.
Sadler will make no scruple I daresay, of doing it in his way for you, or I will get him to
do it for me if you had rarther. I will write to him by this post and let you know the
result'.

*   *   *

4 31st December 1767. To Bentley, Liverpool. ' . . . Sadler has sent two plates of green and
gold. The colour wants strength and beauty but I think it much more genteel and delicate than either black or red, and I doubt not but that they will soon make further
improvements in this colour . . . pray enquire if Sadler has done any more plates with
the crest than those he sent here, which were good for nothing; and if he has not get
him to do 2 doz. good ones'.

*   *   *

5 15th March 1768. Wedgwood is writing of Boulton and his method of decorating enamel
and creamware with gold printing. 'He prepares the Gold himself in the very mode I
recommended to Sadler'.

6 31st August 1768. To Cox. 'I have wrote to Sadler about the dessert service of Pea Green and he does not choose to undertake it but has at present dropped all thoughts of any other colour but red and black so that I would not have you show that printed pattern at present — Messrs Rhodes and Co are to do us the coloured pattern for which reason I have not urged Sadler to do them.'

*   *   *

7 7th December 1768. Bentley (at Burslem) to Cox, London. 'They wrote me from Liverpool in a great bustle about Lady B. Warburton's Arms, which it seems Sadler has persuaded them he can do very well. Please to send the drawings immediately to our house at Liverpool; and the copy of the order hither. Think we may send the ware without further delay. They have a roaring trade at Liverpool. We cannot make bad goods fast enough for them and yet I am afraid we have made more than Mr. Wedgwood would like of that sort lately'. (See letter No. 19, Appendix V.)

[1] The 'Smith and Mason'. No such device as a 'Smith and Mason', which could have been used for this purpose, seems to have been known. To Mr C. Shingler, of the Worcester Royal Porcelain Company, I am indebted for the following explanation. ' . . . Wedgwood is saying that the incorrect engraving must be removed from the copper plate. This is done by first "knocking-up" the engraved lines with a hammer from the other side of the plate and then rubbing smooth the face of the plate with a stone. The hammering part of the process is that of a smith; the stoning part is that of a mason'. This seems to provide a reasonable solution.

Extracts from Wedgwood letters

ROBERT WILCOX

June 1769. Referring to Robert Wilcox, Wedgwood wrote concerning the discharge of twenty painters from Worcester of whom several went to Derby, but were not taken on. 'Some have come to me, one being Wilcox who served his time with Christian and then went to Reid until they failed. Wilcox said his wife was better than himself and showed two heads of her doing in Indian ink — very well done. Wilcox at present employed by Twemlow's but not engaged. I like his appearance much. He seems a sober solid man and has nothing flighty or cox-combical in his dress or behaviour, of which some of his class are apt to contract with small tincture'.

*   *   *

N.D. Referring to Wilcox again. 'His wife and he have got very good wages at Worcester, better he believes that he must ever expect again. They would now be content, he says, both of them, at 25/- per week, which is low enough if they will be tolerably diligent'.

*   *   *

17th September 1769. Burslem. 'Mrs Wilcox is losing her time here as she might as well paint figures upon vases as upon paper, as I am persuaded you will be convinced from the drawings I have sent you If she does such things of herself, what may not be expected of her under the tuition of a Bentley and a Croft? Pray let me know when I shall send her and her good man, for whilst they continue here there is 18/- at least sunk out of 24/-.

*   *   *

20th September 1769. 'I have not yet mentioned to Mr. and Mrs. Wilcox our intentions of having them to town, but I asked Mrs. W. this morning about her living in London. She said she would not like it at all. She had rather live in Staffordshire. I must talk to her again'.

Extracts from Wedgwood letters

MISCELLANEOUS

1 9th January 1768. To Bentley. ' . . . I am often asked here by Mr. Reid's creditors how his affairs are likely to turn out. I wish you would be so good before you leave Liverpool to ask Mr. Clegg how these matters are'.

*   *   *

2 14th February 1767. To Bentley. ' . . . I have received a letter from Mrs Chaffers' partner on the subject you mention. — I am afraid our potters will not be persuaded to think themselves so much indebted in getting high duty laid on Foreign China. For a prohibition I think (it) chimerical to expect until our own factories are able to supply the ladies with that necessary article.'
(Christian was trying to get Wedgwood's support for a Bill to make foreign china, then being imported in large quantities, dutiable. He failed. Wedgwood was pulling no chestnuts out of the fire for Christian. Writing to Bentley a little later, a postscript says 'I wrote my sentiments to Mr. Christian on the china affair!')

*   *   *

3 31st March 1768. To Bentley. ' . . . so briefly I think it will hardly be worth while to take Mr. Dunbibin's works for anything we can employ them. And will not engaging a tile maker at present be rather too early'.
(John Dunbibin and John Latham, potters, of Shaw's Brow, notice of bankruptcy and sale of stock, W.L.A., 25th February 1768. Wedgwood had long thought of making tiles himself and had bought from Sadler some apparatus for the purpose in November 1762. Shortly after this letter was written, he did engage Dunbibin's tile-maker, Billy Nichols.)

*   *   *

4 A letter from Bentley and Boardman in 1769 put Dunbibin's liability to Wedgwood at £33. 12. 0d. Wedgwood reduced it to £20 following a distressing letter from Dunbibin saying that he had paid 20/- in the pound.

*   *   *

5 12th May 1770. To ?. 'I returned from Liverpool last Wednesday when I left all friends well. My stay was so short that I could not meet with any painters to send you that were likely to do any good. Mr. Sadler has engaged those who had offered to us before . . .'.

*   *   *

6 3rd April 1765. (Extract from Wedgwood's Letters, edited by Farrar). 'The last post brought me 5 packets from Sir Wm. enclosing prints of different sorts which he is so obliging to employ his good taste in picking up for me at the Print Shops.'

7 17th February 1772. To Bentley. 'Great care should be taken that the idea of printing does not get abroad, as that may do us more harm than the printing itself can ever benefit us. For if our customers once conceive that we can print figures upon our vases, they will not know where to draw the line betwixt printing and painting and may take it into their heads that we apply the form to everything'.

* * *

8 28th March 1772. To Bentley. 'I have a vast deal to say to you but i it is impossible. But not to lose anything in prefacing, I have first to tell you that I have received a most lofty letter from Mr. Peter P. Burdett, nay, I'll enclose it so that you may know the better how to act if you should happen to see that red fire hot gentleman again. From this specimen of his temper, I had never before heard a word of his character, I should be fully convinced that no connection whatever could be formed with him, but what would have every probability of its being a plague to us . . . We can do without his secret . . . I give my vote most cordially that we have no more to do with him or his secret.

* * *

9 19th April 1772. To Bentley. ' . . . you will percieve that he (P.P.B.) has now added to his pride and conceit a malignity of spirit by endeavouring with his false insinuations to sow discord betwix us, which I did not before suspect him of. I now despise him the more heartily for his wicked attempt, which is as vain as it is mean and malignant. . . . But what do you say to his bill for drawings, attendances upon experiments, etc., Shall we pay it and be thankful that he does not charge us with his expenses to and from London. . . . One might, from any personage less elevated than Mr. Burdett, desire an explanation of the last article, for it seems very extraordinary that we must pay him for experiments made to improve his new invention without partaking of any advantage derived from those improvements'.

* * *

10 No date. Burdett to J.W. The letter referred to in 9. 'SIR, By the waggon from London, you will receive the drawings of dead game, etc., I shall neither take up your time nor my own in expressing my wonder that Mr. Bentley should have authority to tell me that Mr. Wedgwood was a precipitate man who had made some good hits indeed, but that I must not expect to go on with the business I had made so satisfactory a progress in. As matters stand, you have done me an irreparable injury. Overleaf is my charge. I am, Sir,'

* * *

(Account referred to above)

11 Munday's Coffee House,
Maiden Lane, April 16th, 1772.

To Mr. Wedgwood, at Etruria, nr. Newcastle, Staffs.
Dr. to P. P. Burdett.
For making 33 sketches and drawings from Nature of dead game . . 35 gns.
For engraving in a new manner, two human figures . . . . . 8 gns.
For copper, attendance upon experiments and other items . . . . 5 gns.
_____
48 gns.

A note on the Liverpool burgesses or freemen

There were three ways of acquiring the freedom of the Borough, 1, by birth; 2, by gift of the Common Council; and 3, by serving an apprenticeship under indenture to a Freeman within the Borough. The sons of freemen in order to become free, must have been born within the Borough. The Common Council, consisting of some forty members, was elected from the freemen; and the dispute in which Sadler became involved seems to have been caused by the usurpation by the Council of powers belonging to and normally shared by all the freemen.

The Common Council occasionally gave the freedom to public characters who had distinguished themselves in some way, but it is probably correct to say that no freemen were created corruptly for electioneering purposes. On the other hand, it is clear that the practice of selling the freedom was rife for many years until as late as 1792.[1] One historian goes so far as to state that the Corporation raised a considerable part of its income by freemens' 'fines', by virtue of the fact that no one was allowed to carry on any business who was not a freeman.[2] The cost of buying the freedom varied according to the status of the buyer, a merchant paying £20 to £30, a tradesman £5 to £10 and a mechanic perhaps not more than ten to twenty shillings. The same authority tells us that at the beginning of the reign of George the Second, the Corporation raised some £300 to £400 annually in this way.[3]

The rights enjoyed were, 1, To vote at all Elections, parliamentary or municipal; 2, Entitlement to serve on Grand, petty and coroner's juries; 3, To trade without restriction with exemption from payment of the town dues which 'foreigners' would be compelled to pay. Liverpool had freedom reciprocity rights with certain other towns, notably Bristol, Wexford, and Waterford.

---

[1] It has been said that Sadler, who was not a freeman, objected to paying a fine in this way.
[2] *History of Liverpool,* Thomas Baines, 1852, page 407.
[3] Memorandum Book of the Corporation.

BIBLIOGRAPHY

MAYER, JOSEPH. *History of the Art of Pottery in Liverpool.* Repr. 1871.

GATTY, C. T. *The Liverpool Potteries.* 1882.

PRICE, S. *John Sadler, a Liverpool pottery printer.* 1948.

BAINES, THOMAS. *History of Liverpool.* 1852.

STEWART-BROWN, R. *The Inhabitants of Liverpool from the Fourteenth to the Eighteenth Centuries.* 1930.

BEMROSE, WILLIAM. *Longton Hall Porcelain.* 1906.

JEWITT, LLEWELYN. *The Ceramic Art of Great Britain.* 1878.

OWEN, HUGH. *Two Centuries of Ceramic Art in Bristol.* 1873.

METEYARD, E. *The Life of Josiah Wedgwood.* 1865–6.

CHAFFERS, WILLIAM. *Marks and Monograms on Pottery and Porcelain.* 1874. *Ceramic Gallery.* 1872.

TURNER, W. *Transfer printing on Enamel, Porcelain and Pottery.* 1907.

HOBSON, R. L. *Worcester Porcelain.* 1910.

RACKHAM, BERNARD. *Catalogue of the Schreiber Collection.* Vol. I. *Porcelain.* 1928. Vol. II. *Pottery.* 1930. Vol. III. *Enamels and Glass.* 1924. *Catalogue of the Herbert Allen Collection.* 1923.

ECCLES, H. and RACKHAM, B. *Analysed Specimens of English Porcelain.* 1931.

HONEY, W. B. *Old English Porcelain.* 1946. *English Pottery and Porcelain.* 1952.

KING, WILLIAM. *English Porcelain Figures of the Eighteenth Century.* 1925.

LANE, ARTHUR. *Guide to the Collection of Tiles in the Victoria and Albert Museum.* 1939.

SOLON, M. L. *Catalogue of the Sale of the Solon Collection.* 1912.

HEAD, G. W. *The Earthenware Collector.* 1920.

READ, C. H. *British Museum Guide to English Pottery and Porcelain.* 1910.

DYKES, F. C. *Catalogue of Loan Collection to Manchester Art Gallery.* 1924. *Some thoughts on Eighteenth Century English Porcelain.* 1931.

COOK, CYRIL. *The Life and Work of Robert Hancock.* 1948.

MARSHALL, H. RISSIK. *Coloured Worcester Porcelain of the First Period.* 1954.

MACKENNA, F. S. *Worcester Porcelain.* 1950.

BARRETT, F. A. *Worcester Porcelain.* 1953

GARNER, F. H. *English Delftware.* 1948.

CHARLESTON, R. J. *Michael Edkins and the Problem of English Enamelled Glass.* 1954.

ENGLISH PORCELAIN CIRCLE. *Transactions, 1928–32.*

ENGLISH CERAMIC CIRCLE. *Transactions, 1933–54.*

ENGLISH CERAMIC CIRCLE. *Exhibition Catalogue, 1948.*

Magazine articles from *The Antique Collector, Connoisseur, Apollo,* to which reference is made in the text.

INDEX

INDEX

Numerals in *italic* type refer to pages on which footnotes appear. Numerals in **heavy** type refer to the plate numbers of illustrations.

Abbey, Richard, *59*, 100, 149, 156, 157
Acanthus ornament, 52; **12 (d)**, **23 (k)**
Agreement, The Liverpool, 1, 12, 15, 193–5
American Colonies, trade with, 10
  war with, effects of, 9
  petition against, 9
Analysis, 165–6
Angel, John, 60
Aquatinting, 162
Aspinall, William, 123
Attributions, making of, 40

Baines, Thomas, 122
Baker, Henry, *89*, 157–8
Ball, William, 5, *24*, 49, 129, 130, 204
Barnes, Zachariah, 6, 143–7
  border, 73
Barrow, Thomas, 60
Beakers, 54
Beckoning Chinaman, 38, 63, 64; **2(d)**, **10(b)**, **25(b)**
Bentley & Boardman, *8*
Bevelled footrings, 32: **50(k)**
Billinge, Thomas, 88, 91
Bird painting, 93; **14(e)**, **16(f)**, **23(f)**
Biting-snake handle, 51, 52, 54; **21(c)**, **41(d)**, **43(g)**
Black pottery, 131
Block making, 34
Blue grounds, 70, 71; **13(a)**, **14(a)**, **14(d)**, **31(j)**
Blue-and-white ware, painted, 61, 75; **3(c)**, **3(f)**, **5(a)**, **11(b)**, **41(a)**
  printed, 77; **45(a)**, **46(d)**, **47(a)**
Bold, Jonas, 131
Borders, 69, 70
Bottle flasks, 98, 99; **32(b)**, **32(c)**, **32(e)**

Bowen, John 64
Boyer, Mr, 129
Brick making, 1, 2
Bristol-Worcester, 41, 47
Brownlow Hill, 127
Brooks, John, 81, 82
Buckley, Francis, 21
Bucks Society, 31; **37(c)**, **38(b)**
Burdett, Peter Perez, 162–3

Caddick, Richard, 116
Canal transport, 9, 206
Cartlidge, Joseph, 137
Carrickfergus clay, 4
Case, James, 140
Chaffers, Edward, 6, 117, 130–1
  Elizabeth, 117
  Ellen, 19
  Huniball, 117
  Richard, 5, 114–9
Chaffers & Co., 15, 114
  printing department, 88
  types of ware, 118–9
Chamfered edge, 32, 119; **2(b)**
Chinese Imari, 65; **22(c)**
Charleston, R. J., *89*, 99
Christian, Philip, 1, 119–24
  role in partnership, 121
  retail shop, 120
  site of pottery, 122
  junior, 121
Christian's china body, 124
Christian Street, 123
Chubbard, Thomas, 116, 162
Clarkson, Peter, 116
Coffee cans, 32; **5(c)**, **5(d)**, **8(c)**
Conversation Club, 7

Cook, Cyril, 82, 104
Cotter, James, 144
Countersunk bases, 32
Crabstock handles, spouts, 33; **17(b)**
Crazing, 53
Creamware, 8, *85*, 103–4
    printed with Town Arms, *8*
Crisp & Co, Dublin, *4*

D-section handles, 30
Davenport, John, 134
Davis, William, 12, 13
Delamain, Henry, 81, 84
Decline of the industry, 7
Decorators, 'outside', 59, 68
Delftware, manufacture of, 6
    an importation, 3
Delftware painting on china, 68; **11(a)**, **17(c)**,
    17(d), **31(b)**
Dessert services, 55
Directory, Liverpool, 7, *24*
Dishes, 53; **17(c)**
Dobson, John, 128
'Dot' painter, 60; **11(d)**
Double-scrolled handle, 31
Driver, Joshua, 60
Dunbabin, Dunbibin, John, *3*, 141
Duty on foreign china, 7
Dykes, F. C., Collection, 110

Earthenware influence, 6, 24, 34
    lead-glazed, 6
Edkins, Michael, 99
Enamels, 90
Enameller, use of word, 90
Enfield, *A History of Liverpool*, 7
Entwistle, Peter, 21
Evans, Jeremiah, 88, 91, 105, 152–4
Eversion, 35, 36; **3(a)**, **3(e)**, **24(d)**
Eyes, Edward, 19

Factory wasters, 164
Famille rose pallette, 67; **17(e)**, **17(f)**, **18(a)**
Famille verte pallette, 67; **8(g)**
Figures, possibilities discussed, 56–8

Figure painting, 63, 70; **6(c)**, **22(a)**, **31(b)**
'Fine brush' painter, 99; **6(g)**, **7(c)**
Flower painting, 67, 68, 69; **4(b)**, **10(a)**, **13(c)**,
    13(d)
Flaws in paste, 29
Flute lesson, 110; **34(g)**
'Folly', the, 123
Folly Lane potteries, 122, 136
Footrings, undercutting, 31; **34(e)**, **34(f)**,
    50(b)
    wedge-shaped, 50; **50(i)**
Foreign china, effect of competition, 121
Frederick the Great, 88, 89; **35(a)**, **35(b)**,
    35(c), **39(f)**

Gatty, C. T., 19, 20, 21
Gerard, Thomas, 140
Gerrard, Richard, 135, 137
Gibson's Coffee House, 123
Gilbody, Samuel, 88, 89, 125–7; **35(a)**
Gilding, 73
Giles, James, *68*, 71
Glass, manufacture of, 89
    printing upon, 158–9
Glassy porcelain, 49; **21(d)**
Glaze, defects of, 30
Goldfish as decoration, 66, 67; **7(e)**
Gore, John, 149
Green, Guy, 81, 91, 151–2
Greg Collection, 116
Grooving of foot, 35, 44, 45
    handle (see lateral grooving)

Hanbury, Michael, 84
Hancock, Robert, 88, 95, 103–4, 107, 110–1
Harrison, Elizabeth, 194
    John, 116
    Lawrence, 160
Herdman, W. G., 122
Hobson, R. L., on Dr Wall, 13
Holdship, Richard, 13
Holt, Richard, 3
Holt & Gregson MS, 2, 144
Honey, W. B., 12, 84

Imari type decoration, 66; **7(c)**, **22(e)**, **24(f)**

Infirmary building fund, 122
Islington china manufactory, 135
Iron impurity in clay, *28*

Jacobite rose, 69; **13(c)**, **13(d)**
Janssen, Sir Theodore, 81
John Fell Jug, 65, 118: **1(c)**, **1(d)**
Johnson, Joseph, 160–1
    Nathaniel and others, 161–2
Jointed branch painter, 60; **13(e)**
Jones, John, 140
Jumping boy, 63; **24(a)**, **24(d)**

Kiln temperature, effect on translucency, 29
Kingfisher and ducks print, 96
Knotted tree painter, 60; **43(a)**
Kylin pattern, *67*

'Lady and parrot' group, 62, 119; **8(b)**, **8(d)**,
    9(c), **9(d)**
La Cascade, 96, 97, 109–10; **34(e)**, **39(g)**
L'Amour, 111; **39(e)**
Lane, Robert, 123
Lateral grooving, 30, 45; **20(a)**
Lath, Nehemiah, 55
Lawrenson, Thomas, 85, 159
Lead content of porcelain, 31, 166
Limerick delftware, 84, 102
'Liver' as decoration, *52*, 119; **41(d)**
Liverpool, growth of, 10
    freemen, 214
    size of pottery industry, 4
    town Arms, 52, 154
Livesley, John, 114–5, 143
Long-tailed macaw print, 103; **34(a)**, **34(c)**
Lord Street pothouse, 120
Lyes, John, 12, 13, 14
Luffingham, 205

Mackenna, Severne, 13
McNeale, Mr, 128
Marbled blue, 68; **21(a)**
Marks, 165
    on 'scratch-cross' ware, 43

Mask-spout, 32
'Masons Arms', 115, 204
Mayer, Joseph, 12, 16, 18, 19
    bequest to Museum, 20
Mears, Thomas, 133
Mercer, William, 138, 140
Merchants, their interest in potworks, *5*, 144
Meredith, Sir William, 106, 115
Meteyard, E., 106
Milligan, Hugh, 59, 127
Mock Corporation of Sefton, 121
Moss, Liverpool Guide, 86
Moulded wares, 38, 50, 51; **12**(all)
Muggs, export trade in, 2
Mug shape, importance attaching to, 32, 37
    spreading base, 44; **36(c)**, **39(f)**
    bell-shaped, 32, 44; **8(f)**, **26(c)**, **34(c)**

Nelson, Lord, mug belonging to, 67
Nichols, Billy, 205
Note-book, Sadler's, *109*, 148–9
Nield, Dr Newman, 99

O'Kell's pottery, *8*
Oxford Journal, 25
Overlapping scale moulding, 45

Padmore, Richard, 124
    Edward, 125
Parker, G., 90, 150
Parker's pump, 114
Park Lane pottery, 133
Part, John, 141
Patent, Sadler's application, 83, 86
Pencilled ware, 73, 74; **20(c)**
Pennington, James, 49, 132–5
    Jane, 53, 134
    John, maltster, 132
    John, senr, 136–7
        jnr, (1) 60, 142–3
        (2) 134
    Robert, 60, 141–2
    Seth, 10, 53, 138–40
Pennington blue, 133
Pennington & Edwards, 139

Pennington & Part, 138
Pennington pedigree, 132
Pickle dishes, 52; **24(f)**
Picton, Sir James, *19*
Pin-pitting, 30
Pipe clay, *89*
Pipe making, 2
Plan of pottery sites, 22
Plates, 34, 53–4; **3(g)**, **19(a)**, **29(b)**, **31(a)**
    tin enamelled, 34; **42(b)**
Plumper mugs, 4, 115, *117*, 119; **2(a)**
Podmore, John, 123, 125
    Robert, 12, 13, 15, 116, 124–5
        importance of, 15
        oriental ideas, 25
        and Wedgwood, 14, 18
Pole, Charles C., 118
Poll and Squib book, 4, *115*
Polychrome prints, 99, 100
Population figures, *8*
Poole, Joseph, 3
Potteries, number of, 5, 23
Potters, master, 5
Pretender, Young, portrait of, *87*
Prints, classification, 94–103
    colours used, 94
    copying of, 110
    and copper plates, 107
    general review of 111–2
    pirated, 106
    purple, 94–5; **36(a)**
    signed, 93–4
    sources of, 104–7
    reversed, 107
Printing, development of, 87, 103
Privateering, 9

Ravenet, 81
Rackham, Bernard, *26*, 82, 164
Red prints, 203; **38(e)**
Red cow print, 97–8; **32**(all)
    ware, 38–9; **32**
Redcliff Backs factory (Lund), 13
Reid & Co., 5, 127–8
    bankruptcy, *8*, 212
Rhodes, David, 91, 206
Ribbed handles, 35

Rigg & Peacock, *8*
Robinson, John, 79
Rockliff, Mrs, 18, 124
Roscoe, James, 127
    William, 60, 127
Rosson, John, 12, 13, 14, 16, 114
    letter to *Mercury*, 196–9

Sadler, Elizabeth Mary, 19
    John, 81, 83, 85–8, 90–3
        & Green, 91
        and Wedgwood, 87, 91–2
Saltglaze, manufacture of, 3, 6
    printing on, *85*, 205
Saltglaze painting, 63–4; **17(f)**, **18(a)**, **25(a)**, **25(b)**
Sayer, Robert, 104
'Scratch-cross' group, 41
    origin of, 42
    ware described, 44–6; **27**, **28**, **29(c)**, **29(d)**, **30(a)**
    allied wares, 46; **24(e)**
Scrolled handles, 30, 50–1; **8(d)**, **39(e)**
    double 31
Services, 55
Seven Years War portraits, 87, 8, 9; **35**
Shaw's Brow, 4
Shaw, Thomas, 6, 114, 136
Shingler, Cyril, 108
Silver shape, influence of, 51
Smallshaw-Jackson, Mrs, 145
'Smoky primitive' prints, 95; **34(c)**, **34(g)**
Southwark potters, migration of, 3
Soaprock, Chaffers' supply, 17, 26, 119, 202
    difficulty in obtaining, *14*, *25*
    sale of Christian's lease, 17
Spencer, Thomas, 118; **1(a)**
Spiky flower painter, 60, 68; **21(a)**, **21(c)**
Stag hunt design, 74; **6(b)**, **16(a)**, **16(b)**
Staffordshire competition, 7
    warehousemen, 7
Street names, 6
Swan, Jeremiah, 140

Tarleton, Banistre, 161
Tatlock, Henry, 150

Tea party print, 106–7; **38(d)**, **39(d)**
Teacups, handled, 50; **14(b)**, **22(d)**
Teapoys, 54
Teppit, Gauregan, 17
   letters of 20, 202
Thumb, impress on handles, 30
Thwaites & Wilcock, 133
Tiles, Dutch, 82–3, 86
   manufacture of, 3
   printing on, 81, 85, 87
Tilley, Frank, *57*, 89
Tin-glazed porcelain, 34, 165; **42(b)**
Toppin, A. J., 13, *14*, *68*, 82
Translucency discussed, 28–9
Turner, William, 83
Turretted bud painter, 60, 68; **12(f)**, **21(b)**

U-shaped handles, 30; **25(c)**
Undercutting, 31; **11(c)**, **19(e)**, **34(f)**
Wainwright, Jonathan, 144
Wale, Sam, 105, *111*, 203, 209
Walker, Richard, 160
Wall, Dr John, 12, 13
Ware, general features, early period, 28
   later periods, 49, 53
   bowls, 31, 54, 78, 79; **11(c)**, **14(a)**, **40(a)**
   coffee pots, 33, 50; **4(b)**, **15**, **34(a)**
   covers, 33
   crazing, 55
   dishes, 53; **17(c)**
   eversion of rim, 35, 36; **3(a)**, **3(e)**, **34(e)**, **34(f)**
   footrings, irregularity of, 40; **50(e)**

   and bases 31–2, 35–6, 40
   handles, 30–1, 35, 50; **1(d)**, **8(d)**, **11(a)**, **22(f)**, **25(c)**
   jugs, 32–3, 36; **frontispiece**, **1**, **14(e)**, **30**
   polygonal shapes, 38; **3(i)**, **7(c)**, **32(a)**, **32(j)**
   sauceboats, 33–4, 51; **12(d)**, **17(e)** **20(b)**, **33(h)**
   teapots, globular, 33; **15(c)** **36(b)**, **49(d)**
      depressed globular, 37; **13(c)**, **16(b)**, **21(f)**
      fluted, 37–8; **6(c)**, **10(b)**
      palm-tree, 50; **20(e)**, **20(f)**
      hump-handled, 37, 75
Warrington glass works, *54*
Watney, Bernard, 31, *87*
Wedgwood, Aaron, 19
   Josiah, 7, 8, *20*, 207
   and Sadler, creamware printing, 87, 91
   correspondence 203–6
   prices charged, 92
   trading methods, 91
Westropp, Dudley, *3*, 82, *84*
Whieldon-type ware, 18, 117
Wilcox, Robert, 123, 211
Wolfe, Thomas, 53, 134
Woodcuts, prints from, 86
Woods & Co., 131
Worcester Porcelain Company, Partnership Deed, 12
Worcester wares, change of body, 27
   copied, 25–6
   earliest known prints, 27
Wright, William, 137